For if the trumpet give an uncertain sound,
who shall prepare himself to the battle?

Managing the Future of Freemasonry

A book of optimism

David West

*What matters at this stage is the construction of local forms of community within
which civility and the intellectual and moral life can be sustained through the new
dark ages which are already upon us.*

Cover design by Lawrie Morrisson

The quotation on the front endpaper is from *1 Corinthians* 14:8 and that on the title page is from Alasdair MacIntyre's *After Virtue*.

Published 2015 by Hamilton House Publishing Ltd
Rochester Upon Medway, Kent, UK.

ISBN: 978-0-9928572-4-0

Dedication

For Jenny, my wife and dearest to my heart for 47 years.

Thanks

I wish to thank Peter Currie, Glyn Jarrett, Kirk C. White and Lawrie Morrisson for their active assistance and encouragement. I also thank Colombe Anouilh d'Harcourt, Barbara Tesler-Anouilh, Nicolas J. Anouilh and Julie Hamon for permission to quote from *Antigone* by Jean Anouilh.

Author's note

The opinions expressed in this work are entirely my own. They do not necessarily represent the opinions of the United Grand Lodge of England, the Masonic Province of Essex, St Laurence Lodge No. 5511 or any of my brethren. I would like to state quite firmly that this work has no official status whatsoever.

The author

Dr David West gained his first degree in Philosophy from the University of Exeter and his doctorate of and in Philosophy from the University of Leicester. He taught at universities in England and Canada. His later business career included Ford and Xerox. He served on government committees on the future of work, was an adviser to a Cabinet Minister and founded The Working Manager Ltd, creating the core content of its management education process. He is a member of four lodges and four chapters under the English Constitution. His mother lodge is St Laurence No. 5511.

Other books by David West

The Devil, the Goat and the Freemason – a study in the history of ideas

It's no wonder the book has been praised by reviewers on both sides of the Atlantic.

A wonderful, stimulating and provocative book that is a joy to read. It provides a perfect counterpoint to all the pretentious rubbish about Freemasonry that we have suffered so long.

A book everyone should read.

Well written, deeply researched, it dispels the fictions about Freemasonry.

A fascinating book, not only for those interested in the history of Freemasons, but also for anyone trying to reconcile the prevailing scientific and spiritual world views.

A pleasure to read; a serious, insightful book in which the author has a great deal of fun in dealing with the issues that he addresses.

Things to do when you have nothing to do – or how to find those candidates who have been looking for you all this time

Based on the real life experience of St Laurence Lodge No. 5511. It shows how they did it.

This will not only give you interesting and enjoyable work to do; it will also lead you to candidates.

A big thanks to Bro. West for sharing the techniques his lodge has used to prosper.

David West and Lawrie Morrisson are two of the most far sighted and innovative Freemasons in England. Their lodge embraces a constant stream of new ideas and uses all the tools of modern technology to spread the message of Freemasonry. Its website is the envy of the many who seek to follow in the footsteps of St Laurence Lodge and replicate its success.

You'll find many different ways to escape the doldrums that beset many lodges today.

Written as a labour of love, there's lots to like here.

Where there's a will, there's a way – and this book gives you a panoply of ideas for it!

Deism – at the time of the founders of the Premier Grand Lodge

Provides an intellectual and extremely useful introduction to an important underlying movement that was in evidence during the critical period of the development of English Freemasonry.

Ably tackles a topic which during the Enlightenment was offered as a rational alternative to the traditional Christian faith in God.

Non-Masonic

Employee Engagement – and the failure of leadership

Excellent read: very useful research findings and very practical.

One of those books you keep marking with a yellow sticky to refer back to.

For the well-read manager or the newbie, it gives a compilation of critical theory and experience.

Very easy reading style.

You'll never feel again that Philosophy and Ethics are dusty academic topics.

The author, an established Doctor of Philosophy, has worked across a wide variety of businesses trying to improve their managements and this book is really about what he found, what research supports his analyses, and how to fix it. Yes, he has a fix.

Freemasonry is a moral practice. We enable good men to live respected and die regretted.

There are periodic intervals in human experience when the moral life comes under attack. Now is such a time, and we must respond.

We will become a reservoir of social capital, enabling society to preserve the virtue of trust.

We will provide a bastion for the virtues in an amoral world, maintaining a community within which the moral life is lived.

In choosing to become a Freemason, a man accepts an obligation to live according to the virtues of the order. Such a choice cannot be made lightly.

There is no sense in which a man can say, 'I want to be a Freemason but not a good one.'

To be a good Freemason is to exhibit specific virtues. The most important of these are the three grand principles – brotherly love, relief and truth – and the four cardinal virtues – prudence, fortitude, temperance, and justice.

Contents

To minimise footnotes, full references are given in the bibliography.
Where the text gives a source, no footnote is added.

Optimism and the membership problem

Optimism

> *How far that little candle throws his beams! So shines a good deed in a naughty world.*[1]

The golden years of Freemasonry have passed with the departure of a world never likely to return in the lifetime of anyone who might read this book. The world that we face now may seem less than welcoming to the ideals of our order, but I firmly believe that there are still many men in our society hungry for the fellowship and moral meaning that we offer. Our challenge now is to bring our ideals to the attention of a new and different audience.[2] To reach it will require hard work, open-mindedness, creativity, and above all leadership.

I am convinced that a resurgence of Freemasonry is possible. In fact, it is vital to the rebuilding of our society. What I shall say will not always sound optimistic but if we are to rescue our order, we must take an objective look at our problems and the social changes that have caused them. Only by recognising what has brought us to this pass, can we hope to create solutions. We cannot pretend that our problems will simply go away. The optimism that runs through this book depends upon an ability to change.

The membership problem

In late 2014, I received an email from a Mason I have never met. I am an English Mason and my correspondent is a member of three lodges in British Columbia, but we are brothers, despite the 4,700 miles that separate us.

> *Last night my lodge in Vancouver had a short memorial service. Of our members, we had a serving militia soldier, a wounded and decorated veteran of the Korean War, and a long-retired militia Major with 21 years' service. Then we held the customary business followed by our annual installation of officers. We had nobody willing to accept office as Deacons or Stewards. The new Director of Ceremonies was absent due to illness. Our Grand Lodge has provided an optional short form for this sort of thing and we used it.*

> *We had about ten members and two visitors present, the latter taking important ceremonial roles. Two past masters also took part but would not accept election or appointment. Neither is a regular attender: one has business commitments, the other lives several hours' drive away, not counting a ferry trip. Everybody was very happy that the meeting was short. Less than an hour for the whole thing, knocks to knocks. We had a little dinner of very mediocre Chinese food after our board meeting and before lodge. After lodge we had a little dessert, coffee and the formal toasts and I was home before 10.30 to the surprise of my wife.*

---

[1] *Merchant of Venice*, Act V, Scene 1.

[2] In this book, I use the term *audience* to refer to a specific group of men who we seek to attract.

Introduction

A few years ago we consolidated with another lodge and had about 100 members. We are now down to 32. I am now 81 years old, Chaplain in one lodge, Tyler in another and Junior Warden of a third which is going dark in a few days. This is a sad but not unusual picture for Vancouver. Ballooning population and shrinking membership in Freemasonry, concordant bodies and everything else: service clubs, lawn bowling, churches, Legion. No one can make any sense of it.

The current membership problem in Freemasonry has existed for more than sixty years. In that time, we have lost around half our membership worldwide. The membership of the United Grand Lodge of England is no longer the much admired 350,000 and is now closer to half that figure. In 1959 there were just over four million Freemasons in America; by 2014 there were under one and a quarter million, a loss of getting on for three million.[1]

In their important paper,[2] published in 2000, Henderson and Belton drew attention to the fact that worldwide Masonic membership reached its peak around 1960.[3] It is significant that most organisations similar to Freemasonry reached peak membership around the same time. For example:[4]

	Year of peak membership	Decline from peak by 2000
Jaycees	1975	58%
Lions	1967	58%
Elks	1970	46%
Kiwanis	1960	42%
Rotary	1967	25%

All these organisations are concerned with charity, civic action and social responsibility. Their membership experience is much the same as that of Freemasonry, in both timing and extent. While each of the organisations has its own unique features, the similarity of their growth and decline implies a common cause: a significant change in society. In 1950, The United Grand Lodge of England issued 22,500 certificates, a post war peak.[5] Thereafter, the number of candidates declined and the decline continues.

---

[1] The actual figures are 4,103,161 and 1,185,943 for a loss of 2,917,218.

[2] I would like to acknowledge the importance of the article *Freemasons – An Endangered Species?* to this book. The reception that it received at the meeting of *Quatuor Coronati* Lodge was disappointing.

[3] To take some geographically disparate examples, peak membership occurred in Jersey in 1958, in the USA in 1959 and in South Australia in 1961. Source: Henderson and Belton.

[4] US membership figures from Putnam.

[5] The all-time peak came in 1920 with the issuing of over 30,000 certificates. Source: Calderwood.

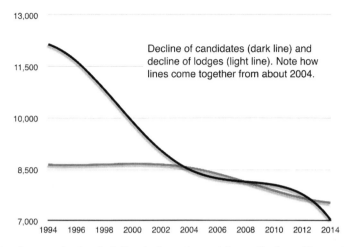

13,000

11,500

10,000

8,500

7,000

Decline of candidates (dark line) and decline of lodges (light line). Note how lines come together from about 2004.

1994 1996 1998 2000 2002 2004 2006 2008 2010 2012 2014

In the first graph, the dark line is the polynomial trend[1] of certificates issued by the UGLE in England and elsewhere. The lighter line is the polynomial trend of the number of lodges. Lodges were able to cope with a decline in candidates for a time. The number of lodges *(light line)* did not respond to decline in initiations *(dark line)* until 2003/4 when the number of certificates (more or less identical to number of candidates) per lodge dropped under 1.0 for the first time. *(See below.)*

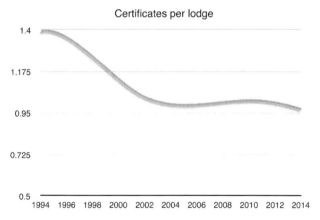

Certificates per lodge

1.4

1.175

0.95

0.725

0.5

1994 1996 1998 2000 2002 2004 2006 2008 2010 2012 2014

This seems to be evidence supporting the commonly held view that a lodge needs better than three candidates in two years to prosper.

---

[1] A polynomial trend is a curved line that is used when data fluctuates. It is useful for analysing gains and losses over a large data set.

The plan of the book

I start with an examination of the years following 1800, a period in which 42% of our lodges were lost. There are uncanny parallels between then and now from which important lessons can be learned. In the earlier 18th century, the ideals of Freemasonry were in keeping with those of our craftsmen and tradesmen brethren. Those ideals were lost during the first part of the industrial revolution and Freemasonry almost died in massive social and economic changes during which the majority of these crafts and trades disappeared.

Eventually, and I think accidentally, Freemasonry found a new source of membership in the blossoming Victorian middle class. Odd as it may seem, given that the period saw two world wars, little changed in the social and moral life of Britain from 1850 to 1950, and the Victorian middle class and its successors sustained Freemasonry for a hundred years. However, during the 1950s a quite sudden change occurred, one which began the end of the middle class.

I shall describe three distinct periods of social change between then and now, each of which has had a deleterious effect on all institutions that require social interaction and commitment, and on Freemasonry in particular. These changes have caused our membership decline and the result of these changes forms the society from which we must recruit today.

I shall then describe the impact of these social changes on the concept of trust. The decline in trust is central to the problems of modern society. It parallels the decline of Freemasonry and both declines share a common cause. I shall argue that the decline in trust offers an opportunity for the resurgence of our order; that we can be a reservoir of social capital, keeping alive the virtue of trust until the wave of barbarism has passed.

I shall then review the philosophical issue of values, the *ought/is* distinction, and examine the absence of ethical principles in today's society. I will discuss Alasdair MacIntyre's account of the virtues and show how this can be applied to Freemasonry. I shall employ the phrase *live respected and die regretted* as a useful way of understanding Aristotle's view of the virtues and use the Masonic word *excellences* as a way of handling what might otherwise be a surprising idea that there are many virtues, often incompatible with each other.

I shall ask what excellences make sense of today's world and argue that there are none. In the absence of any agreed social context, any agreement on *the purpose-to-life* if you will, ethical discussion and the moral life becomes near to impossible. I shall compare our order to the rule of St Benedict, and argue that just as a man can authentically choose to adopt the rule of St Benedict, so he can also choose to become a Freemason, the notion of *authenticity* coming from Jean-Paul Sartre.

4

I shall argue that such a choice is a moral one and that therefore Freemasonry is a moral order, one in which the moral life can be sustained in the face of MacIntyre's new dark age. I shall argue that this is our purpose, our function in society. It is what we are here for. I shall argue that making the serious choice to become a Freemason provides a meaning to life, something that many men are looking for. In providing this, we shall save ourselves.

There are many implications stemming from all this, one of which is that we must cease to listen to the siren voice of PR, and make a positive statement of what we are and what we offer.

I shall analyse the excellences of Freemasonry in some detail primarily because many Masons are unclear about them. If we are to be a community in which the moral life can be sustained in the face of the new dark age, we must certainly know the nature of the excellences or virtues we ask our brethren to sustain. It is also clear that the false gods of PR are seeking to change those excellences and so I shall examine their original meaning in Masonic history. I shall argue that the three grand principles turn out to be the basis of effective management and that if we are true to our principles, we will also exemplify good leadership. I will then describe the management and leadership we require.

This is a book of optimism. I believe that we can achieve a resurgence. More than this, I believe that we can become more relevant to and more important in society than ever before. I will not say that it will be easy and I recognise that resistance will be strong. There are many brethren who would see their lodge go dark, as our North American brethren put it, rather than accept change. Many lodges will go under, but then many always have.

Women's Freemasonry

There are two Grand Lodges in the UK which are solely for women. The UGLE has expressed the view that *except that these bodies admit women, they are … regular in their practice*. This book is about men's Freemasonry but much of what it says could be applied to the Order of Women Freemasons and the Honourable Fraternity of Ancient Freemasons.

Reading the book

The chapters *Values and relativity*, *Morality and context* and *A bastion for the moral life* will be more difficult for some readers than others. These chapters are essentially a matter of moral philosophy which will be new to many Freemasons. I give a précis of the argument beforehand to help, but if it all becomes too much, just skip forward to complete the book and come back at your leisure to review the philosophical bits. They may make more sense then.

Freemasonry and social change: 1800–1850

The condition of England

The Napoleonic War left Britain with a large national debt and to manage this, the government of the day sought to retain income tax, hitherto a temporary measure. Nicholas Vansittart, then Chancellor of the Exchequer, argued that income tax was progressive, pressing more on the rich and thus:

> ... *the least oppressive and the least objectionable of any tax that had ever been imposed.*[1]

He was defeated by a huge majority and the burden of taxation shifted to indirect taxes which pressed more heavily on the poor. With no legal way of expressing discontent, demonstrations and riots broke out, put down by violent repression and the country became all but ungovernable.[2]

> *The King has virtually abdicated; the Church is a widow without jointure; public principle is gone; private honesty is going; society, in short, is falling to pieces; and a time of unmixed evil is come upon us.*   Thomas Carlyle, *Edinburgh Review* 1829

1815 was the *hey-day of aristocratic excess and swagger*[3] and the political leadership, with its cult of amateurism, had no understanding of what was happening. Thomas Carlyle described *The Condition of England* as an issue of two nations, the rich and the poor[4] and in 1819, William Cobbett wrote:

> *Society ought not to exist, if not for the benefit of the whole. It is and must be against the law of nature, if it exists for the benefit of the few and for the misery of the many ... [A] society, in which the common labourer ... cannot secure a sufficiency of food and raiment, is a society ... whose compact is dissolved.*[5]

In France, that society was indeed dissolved by the revolution which resulted in the execution of Louis XVI – and of another 40,000 people across France. Whether or not Louis' consort, Marie Antoinette, actually said *Qu'ils mangent de la brioche,*[6] such a sentiment would have fitted both France and England at the time.

---

[1] *Parliamentary Debates*, First Series, vol. 33, 1816.

[2] Vallance.

[3] Richardson.

[4] Thomas Carlyle, the political observer who made a study of the French Revolution and its causes, *Chartism*, 1839, republished 2012, Ulan Press.

[5] *Political Register*, September 1819; the working-class newspaper started by the fiercely independent William Cobbett in 1799 to press for parliamentary reform. He attacked the rotten boroughs and supported the Swing Riots.

[6] Most commentators say she did not. The phrase is used by Jean-Jacques Rousseau some thirty-five years before Marie Antoinette.

A change in membership?

During this period, our brethren faced the loss of their traditional livelihoods, a loss not only of employment but also of self-respect and status. Urbanisation meant near-slum living conditions, and the loss of contact with families, becoming a stranger in a strange land. Without money to cushion the change, the risk of poverty and the workhouse was very real at a time when to be poor was to be seen as criminal. With an almost complete absence of leadership, it is a wonder that the institution of Freemasonry did not disappear altogether.

Using data from returns made under the *Unlawful Societies Act* of 1799, this graph displays the change in the employment of members of Essex lodges from 1799 to 1899. For example, the number of independent tradesmen reduces almost to zero and the number working in the licensed trade declines by over two-thirds. In 1799, independent tradesmen accounted for about one-third of members of the lodges I have studied and another third were independent shopkeepers and licensed victuallers (small pub owners). Very few could be described as employees, and these included two clergymen, a soldier and an excise officer. By 1899, over half the members were employees, many with jobs unheard of a hundred years before: insurance agent, station master, salesman, broker, engineer and advertising agent. There was a distinct increase in white collar workers.

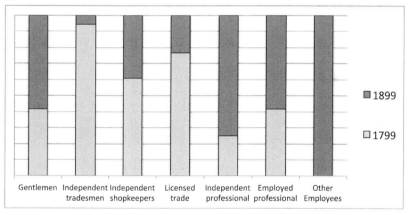

Change in employment by category between 1799 and 1899

This Essex analysis generally accords with David Harrison's analysis of initiates in four lodges in Stockport, Warrington, Oldham and Bolton. He writes:

> ... *the foundation on which these lodges were built seems to have been those active in trading the High Street – the shopkeepers (grocers, butchers, bakers, watchmakers). In the first half of the century, the balance of the sector was innkeepers and in the second half the number of*

merchants and agents rose sharply. It was equally noticeable that the number of industrialists and professionals (solicitors, doctors, clergy, public officials, engineers) rose very sharply in the 1850s ... also noticeable was the decrease in importance of men following a trade ... joiners, farriers, smiths, cordwainers, building tradesmen and ... weavers, spinners, fustian cutters.

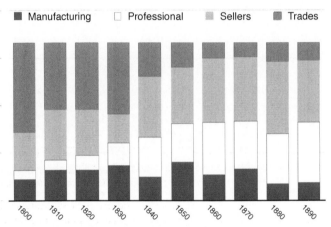

I have constructed this graph from Harrison's data and while his categorisation is a little different from mine, the same picture emerges: fewer traditional tradesmen and more employees and white-collar workers.

Centralisation and urbanisation

Occupations in the 18th century were much the same as in the 17th and certainly as long as Freemasonry had existed there had been little change in the way that people went about earning a living. The industrial revolution changed all that, and at a faster[1] rate in the UK than in other nations.[2] At this time, Britain was becoming the workshop of the world, producing finished goods so efficiently that it could undercut locally made products in almost every country.

The immediate effect of the industrial revolution was to move production from the cottage to centralised and mechanised production facilities, driven initially by water power and later by steam. Thus, industrialisation brought urbanisation.[3]

---

[1] Kennedy.

[2] Matthew Boulton (1728–1809) was called *The First Manufacturer in England* by his business partner James Watt. Boulton founded the Soho Mint and used steam power to drive it. 'Iron-mad' John Wilkinson (1728–1808) ran blast furnaces and rolling mills but is perhaps most famous for his precision boring machine used in the manufacture of steam engines.

[3] Trevelyan writes that in 1820 the City of London was linked up by *an almost continuous line of houses with Hammersmith, Deptford, Highgate and Paddington. For London, like other English cities, had always grown outwards, not upwards.*

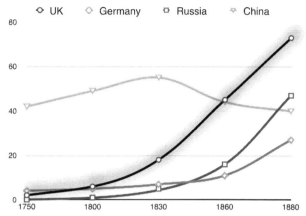

Total industrial output (UK 1900= 100). The total output of the UK exceeds that of China by 1860. The graph turns upward in 1800 in UK but not until 1830 in Russia and 1860 in Germany.

London's population doubled between 1801 and 1850. The Manchester and Salford conurbation grew from 25,000 in 1772 to nearly half a million in 1851. At the turn of the century, 1.4 million people (28% of the workforce) were employed in manufacture and mining. By 1841 that figure had more than doubled to 3.3 million (41% of the workforce).[1]

The impact on Masonic membership

The old trades, so important to the membership of Freemasonry, gave way to mass manufacture and new forms of employment. The gradual growth of the national, if not yet the multinational, company had a similar effect on the shopkeeper, licensed victualer and independent professional. Within the life expectancy of a man born in 1770, these traditional jobs, which were the livelihoods of at least two-thirds of our brethren, virtually disappeared and the countryside emptied as towns drew in those seeking work in the factories.

Disruption was on a grand scale, with a consequent impact upon our order. Between 1820 and 1860, some 252 lodges under the United Grand Lodge of England were lost, 200 of these between 1820 and 1840. To put this into perspective, 252 lodges represented 42% of the total number of lodges that existed at the 1832 renumbering.[2]

---

[1] Data Mitchell.

[2] The list of lodges used to be closed up by removing extinct lodges. The Lodge of Unity (originally known as the Old French Lodge) began as 190 and was renumbered 122 (1755), 96 (1770), 79 (1780), 72 (1792) and after the union of the two Grand Lodges, 96 (1814), 82 (1832) and 69 in 1863.

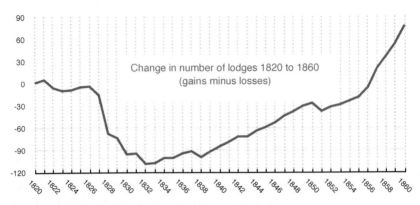

The trough in the number of lodges continued until 1840; not until 1857 did the lodges get back to the 1820 number.[1] There was an increase in the speed of industrialisation around 1830 which coincided with an increase in the number of lodges lost.

It was not as if our brethren left a blacksmith's forge and moved seamlessly to a skilled job in a factory, earning more money and living a better life. They were forced out of their trade by mass manufacture that undercut their prices and they had to leave home to find what they could in the nearest town. Finding another lodge to join was not the first thing on their minds.

Fear of poverty

After the Napoleonic war, prices fell by an average of 0.2% a year.[2] Lower prices did not benefit our brethren because they were matched by a greater decline in wages. In the building trade, wages fell 7% in 1825, staying at that level for another 15 years. The working class has almost never been able to put something aside for a rainy day and such a reduction in wages must have been painful.[3] The only employment category that showed wage growth was that of clerks, more than doubling their earnings between 1797 and 1861.

In the 18th century, an independent blacksmith, baker or a licensed victualler had some ability to manage his own business, but the 19th-century employee was dependent on his employer. The failure of an employer's business, illness or accident could lead families to a slippery slope, at the bottom of which lived the really poor. Around the turn of the century, nearly one person in ten was

---

[1] Data Lane. The data refers only to lodges meeting in England.

[2] Deflation continued, on and off, until the advent of the 1914–1918 war.

[3] Data Mitchell.

receiving poor relief and that must have included many of our brethren. Movement into poverty was easy enough but getting out was next to impossible. Steven King speaks of the ample evidence that:

> *... between 1750 and 1850 both the scale of the poverty problem and its intensity increased. More people became more poor ...*

Charles Dickens

The fear of poverty was constant. The novels of Charles Dickens (1812–1870) may be full of wonderful characters but they are also political tracts in their depiction of the squalid conditions of the poor,[1] and the descent into poverty of middle class men and women is a theme in many of his novels. He often rescues them by use of the artificial device of an inheritance; artificial because Dickens recognised that in real life poverty was usually a permanent state. Dickens himself was haunted by poverty and his own education had been affected by his family's financial troubles. As Simon Callow said:

> *The reason I love him so deeply is that, having experienced the lower depths, he never ceased, till the day he died, to commit himself, both in his work and in his life, to trying to right the wrongs inflicted by society ... From the moment he started to write, he spoke for the people, and the people loved him for it, as do I.*[2]

Oliver Twist (1838) gives us the horrors of Jacob's Island. No creation of the author's imagination, this area was just south of the Thames, east of St Saviour's Dock in Bermondsey. Once a wealthy centre for the timber trade, jobs became scarce when the trade moved downriver to Rotherhithe starting in 1811. During the cholera outbreaks in the middle of the 19th century, half the deaths occurred on Jacob's Island. Despite the increase in national wealth brought by the industrial revolution, average life expectancy at birth rose only slightly, from thirty-five years to forty years by 1850, due to the dreadful conditions that the urban poor endured. With the great influx of people seeking work, any accommodation in London was ruinously expensive and Jacob's Island was just the worst of many similar slums.

The 'undeserving' poor

Gustave Doré, best known for his illustrations of Milton's *Paradise Lost*, also depicted the grim conditions of the criminal classes (the poor) of London. To the rich, the poor were a different race. Samuel Wilberforce preached in 1844:

---

[1] The discovery (July 2015) of annotated copies of the magazine *All the Year Round*, edited by Dickens, shows that he was the author of passionate articles on the mistreatment of the poor. His attack on the *demented disciples who push arithmetic and political economy beyond all bounds of sense* has some resonance today.

[2] *The Guardian*, 4 February 2012.

We look ... every Sunday at our well-filled churches, and we forget, for the moment, in the presence of those we see, the multitudes we see not; whose misery, as well as sin, whose want of room, want of clothes, indolence, neglect or utter wretchedness, are shutting out from our fellowship, and severing from civilisation and religion ... In all our great towns, thin walls separate luxury from starvation. The two classes live in absolute ignorance of each other: there are no points of contact between them ... selfish respectability degrades one set, whilst misery and recklessness, which soon turn to vice and wickedness, weigh down the other.[1]

Slums of London, Gustav Doré

In 1820, the legislation governing poverty in England and Wales was still the 1601 Poor Law. Under this law, *charitable relief* (compare our use of the word in *brotherly love, relief and truth*) was administered by the parish in which an applicant could claim rights: by residence, birth, marriage or apprenticeship, etc. Such relief, which might include food and clothing as well as money, was known as *outdoor relief*.

The cost of such relief was levied on wealthy, and usually unwilling, households and that cost increased dramatically in the first half of the industrial revolution. The wealthy sought to reduce the tax by arguing that relief should not be given to the 'undeserving poor'. They argued that poverty was a matter of bad habits: drinking, gambling and idleness. To mollify the wealthy, the 1834 Poor Law Amendment Act sought to stop outdoor relief, directing that the helpless poor should be sent to what became known as the workhouse, where conditions were made so miserable that only the desperate poor would seek relief.

The word *workhouse* induced fear even in my grandmother, and she died in 1971. While some workhouses were properly operated, many starved their inmates to death. Joshua Hobson's 1848 report on the Huddersfield workhouse said:

---

[1] Bishop Samuel Wilberforce, *Charge*, 1844. Known as 'Soapy Sam', the Bishop was the son of the great anti-slavery reformer, William Wilberforce.

... that the sick poor have been most shamefully neglected; that they have been and still are devoid of the necessary articles of clothing and bedding; that they have been suffered to remain for weeks at a time in the most filthy and disgusting state; that patients have been allowed to remain for nine weeks together without change of linen or of bed clothing; that beds in which patients suffering in typhus have died, one after another, have been again and again and repeatedly used for fresh patients, without any change or attempt at purification; that the said beds were only bags of straw and shavings, for the most part laid on the floor, and that the whole swarmed with lice ...[1]

I have cut short this description which goes on in the same horrifying vein. Huddersfield was not the only example of such evils. After the 1834 Amendment, there was a reduction in the number of able-bodied men seeking relief, if only because the workhouse was an effective deterrent.[2] In practice, outdoor relief continued, based upon the recognition that few of the poor were really undeserving and that poverty had always threatened a large percentage of the population. For example, during the banking crisis of 1796/7, when the land bubble burst and the Bank of England was forced to suspend the exchange of gold for banknotes, 40% of households in the village of Ardleigh in Essex were pauperised. King suggests:

... that up to one-third of any birth cohort from the early 18th century onwards would expect to come into contact with the poor law at some point ...[3]

Social unrest

Nearing the end of the 18th century, people had become disenchanted with government and with the frauds and dishonesties of the electoral system. The 1789 French Revolution came initially as an inspiration to almost everyone. William Wordsworth described his excitement in the *Prelude:*

Oh! pleasant exercise of hope and joy!
For mighty were the auxiliars which then stood
Upon our side, we who were strong in love!
Bliss was it in that dawn to be alive,
But to be young was very heaven!

Richard Price, a member of the Royal Society who died just two years after the start of the revolution, was also inspired by the events in France:

---

[1] http://www.victorianweb.org/history/poorlaw/hudders.html.

[2] Karel Williams has argued for a more positive view of the 1834 *Amendment*, arguing that it offered at least a safety net for the many in need during the immense changes in society.

[3] Local research indicates 38% of households received poor relief in Braintree in 1821 and 40% in Odiham, Hampshire in 1800.

Why are the nations of the world so patient under despotism? Why do they crouch to tyrants, or submit to be treated as if they were a herd of cattle? Enlighten them and you will elevate them. Shew them they are men and they will act like men. Give them just ideas of civil government and let them know that it is an expedient for gaining protection against injury and defending their rights, and it will be impossible for them to submit to governments [which are] *little better than contrivances for enabling the few to oppress the many.*[1]

Thomas Paine, who had motivated the war of independence in America, now supported the revolution in France with his *Rights of Man* (1791) and the government of the day, led by Pitt the Younger, became worried. The response was legislation, not to help the poor but to enable force to be used against any signs of revolution in England. 1792 became known as the *annus mirabilis* of radicalism, a year in which George III found it necessary to issue a Royal Proclamation *Against Seditious Writings and Publications.*

Famously in 1799, Pitt brought in the Unlawful Societies Act *for the more effectual suppression of societies established for seditious and treasonable purposes.* The Act called for a list of names, occupations and addresses of all lodge members to be sent annually to the Justices of the Peace[2] and, as Glyn Jarrett has pointed out, it must have had an impact on the membership of Freemasonry. It is not easy to isolate that impact but the experience of the London Corresponding Society (LCS) is indicative.

LCS was founded by a shoemaker, Thomas Hardy, who was much influenced by Thomas Paine's *Rights of Man.* Its membership consisted mainly of those disenfranchised by the electoral process, and at its peak LCS may have had 80,000 members. In 1794, the leaders of LCS and of other groups who had joined together to seek parliamentary reform, were indicted for high treason. Thirteen were indicted and three were sent for trial. All three were acquitted, but the members were seriously frightened. LCS never recovered.

Mechanisation and its effects

Our brethren faced alarming disruption in their working lives, a constant fear of poverty, poor working conditions and a reduction in wages. Attempts to resist in ways quite normal today, such as public meetings or strike action, were put down, frequently in a brutal manner. To take one example, the productivity of wheat farming consistently increased over the period and, with an oversupply of labour, wages were reduced. This led to the formation in 1832 of the Friendly Society of Agricultural Labourers who refused work for less than ten shillings a week. Wages had already been reduced to seven shillings and they were facing a further reduction to six. The men met at Tolpuddle in Dorset.

---

[1] Price.

[2] The Act was not repealed until 1967 although it had been dead letter for some time.

A local landowner invoked the Unlawful Oaths Act 1797, which prohibited people from swearing oaths to each other[1] and which had been designed to prevent mutinies such as those at Spithead and the Nore. James Brine, James Hammett, George and James Loveless and Thomas and John Standfield were found guilty and sentenced to transportation to Australia. Happily 800,000 signatures meant that in 1836 the Tolpuddle Martyrs returned. Loveless wrote:

> *God is our guide! from field, from wave,*
> *From plough, from anvil, and from loom;*
> *We come, our country's rights to save,*
> *And speak a tyrant faction's doom:*
> *We raise the watch-word liberty;*
> *We will, we will, we will be free!* [2]

Attempts to prevent the introduction of mechanisation and its inevitable effect on wages were as useless in 1832 as they had been earlier under the leadership of Ned Ludd, General of the Army of Redressers. The Luddites had sought to prevent the installation of power looms and frames in the wool and cotton trades. With the 1812 Destruction of Stocking Frames Act, their protest incurred the death penalty.

No radical himself, Byron was one of the few who spoke out against the 1812 Destruction of Stocking Frames Act and the repression of the working men who sought to call attention to their plight. In the House of Lords he said: *When a proposal is made to emancipate or relieve, you hesitate, you deliberate for years, you temporise and tamper with the minds of men; but a death bill must be passed off hand without a thought of consequences.*

The real Ned, if he ever existed, was long dead[3] but one of the many letters written over his name read:

> *… we won't only pray but we will fight, the Red Coats shall know when proper time's come, we will never lay down our arms till the House of Commons passes an act to put down all the machinery hurtfull to the commonality and repeal that to Frame Breakers – but petition no more, and that won't do, fighting must.*

The first half of the 19th century came closer to revolution than any time since the 1642 civil war:

---

[1] This Act is distinct from the Unlawful Societies Act of 1799 although both had a similar purpose.

[2] *Victims of Whiggery*, 1837 pamphlet, reported in *The Uses of Poetry*, Denys Thompson, Cambridge University Press, 1978.

[3] There was a character of the same name around 1779 in Leicester who is said to have broken stocking frames. He may or may not have existed.

1816   *Spa Fields* Islington, seeking electoral reform and relief from hardship.

1817   *Pentrich March,* against unemployment and food prices.

1819   *Peterloo Massacre,* a murderous reaction to a Manchester pro-reform meeting by 750 cavalry, 600 infantry, two six-pounder guns and 400 special constables. 500 were killed, women seemingly targeted.

1820   *Cato Street Conspiracy,* an attempt to form a radical government by blowing up the Cabinet.

1820   *Swing Riots,* agricultural workers destroying threshing machines, led by the fictitious Captain Swing.

1831   *Reform Bill Riots,* against rejection of the Reform Bill in the Lords.

1838   *Chartists,* seeking the vote for every man over 21, with secret ballots.

Political reform

From 1789 to 1914, France experienced four dictatorships, three republics, two monarchies and two empires. Fortunately for Britain, more enlightened Tory and Whig governments eventually enacted a succession of measures against entrenched interests. This reduced the pressure driving unrest and also enabled the next phase of the industrial revolution. In time, far too long a time, legislation achieved everything that the French Revolution had been fought for.

As Tory Home Secretary, Sir Robert Peel established the Metropolitan Police Force in 1829 with a thousand constables. In the same year, under the Duke of Wellington, the Tories brought in the Catholic Emancipation Act. The 1830–1834 Whig government brought in the great Reform Bill of 1832, abolishing most of the rotten boroughs and providing further enfranchisement. They also restricted the employment of children with the first of the Factory Acts in 1833, brought in the Slavery Abolition Act in the same year, and amended the Poor Laws in 1834. Prime Minster for a second time in 1841, Peel extended the Factory Acts and repealed the Corn Laws which had prevented the import of corn from abroad. The repeal divided the Tories and Peel resigned. The Whig government under Viscount Melbourne enacted Municipal Reform (1835) to establish local government elected by ratepayers and further reduce the rotten boroughs.

Nevertheless, to the ordinary man in the street and indeed our brethren, it must have seemed that their whole world was in flux: massive changes in the nature of work, movement from country to city, social unrest driving political change, extreme poverty combined with extreme wealth – and leaders with feet of clay.

Absence of leadership .

George IV (regent 1811, king 1820–1830) was obese, selfish, addicted to opium and oblivious to what was going on away from his court. Victory in the Napoleonic Wars had been gained without his involvement or, it seems, much interest. He was far more taken up with fashion; one of his favourites, Beau

Brummell (1778–1840), claimed to take five hours to dress and to have his boots polished with champagne.

1820, the year of George's coronation, was more notable in the public mind for his attempt to divorce his estranged wife, Queen Caroline, using a parliamentary bill to show that she was guilty of adultery. The debate was salaciously reported by the newspapers of the day, the King claiming that he and the Queen never had sex after the second night of the marriage and that he had *to conquer* [his] *aversion and overcome the disgust of her person.* In response, the Queen claimed that her husband was so drunk that he spent most of the wedding night in the fireplace, *where he fell, and where I left him.* The populace was firmly on the side of the Queen and celebrated in the streets when the bill was withdrawn.

Masonic leadership

The absence of leadership shown by the King was reflected in Freemasonry. Lodges can do quite well on their own, up to a point, but there is always a need for central leadership to administer, educate, inspire, reward and advise. During periods of great change, great leadership is required. Such leadership was desperately needed by lodges during this period, but was not forthcoming.

I will take three Provinces as examples and examine the involvement of their Provincial Grand Masters (PGMs) and the regularity of meetings of Provincial Grand Lodges (PGLs). Such meetings are not significant in themselves but their occurrence is a useful indication of the involvement and commitment of the PGM and the Provincial Executive.

The Essex experience

Keith Buck reports that in 1814 there were fifteen lodges in Essex. By 1832, there were four. In 1815, the PGM, William Wix, presided over what seems to have been a successful meeting of PGL, the minutes of which indicate a decision to hold future meetings twice a year. No further meetings occurred and in 1823 Wix resigned, leaving the county to live in Kent. His deputy left in the same year. The next PGM, William Honywood MP, was offered the position in 1824 but delayed acceptance until 1828 and then only when a deputation of Essex Masons invited him to make a decision on the spot. His installation as PGM never took place; a sick man, he died in 1831. His deputy had been appointed in 1827 but did very little either and moved away in 1832. In effect, there was no PGM between 1823 and 1836 when Rowland Alston was appointed, with one son as his deputy and another son as Provincial Grand Secretary, although the two did not overlap in office. Whether such nepotism was right or wrong, at least some leadership was available to a Province which had received none since 1815.

The Lincolnshire experience

The story of the Province of Lincolnshire is much the same. The Rev. William Peters had been PGM from 1792 until his death in 1814 but appears to have played no part in the life of the Province.[1] As William Dixon writes:

> *Lincolnshire provincial records show scarcely any attendance on the part of PGM.*

He was followed by William Henry White,[2] described by Dixon as:

> … *an entire stranger* [who was] *never installed, never attended a meeting and never interfered or took any interest whatever in the Province.*

As the Essex experience shows, this seems to have been common. Dixon again:

> [As] *was always the usual custom throughout the country; the provincial grandmaster's duties* [were] *deemed at an end with the appointment of an efficient deputy.*

That *efficient deputy*, the Rev. Matthew Barnett, had been a founder of the first lodge in Lincolnshire in 1787, and had been appointed Deputy PGM in 1793. He continued in office for another forty years by when he must have been getting on for 80. With the best will in the world, it is difficult to conceive how anyone at an advanced age, born before the industrial revolution took hold, could provide leadership in the middle of massive social and economic changes, entirely on his own. As Dr George Oliver reports:

> *Neither Bro. Peters nor Bro. White ever held a Provincial Lodge in my time.*[3]

That is true enough. For twenty-one years, 1793 to 1814, there were only seven meetings of PGL, and none after 1806. (Oliver was initiated in 1801.) From 1815 to 1826, a period of fourteen years, there were just three, all after White had left the county. No more meetings were held until 1832, when the next PGM, Charles

---

[1] He was also Deputy Provincial Grand Master of Nottinghamshire; held five or six 'livings' and was a popular portrait artist who charged, it is said, 80 guineas a portrait (about £8,000 today.)

[2] Not the Grand Secretary of the same name.

[3] From his oration after receiving a *testimonial & a silver cup and service of plate contributed to by Freemasons in all parts of the world* in 1844. *The Builder,* December 1919. Reported by masonicdictionary.com.

Tennyson d'Eyncourt,[1] was installed. He had been appointed six years earlier but, in keeping with the times, seemed in no hurry to get his installation organised. Thereafter, meetings were held almost annually from 1832 to 1859. How much of this was due to the PGM is an open question, for Dixon writes:

His speeches on the rare occasions when he presided at PGL were eloquent and interesting.

No doubt the Lincolnshire Masons would have preferred that his attendance was usual instead of rare and his speeches inspirational and motivational rather than eloquent and interesting. Oliver wrote of d'Eyncourt's management:

Masonry during this time declined so much there was scarcely an efficient Lodge in the province; the Barton, Grantham, Grimsby and Sleaford Lodges had entirely discontinued their meetings. Even the Lincoln and Boston Lodges were feeble.[2]

During this period, Lincolnshire experienced zero growth of lodges but the opportunity of new membership was there if there had been leadership to grasp it. Lincoln had a population of 7,000 in 1800. By 1900, the city had over 50,000 inhabitants. In 1828, Lincoln was lit by gas. In 1842, Clayton & Shuttleworth, iron founders, started making steam engines. The railway arrived in 1846.

The Sussex experience

The Province of Sussex had managed to double its number of lodges between 1810 and 1830 and then lose all the gain in half that time. Its story is another of absentee landlords, the most obvious being the Duke of Richmond. For the whole of his tenure, he was abroad in Ireland, Brussels and Canada,[3] where he had been appointed Lieutenant Governor and where he died, having been bitten by a rabid fox. Even had he been active in the affairs of the Province, he may not have been of much use, being described as:

… buttoned up tight about affairs and scarcely communicative … Everything is done by interim secretaries.[4]

His successor, appointed in 1823 after another delay of four years, was his son[5] who held just one PGL meeting in 1827:

---

[1] A snob who added the last name to appear to be of noble blood. He also rebuilt his home to look like a castle. He sought and initially failed to establish a title for himself. His older brother was the father of the poet. Charles was suitably infuriated when the poet became Alfred, Lord Tennyson. He eventually succeeded in gaining a baronetcy.

[2] Oliver, quoted by Dixon.

[3] I estimate that it would take three weeks at best for the PGM to reach Sussex from Ontario.

[4] Halpenny. Entry by George F.G. Stanley, quoting Bishop Plessis, Archbishop of Québec.

[5] A brave soldier, severely wounded in 1814, (the musket ball in his chest was never removed) he was ADC to Wellington, MP Chichester 1812–1819, active in House of Lords, Privy Council 1830, Postmaster General 1830–1834, Lord Lieutenant of Sussex 1835–1860.

... [when] *it would appear that it was intended that the PGL should assemble triennially but, strange to say, no meeting was held for 27 years.*[1]

One of the Sussex deputies was living abroad due to ill-health and on his death, no replacement was made for nine years.

Figurehead or leader?

It is little wonder that so many lodges went under, even if private lodges did make valiant efforts, including the Angel Lodge who in 1834, their hundredth year, initiated James Webb, wonderfully described by Buck as:

> *... by repute the ugliest man in Brightlingsea* [and] *an indefatigable Mason. He ... was said to walk to Colchester and back for Lodge meetings, a round trip of twenty miles.*

Grand Lodge obviously saw the PGM as nothing more than a figurehead, which seems to contradict Kearsley's view that following the Union:

> *Provincial Grand Masters were now required to hold regular meetings at least once a year and to appoint officers.*

This did not happen and it would appear that Kearsley's description of the status of PGMs before the union – that they were *appointed in somewhat whimsical fashion* – continued, to the detriment of the Craft. It was clear that lodges in the Provinces wanted a leader, and individual lodges felt forced to take action when Provincial Grand Masterships were vacant, or when those appointed were absent, dilatory or plain bored. In Essex, the Angel Lodge and the Lodge of True Friendship tried to get things moving as did the Royal Clarence Lodge in Sussex. The short lived Doric Lodge in Lincolnshire sought to reduce the costs of Freemasonry to make it more available to working men, but suffered for its attempt.

The PGMs chosen by Grand Lodge may have been the great and good but this meant that the affairs of Freemasonry figured low in their priorities. Charles Tennyson d'Eyncourt was a professional politician: MP for Grimsby, 1818; for the pocket borough of Bletchingley in 1826; for Stamford in 1831, and then for the Metropolitan Borough of Lambeth in London, well away from Lincolnshire where he was PGM. Busy supporting constitutional and municipal reform, he aided Queen Caroline in the divorce proceedings, but still became a Privy Councillor and an Equerry to the King. He was high steward of Louth, Deputy Lieutenant of Lincolnshire, fellow of the Royal Society and a magistrate.

Dixon wrote of him:

> *... our Right Worshipful Brother would have made a most excellent Prov. G. Master had he, in the words of the Old Charge, 'been resolved against all politics' ...*

---

[1] Francis.

Contrast d'Eyncourt's record, as reported by Dixon, with that of Colonel James McQueen who, on becoming Deputy PGM of Sussex, showed that he had at least thought about leadership: *Let me crave your indulgent consideration on the difficulties that attend my position ... having sustained a lapse of twenty-seven years without assembling ... had it not been for the unceasing and zealous exertions of several energetic and worthy members of the Craft ... our Grand Lodge might have continued ... in comparative abeyance ... I stand before you a stranger, sensible of the difficulties which beset my path and desirous to the best of my ability zealously and impartially to carry out the duties of my office. The first step I have to take is, I fear, one that may lay me open to misconception, and an imputation of partiality, viz. the appointment of officers, as I deem it prudent to surround myself with brethren long known to me for their zeal, ... Let us consider this year as one of probation, in order that we may fairly relaunch our long-stranded Institution, unruffled by waves of anger or envy, and united in the strongest bonds of brotherly love ... and as we progress in... I shall be better able ... to select brethren from other Lodges.*

Very clearly, the job required much more time than d'Eyncourt was willing to give it and he was appointed simply because he was a friend of the Duke of Sussex.

The lack of leadership was not limited to Essex, Lincolnshire and Sussex.[1] Shelley was not given to understatement in either his life or his opinions but it is hard to entirely disagree with what he wrote just after the Peterloo Massacre:

An old, mad, blind, despised, and dying king,
Princes, the dregs of their dull race, who flow,
Through public scorn ... [2]

The Duke of Sussex

During the Grand Mastership of the Duke of Sussex, more than 200 lodges in England were lost. The Duke was a complex and even contradictory character. The sixth son and ninth child of King George III, his early adult years were spent abroad. Indeed, until 1806 he was rarely in England and it was in Rome in 1792 that he met and married Lady Augusta Murray. Just before their first son was born, the King declared their marriage void.[3] In 1831, after Lady Murray had died, he married Lady Cecilia who was never recognised as the Duchess, although achieving some recognition later by Queen Victoria.

Money was difficult. The Duke espoused liberal political views which did not please his father nor the later King William IV, and he did not receive the well-

---

[1] According to Armstrong, Sir John Grey Egerton, PGM of Cheshire 1810-1825, had also *greatly neglected his duties*.

[2] Poem entitled *1819*.

[3] Under *The Royal Marriages Act*, 1772, the King could veto all Royal marriages until the royal person reached the age of 25. The act was brought in because William, Duke of Gloucester and Henry, Duke of Cumberland married commoners.

paid sinecures Royal Princes normally held.[1] Fulford reports the Duke's excursion to Howick from Newcastle to lay the foundation stone of a new library, at a time when there was little canvassing except during elections:

… the massive figure of the Duke of Sussex, standing up in his carriage beaming and bowing as he drove through a blaze of blue and orange,[2] scandalised and frightened the Tories who were sourly peeping at him out of their windows.[3]

When the 1832 Reform Bill appeared to be in danger in the House of Lords due to Tory opposition, he went to see King William IV[4] at Windsor to argue that the necessary number of Whig peers be created to ensure the bill's passage.[5] The King was furious and refused to see the Duke again.[6] For this and for his marriages, he was seen as the least important of the Royal Family, which must have been hurtful. This was a great pity because the Duke was interested in science and the arts. President of both the Royal Society and the Society of Arts,[7] he had a library of fifty thousand books and laid the foundation stone of the University of London. He enjoyed singing and amazed a lady who congratulated

---

[1] He received just the £18,000 government grant, equivalent to about £2 million today. Under William IV, he was made a Ranger of a Royal Park but he fell out with that King also.

[2] The Whig (more commonly buff) and Hanoverian colours.

[3] Gareth Davies provides a more detailed account of the event, the booze-up of the century.

[4] William IV, third son of George III, who never expected to become king, gets a bad press. He was a Freemason and he also saw active service in the Navy, eventually retiring as a Rear Admiral under Nelson. William was easy-going and informal, even ready to use public transport. He offered the government the use of Buckingham Palace when the Houses of Parliament were burned down. Against all this, he opposed the abolition of the slave trade.

[5] In the end, Lord Grey and Robert Peel, from opposing parties, combined to get the bill passed.

[6] The disagreement was patched up later but further disagreements occurred. For example, King William IV refused to appear in the Lords to give his consent in person to the 1834 Reform Bill, only to discover later that the Duke did appear and in full fig, complete with the Star of the Garter.

[7] Which became the *Royal Society for the encouragement of Arts, Manufactures and Commerce* in 1908.

him on his voice, saying: *I have the most wonderful voice that was ever heard – three octaves.*[1]

He stood *6 foot 3 inches tall and was corpulent by any standards.*[2] He suffered from asthma for the early part of his life and later developed cataracts which could not be operated on until they entirely covered his eyes. The operation was a new process, dangerous but successful. Towards his end, he suffered from a bacterial infection of the skin, a condition similar to cellulitis. He tried to treat it by living on turtle soup and orange ices but died in his bed in 1843. At his own request, he was buried in Kensal Green cemetery, not with the Royal Family at Windsor. His second wife was later buried beside him.

Fulford provides an epitaph that there ... *was laid the finest product of the Whig tradition.* Ever ready to lend his name to philanthropic ventures, it was only in the latter part of his life that his commitment to the Whig cause finally saw success. Fulford writes:

> *The years from 1830 to 1843, in which he lived to enjoy his triumph, made some amends for a life which would otherwise have been at best curious and in all probability futile.*

His leadership

Described in contradictory terms as tolerant, liberal, intellectual, autocratic, hands-on, vain, eccentric and wayward, a contemporary source wrote of him:

> *A man of superior talents, [it] would overstate his abilities to say he is a first rate man ... intellectual resources above mediocrity ... speeches remarkable for the ardent love of liberty ... excels at putting obvious truths into popular form ... makes his views as clear to others as they are to his own mind ... no one yet mistook the drift of his argument.*[3]

The picture arises of someone bright enough but not brilliant, self-opinionated, perhaps uncreative, pompous and a poor listener with a liberal conscience. He obviously liked to be different. Sandbach describes him as having a:

> ... *progressive inegalitarian outlook ... a highly developed sense of his own position ... a liking for autocratic power, wielded with a firm but generally courteous hand.*

Masonic writing about Royal Masons all too easily becomes hagiography. The truth about the Duke seems to be that, despite his success in forcing through the Union with his brother, Prince Edward, Duke of Kent and Strathearn, he lacked day-to-day leadership skills, being given to over-attention to detail and the use of edicts which often, if not usually, rebounded on him. His time was divided among

---

[1] Fulford.

[2] Bereseiner.

[3] Sandbach.

his many interests and Freemasonry was not the most important of them. Indeed, he seemed not to take it seriously. When the idea arose of inviting Robert Owen, the social reformer and founder of the cooperative movement, to become a Freemason, the Duke replied:

> *No, by all that is good, were he to witness our ceremonies he would make us all to appear fools. His subjects are of a character too serious and extended for him to be occupied with our trifling amusements.*[1]

His priorities

Within Freemasonry, he allowed himself to be caught up in minor matters, for example the design of a jewel for the stewards of the Boys' and Girls' Institutions. Instead of delegating, he became personally involved in a committee to revise the RA ritual which, predictably perhaps, came to little. Indeed, Kearsley's analysis of the priorities of Grand Lodge post-Union seems to indicate it had little awareness of the world outside Freemasonry. Re-decorating lodge rooms, renumbering lodges, agreeing rank and regalia and arranging a new coat of arms, all these were no doubt desirable but they do smack of fiddling while Rome burned.

Kearsley argues that charity jewels were developed during his Grand Mastership but unfortunately the charities were the pivot of the conflict between the Duke and Robert Crucefix. Some commentators take the view that he opposed Crucefix's creation of the *Asylum for Aged and Decayed Freemasons* because he had not initiated it, but Kearsley writes:

> *The Duke felt that it would encourage men to join Freemasonry for the charity they would get out of it … He thus strongly opposed the idea.*

The Duke may have been right that his scheme of annuities would have been more effective than spending on a building, but creating a win/lose is always a bad way to manage. Facilitating an agreement would surely have been his best contribution. Seeking relief for brethren and for distressed men and women outside Freemasonry would have focused the order on what was happening in society and given it a relevance it clearly lacked.

The Duke surely did not need the continued and silly squabbles between Antients and Moderns but he did not handle these with any tact. His autocratic response to the would-be Antient rebels led to the formation of the breakaway Grand Lodge of Wigan, which sought to keep alive the Antients' ceremonies until as late as 1913. Neglect on the part of yet another Provincial Grand Master was a major part of the cause.[2]

---

[1] Ridley.

[2] Harrison.

24

Kearsley argues that the Duke was not always autocratic and quotes his 1813 letter to the Count Jacob Pontusson de la Gardie: *One must advance stepwise and without wronging the individuals; that is the landscape I have created for my moral and political life.* However, given the context that Belton provides, the letter concerns another of the Duke's whimsical ideas, to get English Masons to adopt the Swedish system. The letter is an attempt to excuse himself for his delay in implementing the system.

What brethren need in times of great change, then as now, is help in understanding what is happening and advice on what to do about it. In the Duke's situation, more openness and explanation in decision-making was required. The need for a different approach to leadership was clearly seen in the popularity of Crucefix's *Freemasons' Quarterly Review.* That publication, much to the Duke's displeasure, provided a speedy account of what went on in Grand Lodge, publicised the activities of those orders beyond the Craft, and set out to arouse debate concerning decisions of the Masonic hierarchy.

A child of his time

Bernard Cornwell's historical novels[1] are always a good read but he does give his heroes anachronistic social opinions and motivations. In the same vein, I may be justly accused of anachronism in arguing that the Duke's leadership style was inappropriate. Autocracy was no doubt the normal mode of behaviour at court and the Duke was no different from any other royal personage but autocratic commands are usually dysfunctional, especially when they are transmitted through failing local management.

As Bro. James puts it in his 1962 Prestonian Lecture:

> *The Duke was getting old, his illnesses were prolonged and painful, ... his veteran advisers had all passed away ... No wonder he became ill-tempered. The Grand Master was a changed man; he was hectoring, unjust, despotic; it was not a pleasant sight. Though many fine things were said of him at his passing, his demise brought relief to the Fraternity.*

Those who cannot remember the past are condemned to repeat it.[2]

In this chapter, I have described the social, economic and legislative changes that affected our order in the first part of the industrial revolution, a time which might have turned bloody in Britain, as it did in France. Its impact upon our order was almost fatal. In the 19th century, our brethren were faced with:

---

[1] In addition to his acclaimed *Sharpe* novels, I highly recommend his Arthurian trilogy: *The Winter King, The Enemy of God* and *Excalibur.*

[2] George Santayana, *Reason in Common Sense*, first published 1905.

- Mechanisation causing loss of skilled trade livelihoods that in many cases went back for generations.
- A change in the nature of work from owner/tradesman to employee with a loss of self-respect and status.
- Rapid urbanisation bringing a poor quality of life in near-slum conditions.
- A rash of jobs that were often temporary as companies grew, moved, were taken over or went out of business.
- A reduction of earnings and a constant fear of the workhouse, with the poor seen as criminals.
- An increasing gap between rich and poor; the poor being kept out of sight and protest harshly put down.
- Legislation against joint action by workers trying to protect themselves.
- Social unrest, repression and a fear of revolution.

All this occurred with an almost complete lack of leadership at all levels. In the 1800s, Freemasonry walked blindfold into a perfect storm. Recovery did take place but only as a fortunate accident. We are about to find that history has repeated itself and it should be unnecessary to state that we cannot rely on serendipity again.

Could something have been done?

There was an enormous gap between rich and poor during the 1800s, as now, and many senior brethren were among the rich, including some I have mentioned. Charles Tennyson d'Eyncourt was the sole beneficiary of his father's legacy of 2,000 acres. The 5th Duke of Richmond owned Richmond House in Whitehall, Goodwood House in Sussex and inherited vast estates in Scotland.[1] The 'wealthy' William Wix lived in Lloyds House on Bishops Down near Tunbridge Wells, a house worth perhaps about £5 million today.

Such wealth was not limitless, but private lodges could have been supported – with information, advice and encouragement if not money – certainly not left to their own devices. Something could have been done, should have been done, but little was done. It seems that the leadership was isolated from the situation of the ordinary Mason, perhaps because of their wealth, and the membership that had sustained Freemasonry at least since the 1780s just disappeared. It looked as if Freemasonry had come to an end.

---

[1] The third and fourth Dukes had left large debts.

Freemasonry and social Change: 1850–1950

Recovery

What kept our order going was the dedication of the ordinary Mason and what eventually saved it was the advent of a new source of membership which arose around 1850. The middle-class identity, *a clearly defined consciousness based upon the notions of respectability and self-help* as Callum Brown puts it, found an echo in the ideals of Masonry. Then in 1874, the popular Albert Edward, Prince of Wales, became Grand Master and made Freemasonry fashionable. In 1882, Lord Brooke, later the Earl of Warwick, became Provincial Grand Master of Essex. Buck writes:

> Lord Brooke inspired the Province with … vigour and élan and annual meetings often became gay social occasions much enjoyed by the brethren and their ladies.

Inspire is a good word to hear attributed to a leader.

The Victorian middle class

To understand the middle class and its disappearance in modern times is to understand our membership, why we have lost so much of it and why we have such difficulty in replacing it. It may often get a bad press but the Victorian period was not only the most innovative technological time in British history, it also made startling improvements in literacy, medicine, education, democracy and the press. For many people, Victorian buildings still represent the best of public architecture. Donna Loftus writes of:

> … the massive expansion of local government and the centralised state, providing occupations for a vast strata of civil servants, teachers, doctors, lawyers and government officials as well as the clerks and assistants which helped these institutions and services to operate.

The white-collar worker became increasingly valued.

> Between 1881 and 1911 the number of doctors doubled, the number of government clerks trebled and there were five times as many scientists. Most impressive perhaps was the increase in the number of clerical and support jobs – for every new solicitor or barrister there were two new legal clerks …[1]

Suburbia

The Victorian middle class carved out specific areas for their lives, progressively moving away from the city centre into suburbia. The middle class suburban villa

---

[1] Gunn & Bell.

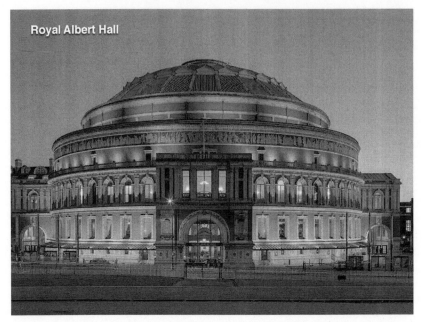

Royal Albert Hall

was not just a place to eat and sleep; the historian, Francis Thompson, writing of the houses built increasingly from the 1860s, says that it was only there that:

> ... the family could distance itself from the outside world in its own private fortress behind its own garden fence and privet hedge and yet could make a show of outward appearances that was sure to be noticed by the neighbours, that the suburban lifestyle of individual domesticity and group-monitored respectability could take hold.

The Victorian villa housed the middle-class values of thrift, respectability, responsibility and self-reliance and the railways took these values further and further afield. Commuting is not a 20th-century invention. The railways grew rapidly from their inception in 1825. By 1840 there were nearly 1,500 miles of track and by 1860 the mileage had increased to over 9,000. There was steady growth through to the peak mileage of 20,500 miles in 1927, after which the railways began to decline, almost fatally destroyed by Beeching's amateurish and egotistical use of statistics in the 1950s.

Civic involvement and aspirations

The middle class even had disposable income. The concerns and priorities of Dr John Heaton, who moved into a Leeds suburban villa in 1856 make fascinating reading. He wrote in his diary[1] of the home improvements he undertook and of the musical evenings, children's parties and family excursions that took place. His relationship with his wife was marked by a loving domesticity but much of Heaton's time was spent outside the home, not only at work but also in civic improvement. He was a member of both the Yorkshire Education Board and the Leeds School Board and President of the Leeds Philosophical and Literary Society. He belonged to the Leeds Conversation Club and the Leeds Improvement Society, the latter campaigning for a College of Science and for the building of a Town Hall. He speaks of the achievement of the Leeds Art Gallery with some pride.

In the 1880s, the entire income of a working-class family would be about £78 per year. The male earner in families who could afford to be neighbours of the Heatons had an income of more than three times that and their income was increasing year on year. The Victorian middle class had money for cultural and aesthetic aspirations which, in their minds, went along with moral education.

Part of the Victorian middle class self-image was being seen as a professional person and new professional bodies appeared around this time: the Society of Teachers[2] in 1846, the Institute of Actuaries[3] in 1848, the Chartered Banker Institute in 1875, the Institute of Chemistry[4] in 1877 and the Institute of Chartered Accountants[5] in 1880. Most of these bodies gained a Royal Charter soon after their foundation. Membership, especially of a Royal body, conferred respectability and status and for many who were not members of a profession, and for some who were, Freemasonry achieved a similar aim.

> Popular at the time was the writing of Samuel Smiles, particularly his book, *Self Help.*
>> *The spirit of self-help is the root of all genuine growth in the individual ...*
> Smiles expresses great admiration for character and argues that:
>> *Character consists in little acts, well and honourably performed; daily life being the quarry from which we build it up, and rough-hew the habits which form it ... Mind without heart, intelligence without conduct, cleverness without goodness, are powers in their way, but they may be powers only for mischief.*
> I have found no evidence that Samuel Smiles was a Freemason and it is unlikely that his writing affected the 19th century ritual books. The similarities between his work and the ritual are just evidence of the close accord between Victorian and Masonic values.

---

[1] Payne.

[2] Royal Charter 1849, now the *College of Teachers.*

[3] Royal Charter 1884.

[4] Royal Charter 1885.

[5] Founded by Royal Charter 1880.

Philanthropy

Although a later and more cynical age has cast doubt on the motivations of Victorian philanthropy, what cannot be doubted is its extent. It has been said that the income of the London charities alone amounted to over £2 million in 1874 and exceeded £3 million by 1893 (today £320 million), a figure that represented fully one-third of the amount spent by the *Poor Law* authorities. Melvyn Bragg has reported that the amount contributed to charities in aid of the poor exceeded government expenditure on what is today known as welfare. Such charity work was overwhelmingly Christian. Bragg writes:

> *The theory that poverty is the result of a lack of will and virtue, that indolence and sluttishness and drunkenness and crime render you undeserving of help until you take the path of reform through religion is now, in most of the English-speaking world, spoken of, if at all, with a shake of the head or with contempt for those misguided Victorian days.* [This] *does not detract from the determination and the faith of those women who with broom, scrubbing brush and pail and the King James Bible, went into the sewers of society on a mission to save souls by way of mending and redirecting ruined lives.*

Victorian philanthropy took many guises. From 1841, the Metropolitan Association for Improving the Dwellings of the Industrious Classes sought to build homes for the poor. In what it called *five percent philanthropy*, the movement asked wealthy donors to invest money at a below-market rate of return, and they did.

The Cooperative Movement, almost destroyed by incompetence and greed in 2011, started in Rochdale, Lancashire in 1844. Angela Burdett-Coutts, advised by Charles Dickens, created the Columbia Market in 1869. She also funded churches, schools, housing schemes and even drinking fountains for dogs. John Passmore Edwards, Liberal MP and editor of *The London Echo*, was active in movements for the abolition of capital punishment, the suppression of the opium trade and political reform. He endowed the Whitechapel Art Gallery and the London School of Economics and Political Science as well as twenty-four libraries around London and in Cornwall where he was born.

Later Victorian employers built their own model (meaning *ideal*) villages to house their workers: Bournville, Birmingham (1893) was built by the Quaker Cadbury brothers; Port Sunlight in the Wirral (1899) built by the Congregationalist William Lever. The Cadbury brothers created a pensions scheme, a workers committee and an employee medical service while William Lever provided an open-air swimming pool, an art gallery, schools, a concert hall and allotments.

The total amount donated to charity in 2011/12 is estimated at £9.3 billion; a £2.3 billion decrease compared with the previous year in real terms. In £sterling there is more charitable giving today than in Victorian times, but then Britain today is immeasurably richer and there are a lot more people. If one makes allowance for inflation, population and GDP, the Victorians seem to have been around twenty times more philanthropic than people are today.

The salaried middle class

While members of the early Victorian middle class had largely consisted of what we might today call the *upper* middle class, as time went on the label of *middle class* became associated more with the salaried white-collar workers who followed their predecessors out, and further out, into the suburbs. They worked harder for their status, leaving at home not ladies managing servants, but full-time housewives.

House prices actually fell in the 1920s and 1930s; a typical semi-detached in Middlesex cost about £700; one further out no more than £450. In 1935, mortgage repayments would have been 25% of income for a clerk like Bob Harper *(right)*, first Master of my mother lodge.

In the 1920s, the long frock coat of the Victorian period gave way to the morning suit, worn by many Masons today, but while the financial standing of salaried middle class men would have in no way equalled that of Dr Heaton, their values were much the same. They were courteous and civil but reserved. Etiquette, manners and dress mattered a great deal.

Moral rectitude was important and moral respectability even more so: one not only had to be good but be seen to be good. Frugality and temperance were newer virtues as were limitations on what could be discussed in polite company: no politics, religion or money, and definitely no sex.

The sociable 1930s

The Caravan Club reached its pre-war peak in 1939 when 201 outfits turned up for the National Rally in Northampton. Cycling clubs date from the 1890s but bicycles were recognisably modern by the 1930s. Victor Silvester won the first World Ballroom Dancing Championship in 1922. Contract Bridge dates from the 1920s.

In the 1920s and 1930s, a more sociable middle class appeared, still holding to the same virtues but more relaxed about them. Social histories of the period talk of regular whist drives, dances and musical activities organised by the local residents' association. There were tennis, cricket, cycling, amateur dramatic and even motor clubs in addition to activities based on the many different church denominations.

Measured in terms of baptisms per 1000 live births, the Church of England baptism rate makes an allowance for changes in population and birth rate and is thus a useful measure of minimal religiosity: attendance at church at least for

■ Baptisms per thousand live births

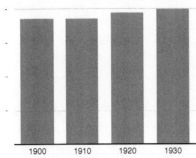

hatches, matches and dispatches. 70% of live births were baptised in the 1930s, a slight increase in religiosity over 1900. Religious belief was still the norm and children still went to Sunday School. Middle-class men would have responded immediately to the charge after initiation:

As an individual, I would further recommend the practice of every domestic as well as public virtue. Let prudence direct you, temperance chasten you, fortitude support you and justice be the guide of all your actions.

Very middle-class sentiments, in fact. Temperance in Victorian times commonly referred to abstinence from alcohol, although this is not its root meaning nor its meaning in the four cardinal virtues as I will show later.[1]

The true gentleman

Cardinal Newman's description of the true gentleman in his 1852 book, *The Idea of a University*, captured at least the self-image of the Victorian male and may have partly created it. He writes that the true gentleman:

… is tender towards the bashful, gentle towards the distant, and merciful towards the absurd; he can recollect to whom he is speaking; he guards against unseasonable allusions, or topics which may irritate; he is seldom prominent in conversation, and never wearisome. He makes light of favours while he does them, and seems to be receiving when he is conferring.

He never speaks of himself except when compelled, never defends himself by a mere retort. He has no ears for slander or gossip … and interprets every thing for the best. He is never mean or little in his disputes, never takes unfair advantage, never mistakes personalities or sharp sayings for arguments … He has too much good sense to be affronted at insults, he is too well employed to remember injuries, and too indolent to bear malice.

Such a description would have fitted very nicely (in the sense of that word meaning *exact*) with the self-image of the Victorian, Edwardian and even later Freemason. It would not have fitted many men in the society that followed.

---

[1] Temperance movements against alcohol stem from the 1820s. The wonderfully named Band of Hope started work in 1833. Pete Corrigan and his Band of Hope still play superb Dixieland jazz at the Queens Theatre in Hornchurch, Essex, UK. I don't think they are teetotal.

Now gone away

As a recruitment source, the middle class could not have been bettered. By 1911, there were 900,000 white-collar workers and by 1951, two and a half million, increasing from 5% to 11% of the workforce. There were few attacks on the Craft and, before WWII, Freemasons appeared in public, their activities being publicised in newspapers. Freemasonry was seen as part of the establishment and middle-class men aligned themselves with it for that very reason. We must now recognise that this middle class has largely gone away.

Rock 'n' roll may be partly to blame. Both Elvis Presley's *That's all right, Mama* and Bill Haley's *Rock Around the Clock* were released in 1954 even if the 1956 film of the same name had greater impact. In 1955, the top four singles were recorded by Tennessee Ernie Ford (*Sixteen Tons*), Slim Whitman (*Rose Marie*), Ruby Murray (*Softly Softly*) and Eddie Calvert, the man with the golden trumpet (*Cherry Pink and Apple Blossom White*), whose other number one, *Oh Mein Papa*, had been released a year earlier. In 1963, the first and second in the top ten for the year were from the Beatles (*She Loves You* and *From Me to You*) and the third and fourth from Gerry & the Pacemakers (*How Do You Do* and *I Like It*). The sixth was Gerry again with *You'll Never Walk Alone*, which really should be a Masonic anthem.

Freemasonry and social change: overview 1950–present

In 1950, the Grand Master was probably murdered. Edward William Spencer Cavendish, 10th Duke of Devonshire, died of a heart attack at age 55 while being treated by John Bodkin Adams, a probable serial killer.[1] The next Grand Master, Roger Lumley, 11th Earl of Scarbrough, took the stage with little preparation.

History repeats

The similarities between the uncertainties of the 1820s and of today are uncanny.

1820s' uncertainties	Today's uncertainties
Mechanisation causing loss of skilled trade livelihoods that in many cases went back for generations.	Downsizing, increased use of IT, the end of the clerical worker. Management redundancies.
Change in the nature of work from owner/tradesman to employee with a loss of self-respect and status.	The end of middle class careers, managerialism, increase in women entering the workforce.
A rapid urbanisation bringing a poorer quality of life with the ever present risk of descent into the slums.	Greater commuting distances, longer hours without pay, working families needing benefits, food banks.
A rash of jobs that were often temporary as companies grew, moved or went under.	1.3 million people underemployed. Zero-hours contracts, part-time work, greater 'self-employment'.
Uncertainty and reduction of earnings with a fear of the workhouse; the poor seen as criminals.	Reduction in benefits, worsening terms and conditions. Poor as 'scroungers'. Fear of redundancy. End of company pensions.
Increasing gap between rich and poor. The poor out of sight with protests being harshly put down.	Increasing gap between rich and poor. Unions no longer a force to protect working people.
Social unrest, civil disobedience and fear of revolution. legislation against joint action.	Attacks on trades union, reduction of employment protection, protest marches.

The second half of this period has brought about conditions oddly reminiscent of the pre-Victorian era. Just as then, pay levels for the ordinary folk in the UK declined – by nearly 9% in real terms 2010–2014 with real wages falling every year following the banking crisis. One in five workers had taken a pay cut.[2] In 2014, 1.3 million people were in part-time jobs but needed full-time work and 1.4 million people were on zero-hours contracts, mostly younger workers.[3] 65% of employees said that the amount of work they were expected to do had increased. 34% said that they were expected to work unpaid overtime.[4] As in the 1800s, many Freemasons worked longer hours for less money in fear of losing their jobs.

---

[1] More than 160 of Adams' patients died in suspicious circumstances.

[2] 2014 *British Social Attitudes Survey*.

[3] The UK Government Office for National Statistics reported that in 2105 such contracts were used by about 10% of all companies, a figure which rose to 50% in catering and retail.

[4] *YouGov*, 2014.

34

While the one-nation Toryism of the 1950s, and the social democracy of the 1960s and 1970s seemed to be leading towards a more egalitarian and caring state, from 1980 such decency was replaced by greed on the one hand and fear of poverty on the other. In the 1800s, an *aristocratic excess and swagger* caused a disgust of leadership. A similar disgust has been caused in later years by the discoveries of dishonesty within the finance industry, expenses fiddling and cash-for-access in parliament, sex crimes among media personalities and too many other sins against decency to mention. By 2000, respect for senior management had declined to an all time low. The establishment had shown that it could not be trusted. Life became harder edged and uncaring with fewer spiritual values.

Most of the men that we sought to recruit and retain had less time, less money, less energy and less security. Brethren could not commit *to regular attendance at the Lodge of Instruction* because they simply didn't know what demands their employers would put on them. These changes went along with other uncertainties resulting from changes in religious belief and the role of the sexes. Reversing the failure of leadership in 1820, it falls upon today's Masonic leadership to help our brethren through these changes.

Three phases

I shall consider the period from 1950 to the present in three phases. The first, *The end of rules*, concerns the flowering of social democracy and the primacy of the individual. From the mid-1950s to the 1970s, there was a rejection of the establishment which included almost every cow previously held sacred, including Freemasonry. It was a delayed reaction to the privations of WWII, occurring only when prosperity returned. When it did, the Prime Minister Harold Macmillan announced *You never had it so good!*

The second phase, *Show me the money*, was a reaction to the first and a partly successful attempt to turn back the clock. The title is from the 1996 film *Jerry Maguire*. Anything but one-nation Toryism, there was a meanness about the years from 1980. Its focus on money, an outcome of Thatcherism, was not an environment in which Freemasonry could flourish. Brotherly love, relief and truth do not fit with greed and self-interest.

These vices were not what Margaret Thatcher intended to create but they do typify the third phase, *The end of decency*, a classic example perhaps of the law of unintended consequences. If the idealism of the 1960s and 1970s seemed to be leading towards a more caring world, the counter-revolution from 1980 onwards, and particularly from 2000, produced the opposite and created a vacuum in the moral life. In these three phases lie the reasons for the decline in Freemasonry – but in the third phase an opportunity for its renaissance.

Phase 1 – The end of rules: 1950–1970

As Callum Brown has remarked:

> ... *the 1950s was in fact a deeply old-fashioned era, so old that it has often been described as the last Victorian decade.*

Intoxicating times

Good or bad, the main effect of this period was the loosening of the rules and structures that had governed Britain since the rise of the middle class in the 1850s. Some of this was deliberate, for example the introduction of social democracy as a result of the sacrifices made in WWII, and some of it was unforeseen, like rock 'n' roll. Looking back on this decade from 60 odd years on, when so many of our brethren had not even been born, it is important to emphasise what a dramatic change it was. Jazz had its earthy rhythms and young girls had long swooned over bobby soxers, but in rock 'n' roll there was not only a beat but a revolution. Its early lyrics at first expressed barely disguised sexual desire but its later lyrics became fused with the protest movement, gaining a powerful political content. Poetry had often been political, as we have seen in Wordsworth's early fascination with the French Revolution, but the poetry of *the old sheep of the Lake District*[1] was not driven by a pounding electric bass guitar.

To live through *the end of rules* was an intoxicating experience which gave hope for a new world, but it was not one in which an autocratic, structured, hierarchical and Victorian order like Freemasonry would thrive. Nevertheless, there were exciting dreams to be part of. Everywhere, everything held such promise of a better and fairer world. One might well quote Wordsworth again:

> *Bliss was it in that dawn to be alive, But to be young was very heaven!*

Globalisation at that time meant global friendship and understanding, not manufacturing companies chasing ever lower rates of pay. There was a revolution in values, a new emphasis on the primacy of the individual and an increase in individual freedoms. Above all, there was a rejection of the old establishment, of *the man* and of *law 'n' order*. There was a wave of frustration and even anger against what had gone before. Graffiti on the garden wall of a doctor's surgery near where I lived read *Smash the hierarchy!* in dark paint that took many years to fade.

A new order appeared in working life and control was rejected in favour of engagement of the spirit. Rank no longer implied knowledge, and the process known as organisational development (OD) sought to break down hierarchical decision-making and to build an organisational life fuelled by interpersonal trust

---

[1] As Rumpole fondly called him in John Mortimer's novels.

and collaboration. Part of this revolution was feminism which had stuttered earlier but now began to change relationships and the use of time.

Claiming their just desserts

You will see a state of prosperity such as we have never had in my lifetime – nor indeed in the history of this country. Indeed let us be frank about it – most of our people have never had it so good.[1]

Famously, this is Harold Macmillan, British Prime Minister from 1957 to 1963. *Supermac*, as he was dubbed, made full employment his aim as part of his one-nation Tory beliefs and the 1950s did indeed see economic improvement. Rationing ended in 1954 and there was a definite increase in the standard of living. Growth, which had begun around 1950, brought rising wages and near full employment; most people felt better off than ever before.

> Stemming from Disraeli, one-nation Toryism holds that one part of society cannot move forward at the expense of another and thus all members of a society have obligations to all other members. Special duties fall on the rich; indifference to the suffering of the people causes instability in society and makes revolution likely.

This economic success was based on overseas trade: earnings from exports and overseas investments. This produced strong consumer demand, but companies failed to make productivity and overseas marketing investments with the result that wage inflation took hold. However, while it lasted, Britain enjoyed more money, more choice, better housing as well as the new welfare state implemented after the war.

The working class had suffered privation ever since the depression in 1932, and now felt they deserved their piece of the action. Macmillan may have been a patrician Tory but, from 1931 to 1945, he was MP for Stockton-on-Tees, a depressed northern industrial and market town. Before the constituency was abolished, it served from 1961 to 1983 as the seat of Bill Rogers, one of the gang of four founders of the Social Democratic Party. Such a constituency was never to be important again.

Social democracy

At the beginning, as if the genie had been let out of the bottle, everything seemed ready to change and the politics of the time reflected that. Social democratic legislation had a new focus on the underclass, but it also removed behavioural constraints. Just as in the 1830s and 1840s when legislation was brought in to avoid social unrest (if a little late), so in the 1960s many of the causes and

---

[1] Quoted in *On this Day*, BBC, 20 July 2005.

President Johnson with Dr Martin Luther King at the signing of the Voting Rights Act 1965.

movements were assimilated into the mainstream. In the USA, Lyndon Johnson, President 1963–1969, managed to put through his *Great Society* legislation: an attack on poverty, ending segregation and extending civil rights, welfare and education as well as subsidies for the arts. In Britain, Harold Wilson (1964–1970 & 1974–1976, followed by Callaghan to 1979) legalised abortion, decriminalised homosexuality, abolished capital punishment, extended the Race Relations Act, and introduced equal pay legislation and the Employment Protection Act with statutory maternity leave.

The increase in individual freedoms was celebrated at events that have become legendary. The Summer of Love hit LA in 1967, the same year that the Beatles released *Sergeant Pepper's Lonely Hearts Club Band*. Their 1966 *Revolver* has been described as the distillation *of an LSD trip into a three-minute song*.[1] Woodstock 'happened' in 1969. The critic Charles Marowitz wrote of the 1968 London production of the rock musical, *Hair*:

> *Without Vietnam and the American repugnance to that war, the show would never have come into being. It is almost entirely nourished by the current generation's hatred of what its 'senior citizens' have allowed America to become.*

The twenty-year-long Vietnam war aroused widespread rejection of the military-industrial establishment. President Dwight Eisenhower (Supreme Commander of

---

[1] *Rolling Stone* magazine.

the Allied Forces in Europe aduring World War II) in his 1961 farewell address to the nation, said:

> *In the councils of government, we must guard against the acquisition of unwarranted influence, whether sought or unsought, by the military industrial complex. The potential for the disastrous rise of misplaced power exists and will persist.*

The war in Vietnam had begun as a Vietnamese war of independence from France and ended as an American war against what paranoia saw as creeping communism. As a vehicle for dissent, little came near it. Public opinion gradually hardened and by 1967 two-thirds of Americans thought the war a mistake. In 1973 Richard Nixon ended American involvement.[1] *Make love, not war* for a while replaced *my country, right or wrong* and flower power[2] was the response to the violent attacks made on those who opposed the war. If you were going to San Francisco, you were advised to wear a flower in your hair because *you're gonna meet some gentle people there.*[3] Environmentalism was born.

It was an idyllic and indeed idealised time, its essence being *whatever turns you on*, and that did not always mean drugs. Do your own thing; be your own person free from external and, what seemed at the time, meaningless rules, as long as you do not cause harm to others. Abbie Hoffman summed up his views at the time:

> *I believe in the redistribution of wealth and power in the world. I believe in universal hospital care for everyone. I believe that we should not have a single homeless person in the richest country in the world. And I believe that we should not have a CIA that goes around overwhelming governments and assassinating political leaders, working for tight oligarchies around the world to protect the tight oligarchy here at home.*[4]

Anger, protest and laughter

Major theatrical events took place in the late 1950s and 1960s. John Osborne's *Look Back in Anger* came to the stage in 1956, and Arnold Wesker's trilogy (*Chicken Soup with Barley*, *Roots* and *I'm Talking about Jerusalem*) followed from 1958. In films, *Billy Liar* (with Tom Courtenay) came out in 1959, *Saturday Night and Sunday Morning* (with Albert Finney) in 1960, *The L-Shaped Room* (Leslie Caron and Tom Bell) in 1962 and *This Sporting Life* (Richard Harris) in 1963, all films of anger and frustration. The 1960s also saw the rise of satire, with *Beyond the Fringe* and *That Was The Week That Was*. The magazine *Private Eye* was first published in 1961.

---

[1] By 2000, Vietnam had re-established relations with the rest of the world. In 2010, it was seen as having the world's highest potential source of growth and profitable investment opportunities.

[2] In the UK, most memorable for the cover of the Beatles album, *Sergeant Pepper*.

[3] First released by the Mamas and the Papas in 1967.

[4] Quoted by John T. McQuiston in his obituary of Hoffman, *New York Times*, April 14, 1989.

The Aldermaston marches organised by the Campaign for Nuclear Disarmament became an annual event and were a foretaste of the student protests in 1968. Unlike the 1830s and 1930s, the marchers and the protestors were not drawn from the dispossessed. In 1965, 80% of the marchers were white-collar workers and professional people.[1]

Management philosophy

The theories of Frederick Taylor's *Scientific Management* in manufacturing, and of French mining engineer Henri Fayol in business administration, had held sway since the 1920s. Both were about top-down control. *Scientific management* assumed that workers were incapable of rational thought and that intelligent people (like Taylor) were required to analyse the best way to do a job of work, to break it down into its constituent parts and then instruct workers, in minute detail, how to do it. Taylor (1856–1915) wrote of workers in Bethlehem Steel's pig-iron plant:

> *When* [the manager] *tells you to pick up a pig and walk, you pick it up and walk, and when he tells you to sit down and rest, you sit down. You do that right through the day. And what's more, no back talk.*

He explained that workers had just enough brain to be trained, that the:

> *... workman who is best suited to handling pig iron is unable to understand the real science of doing this class of work. He is so stupid that ... he must consequently be trained by a man more intelligent than himself into the habit of working in accordance with the laws of this science before he can be successful.*

Perhaps the most famous exponent of Taylor's ideas was Henry Ford.[2] He is said to have complained that whenever he hired a pair of hands, an unnecessary mind came with it. The problems that Ford Motor Company encountered in the transition from the Model T to the Model A and the V-8 have been attributed to Ford's authoritarian management style.

Henri Fayol (1841–1925) famously said that it was the job of management to *plan, organise, direct, co-ordinate and control*. He argued for one single controlling mind to generate a plan for all to follow; that the right to give orders and the power to exact obedience must be vested in management and that the formal chain of command must run seamlessly from top to bottom of the organisation.[3] The

---

[1] Gunn & Bell.

[2] Whether he had heard of Taylor or not. It is worth noting that Henry Ford paid higher than normal wages to retain workers he had trained.

[3] Compare this with John Lewis who state: *Our democratic network of elected councils, committees and forums gives Partners* (employees) *a real say in our decision-making processes, and allows us to challenge management on performance and have a say in how the business is run.*

views of Taylor and Fayol were treated as common sense through to 1950 and are still the basis of indifferent management practice to this day.

Organisational development

However, even business management changed in the 1960s. One cause of this was the increase in higher education. In a seven year period, the number of men and women graduating from UK universities doubled to more than 50,000. There was a larger proportionate increase in the number of higher degrees awarded.[1]

In the 1960s and 1970s, the practice of OD, led by Warren Bennis, Bill Reddin and Robert Blake, offered a new world of work. While Fayol and Taylor were engineers, the OD practitioners were psychologists. Bennis saw that existing management methods rarely actually solved problems because the organisation followed established routines which did not get to the underlying issues. He set out goals of real change including:

> *Creating an open, problem-solving climate throughout the organisation.*
> *Recognising the authority of knowledge and competence as opposed to rank.*
> *Getting decision-making and problem-solving as close to the information sources as possible.*
> *Building trust among persons and groups throughout the organisation.*
> *Maximising collaborative efforts.*
> *Increasing a sense of ownership throughout the workforce.*
> *Growing self-control and self-direction for people within the organisation.*

Douglas McGregor *(left)* argued that management behaviour is dependent upon the manager's philosophy of human beings in their relation to work. Some managers take the view that people dislike work and will avoid it if they can; that they must be coerced to put in the required effort, offered inducements and threatened with punishment. McGregor called this *Theory X.*

Other managers see work to be as natural as play and hold that people have a capacity for self-control, that they are self-motivated by self-esteem and achievement, and that few organisations make full use of their employees' abilities. The increase in higher education created a large number of employees of which this *Theory Y* was clearly true.

---

[1] *Education: Historical statistics, Standard Note: SN/SG/4252,* 2012, Paul Bolton, House of Commons Library.

The *Human Relations* movement (with its roots in the Hawthorne experiments of the 1930s) was directly opposed to command and control and its new emphasis on delegation and creativity was a heady brew. In the 1960s, it became mainstream and its names and theories became legends of management: Abraham Maslow and the *hierarchy of needs* (1943), Kurt Lewin and *T-groups[1]* (1946), Frederick Herzberg and *hygiene and motivating factors* (1959) as well as McGregor (1960).

Increase in personal freedoms

While pornography is the curse of the internet generation, it was really a Victorian invention, 1880 being taken to be the date when photographs could be printed inexpensively. Nevertheless it was in 1960 that the contraceptive pill was licensed, the same year in which Penguin published the first unexpurgated version of *Lady Chatterley's Lover.* Opening the famous obscenity trial, prosecution counsel, Mervyn Griffith-Jones, amazingly asked the jury whether the novel was *something you would wish your wife or servants to read.* The question was a watershed: one moment a serious question and the next an object of ridicule. It was as if one era gave way to another within the length of a sentence.

While pre-marital sex was daring in the 1960s, by 2014 only a quarter of the population disapproved.[2] Marriage was no longer seen as the only sexual or loving relationship.[3] In the public consciousness, the gay movement began in 1969 as a reaction to the riots against a police raid in New York City. The first Gay Pride March took place in 1970. Attitudes towards gay relationships changed markedly after the *Sexual Offences* Act of 1967.

Feminism

A signally important phenomenon during the whole of this period has been second- and third-wave Feminism. I discuss this in the first phase but of course this movement has spanned the whole period and is still developing. Feminism has roots at least as long ago as the 14th century. In my book *The Goat, the Devil and the Freemason,* I mentioned Christine de Pizan (1364–1430), most famous for her attack on the mid-13th century narrative poem, *Le Roman de la Rose,* itself best described as a pornographic manual of courtly love. Being the daughter of a doctor and a mother of three, Christine de Pizan objected mildly to the unnecessary detail, asking *Doesn't everyone know how men and women copulate naturally?*

---

[1] T-groups have no agenda. Participants discuss their feelings and responses to other participants, learning how what they say and do affects others. It would not have interested Taylor or Fayol.

[2] *British Social Attitudes* 2014.

[3] There remains strong support for monogamy; nearly 90% of the population, a figure consistent since 1983, think extramarital sex is wrong.

but much more to the poem's justification of rape.[1] Mary Wollstonecraft (1759–1797) is known today for her *Vindication of the Rights of Woman* in which she argued that women were not inferior to men, and only appeared so because they were not given the same educational opportunities. The most famous 20th-century feminists were Emmeline and Christabel Pankhurst, who campaigned for women's suffrage, which was achieved in the UK in the same year that Marie Stopes published *Married Love*, banned as obscene in America.

So feminism is not a new subject nor was it new to our earlier brethren, but it did not affect male society much until the 1970s with the rise of what has become known as *second-wave* feminism. In *The Female Eunuch* Germaine Greer argued that the traditional, and especially the suburban, family demeaned and sexually repressed women, treating them as if they were eunuchs. Contrast this with the *loving domesticity* of Dr Heaton's Leeds villa. Like Mary Wollstonecraft, Greer objected to the way that girls were taught to be submissive and it is hard to argue that women have not been treated abominably when, for example, medical insurance companies in the USA refuse to cover conditions arising from pregnancy, claiming that this is not discrimination because their refusal applies to all pregnant persons, male and female.

Having got to grips to some degree with the first two phases of feminism, men have been taken aback by the third wave, which to the outsider looks like pre-feminist behaviour in its:

> … *re-adoption by young feminists of the very lipstick, high heels and cleavage proudly exposed by low-cut necklines that the first two phases of the movement identified with male oppression.*[2] *Pinkfloor expressed this new feminism when she said, 'It's possible to have a push-up bra and a brain at the same time.'*[3]

Naomi Wolf, best known for her 1991 book, *The Beauty Myth*, is quoted as saying:

> … *I conclude that the enemy is not lipstick, but guilt itself; that we deserve lipstick, if we want it, and free speech; we deserve to be sexual and serious – or whatever we please; we are entitled to wear cowboy boots to our own revolution.*

Men need to recognise that women do not dress for men but for other women.

---

[1] Writing at a time when women were not thought of as independently capable beings, Christine de Pizan was a phenomenon. She was married off at fifteen but after a short and happy marriage was widowed and left with her children, her mother and a niece to look after. Her change of fortune obliged her to *take on a man's responsibilities in the world* as she puts it. She supported her dependents by copying manuscripts and started to write, becoming a notable literary figure. Her *Book of the City of Ladies* and *Book of the Three Virtues* both enjoyed success well into the 16th century.

[2] Rampton.

[3] Quoted in Rampton.

Women and work

At one time, women's jobs were seen largely as temporary: ceasing when marriage brought children. Even as late as the mid-1980s, getting on for half of British people still thought of the man as the breadwinner and women in a supportive and caring role. By 2012, women formed nearly half the workforce, and 87% of people said that women could quite properly choose a career over family duties. Must women choose between breaking the glass ceiling or wearing the glass slipper? Christy Krumm says that as a teenager she felt an ambivalence:

> *On the one hand, the idea of girl power was exciting and fun. It made me grateful to the generations of women who had fought to give me the right to vote, earn a degree, and make the same salary as my male colleagues. Yet, on the other hand, I liked it when men I dated opened the car door for me. Was I allowed to want both?* [1]

Sabrina Schaeffer, executive director of the Independent Women's Forum, argued that gender roles help both men and women navigate the often rough waters of courtship, marriage and sex; that ignoring such roles creates confusion.

Feminism and Freemasonry

There is no doubt that feminism has created significant changes in the male role and self-perception. When the Titanic sank, 75% of females survived while 80% of males died but this world, and the one in which Freemasons treat their Good Ladies to an annual Ladies' Festival, is a long way from Elizabeth Peters' remark:

> *I disapprove of matrimony as a matter of principle … Why should any independent, intelligent female choose to subject herself to the whims and tyrannies of a husband? I assure you, I have yet to meet a man as sensible as myself!* [2]

And from Ayaan Hirsi Ali's view that:

> *As a woman you are better off in life earning your own money. You couldn't prevent your husband from leaving you or taking another wife, but you could have some of your dignity if you didn't have to beg him for financial support.* [3]

University of London research indicates that in 2013, as a result of underemployment, unemployment and self-employment, fathers' time with their children had increased by 700% since 1960. Women may have long felt their work/life balance to be out of kilter, but men began to think they were now asked to play too many roles, struggling to meet the increased range of demands made

---

[1] *How To Expect Chivalry From Men In The Age Of Feminist Thinking*, yourtango.com.

[2] Elizabeth Peters, *Crocodile on the Sandbank*, an historical novel set in 1884-85, Grand Central Publishing, 2013, (first pub. 1975).

[3] Ayaan Hirsi Ali, *Infidel*, autobiography of a Somali-born Dutch activist and politician, Atria Books, 2008, (first pub. 2006).

of them. In a reversal of pre-feminism, many men saw the world as dominated by women and felt handcuffed by political correctness; two-thirds concealed their opinions of male/female relationships.[1]

The male companionship of the lodge began to serve a new purpose – that of providing a haven away from the gender confusion.

It is important to both sexes that the truth is not lost in the discussion. The claim that crimes against women peak on Super Bowl Sunday in the USA is untrue. The number of such unpleasant events that take place on Super Bowl Sunday is not statistically different from any other day. The claim that 3 to 4 million women are violently abused every year by husbands and partners in the USA is also untrue. The figure, which is horrifying enough, is more like 100,000. The evidence is that 84% of US families are non-violent and that even among the remaining 16%, half the violence is by women against men. One radical feminist argues that rape happens to 50% of women at least once in their lives. The figure usually cited is 25%. In fact neither 50% nor 25% is correct. A Harris Poll on women's health, which elicited answers to personal question such as suicide attempts, use of hard drugs and sexual abuse while growing up, also asked whether respondents had ever been the subject of sexual assault. Only 2% said yes. Rape, assault and violent abuse are absolutely unacceptable but gross exaggerations of the frequency of such events does nothing to help men and women understand each other during the shift of relationships between the sexes.

Good things and good people

The *end of rules* involved a rejection of the old ways and our institution was undoubtedly seen as part of the establishment. Perhaps for the first time, Freemasonry had become counter-cultural. The flow of younger candidates began to dry up and the seeds of our decline were sown. Nevertheless, this period was very much about values and showed how much men and women will respond to ethical ideals when they can see them clearly.

What followed was the destruction of those ideals but there is still good in the world. Overleaf is a list of good things and good people. As Fidel Castro said, *Un mundo mejor es posible.*

---

[1] *Daily Telegraph*, 26 March 2008.

Good things

Antarctic Treaty System
Bacon sandwiches
Crowd funding
End of page 3
Eradication of smallpox
First non-white US president
First planet seen around a star other than the sun
Gene sequencing

GPS
High yield rice
The iPad
Large Hadron Collider
Love Actually
MRI scanning
Malarial vaccine
Mars Curiosity
Médecins Sans Frontières
Morecambe & Wise

The Orchestra of the Age of Enlightenment
Paradise, Nova Scotia
Protease inhibitors
The Rolling Stones
The Royal Shakespeare Company
Stem cell research
Ten million people protest the Iraq war
The worldwide web

Good people

Seve Ballesteros
Bono
Sir Richard Branson
Sir Bobby Charlton
Jon Crudas
Sir Bob Geldof
Ian Hislop

Dame Margaret Hodge
Dame Kelly Holmes
Alan Johnson
Henry Longhurst
Nelson Mandela
Angela Merkel
Paul Newman

Sir Terry Pratchett
Sir Simon Rattle
Dame Anita Roddick
Dame Maggie Smith
Baroness Warnock
Sir Bradley Wiggins
Victoria Wood CBE

You should create your own list. It is worth doing to recognise that there are still good things and good people about.

Phase 2 – Show me the money: 1980–2000

The counter-revolution

Rock historian Sean Egan described the Rolling Stones in 1964 as *representatives of opposition to an old, cruel order − the antidote to a class-bound, authoritarian culture.* Joe Cocker's 1969 Woodstock performance of *With a little help from my friends* was eight minutes of passion, an anthem to brotherly love, but in the same year the Stones' *Gimme Shelter,* on the album *Let it Bleed,* was being described as a song *to symbolize … the death of the decade's utopian spirit.* Mick Jagger himself called it *a kind of end-of-the-world song, really. It's apocalypse.*[1] The revolution was over. Bill Clinton said:

> *If you look back on the sixties and think there was more good than bad, you're probably a Democrat. If you think there was more harm than good, you're probably a Republican.*[2]

The historian William Chafe noted that even in 1967:

> *… the shrill attacks on 'establishment' values from the left were matched by an equally vociferous defense of traditional values by those who were proud of all their society had achieved. If feminists, blacks, antiwar demonstrators, and advocates for the poor attacked the status quo with uncompromising vehemence, millions of other Americans rallied around the flag and made clear their intent to uphold the lifestyle and values to which they had devoted their lives.*

Reagan and Thatcher

The reaction that Chafe spoke of came to fruition in 1981 when Ronald Reagan became President of the United States, two years after Margaret Thatcher had become the British Prime Minister. The two created a close relationship. Both attempted to reverse the policies of their predecessors, reducing taxation and government spending. Both believed in *trickle-down,*[3] the theory that reduced taxation for the wealthy would produce spending to provide jobs for the poor. Thatcher said:

> *My policies are based not on some economics theory, but on things I and millions like me were brought up with: an honest day's work for an honest day's pay;*

---

[1] Quotes from *Rolling Stone* magazine.

[2] Speaking at *BookExpo America* in Chicago, June 3, 2004.

[3] Arndt: *Trickle-down is a myth which should be exposed and laid to rest.*

live within your means; put by a nest egg for a rainy day; pay your bills on time; support the police.[1]

Of course, that is not how the rich become rich nor are home economics similar to government economics. Nevertheless, what she said was an earnest of her and Reagan's intentions.[2] While Thatcher sought to reduce the costs of social services, education and housing, Reagan saw economic dangers in health programmes:

One of the traditional methods of imposing statism or socialism on a people has been by way of medicine. It's very easy to disguise a medical program as a humanitarian project . . . Now, the American people, if you put it to them about socialized medicine and gave them a chance to choose, would unhesitatingly vote against it. We have an example of this. Under the Truman administration it was proposed that we have a compulsory health insurance program for all people in the United States, and, of course, the American people unhesitatingly rejected this.[3]

This was very largely true; when Obamacare[4] was finally introduced, it was only in a watered-down state.

Inflation and divisiveness

Of course, Thatcherism was a reaction not only to the social and philosophical changes of the 1960s but also to the damaging inflation of the 1970s. It had taken off at the beginning of Edward Heath's Conservative government in 1970, peaking at nearly 25% by 1976, and was put down to various factors including decimalisation, a sudden rise in oil prices and a wage/price spiral caused by over-powerful trades union and a loose monetary policy.

A commonly accepted explanation is that the culprit was the inability to measure spare capacity in the economy. The Taylor Rule holds that central banks should raise interest rates when (a) inflation is above target or (b) demand exceeds capacity and vice versa. Successive governments had been unable to see that growth in capacity had slowed, again due to the lack of investment in productivity. Governments drew the incorrect conclusion that slow growth indicated a lack of demand and tried to stimulate it by increasing money supply, hence inflation.

Heath had attempted to reverse the rise of unemployment in the 1972 recession by reflating the economy, seeking to control the resultant inflation by a prices and incomes policy.

---

[1] Quoted in the *News of the World*, September 1981.

[2] Reagan did cut income taxes but he also tripled the Federal debt by increased government spending. It is not clear that trickle-down had any beneficial effects at all. Since the income of the top 1% of earners in the US trebled, and any trickling seems to have been upward.

[3] Radio address on *Socialized Medicine*, 1961.

[4] *The Patient Protection and Affordable Care* Act 2010.

This failed when a miners' strike led to the government imposing a three-day week for the first three months of 1974 and Heath lost the ensuing election.[1] As a reaction to this experience of inflation both UK and US governments adopted an overtight tight monetary and fiscal policy which caused the recession from 1979 to 1981. The number of unemployed in the UK rose to over 3 million, a level not seen since the 1930s.[2]

Thatcher once famously said that there is *no such thing as society*:

> *There are individual men and women, and there are families. And no government can do anything except through people, and people must look to themselves first.*[3]

Unlike the aims of one-nation Toryism, Mrs Thatcher accepted unemployment as part of her armoury against the trade unions.[4] As Fryer and Stambe write, in *Neoliberal austerity and unemployment*, unemployment is useful because it:

> *... provides a pool of potential workers unable to be unwilling to do the most boring, dirty, dead end, menial, underpaid, temporary, insecure, stressful jobs* [and] *provides competition for jobs from desperate jobseekers allowing employers to drive down wages and working conditions.*

> The Telegraph reported the National Archive release of papers on the 1984 miners' strike: Early in the strike Mrs Thatcher voiced concerns that officers were 'not carrying out their duties fully' because few picketers were being arrested, and she and her Ministers agreed that forces should adopt a 'more vigorous' approach. ... After the 'Battle of Orgreave', June 18, 1984, when many police officers and pickets were injured ... South Yorkshire police authority asked the local chief constable to cease deploying officers to future pickets at that plant.

The result of Thatcher's actions was to make the rich richer and the poor poorer. She reduced tax rates for high earners from 83% to 49% to provide greater incentives, as she saw it, but reduced the ability of the trades union to act as a counterbalance. She sold off publicly owned enterprises to reduce the role of the state, unwittingly creating private as opposed to public monopolies and reduced

---

[1] Paul Mason views 1973 as a phase change in the Kondratieff cycle sparked off in 1971 by Nixon unpegging the dollar from gold. This set off the stock market crash of 1973, itself exacerbated by the Arab-Israeli war and the resultant oil embargo.

[2] Industrial action has not disappeared. The Office for National Statistics, *Annual Article 2014*, reported: *The number of working days lost due to labour disputes in 2014 was 788,000 compared with 444,000 in 2013. The 2014 figure is more than the average in both the 2000s and the 1990s, but less than the 1980s.*

[3] Interview for *Woman's Own*, 1987.

[4] Mason argues that the destruction of the unions was the real aim of the neoliberalism of Pinochet, Thatcher and Reagan. *Its guiding principle*, he writes, *is not free markets, nor fiscal discipline, nor sound money, nor privatization and offshoring – not even globalization. All these were by products or weapons of its main endeavour: to remove organized labour from the equation.*

controls on the finance industry, leading to the banking crash of 2007/8. Thatcher wrote of her admiration for Michael Novak, best known for his book *The Spirit of Democratic Capitalism*, noting that:

> ... *what he called 'democratic capitalism' was a moral and social, not just an economic system, that it encouraged a range of virtues and that it depended upon co-operation* ...[1]

Using documents released from the National Archives in 2014, the *Guardian* reported that Sir Robert Armstrong, cabinet secretary, had voiced strong concerns in March 1986 over the signs of a 'loadsamoney' culture developing in the City of London on the eve of the deregulation of the stock exchange. Sir Robert spoke of the increasing disquiet those who dealt with the City, not just over the levels of remuneration but the corners being cut and money being made in ways bordering on the unscrupulous.

Greed

Far from encouraging virtues, Thatcher's actions made greed good. Ivan Boesky, speaking at University of California, Berkeley in 1986, is reported to have said:

> *Greed is all right, by the way. I want you to know that. I think greed is healthy. You can be greedy and still feel good about yourself.* [2]

Boesky was later imprisoned for insider dealing, fined $100 million and banned from working in the financial sector ever again. As Dante wrote, avarice:

> *O'ercasts the world with mourning, under foot,*
> *Treading the good, and raising bad men up.* [3]

The earlier vision of social democracy and cohesion had passed but the individualism that was part of it had not; the reduction in regulation led to white-collar lawlessness. The new ideal became the individual who became rich. The income of the American top 1% increased by about 250% between 1980 and 2000 while that of the remaining 99% increased by less than 1%.[4] As Thatcher said: *Nobody would remember the Good Samaritan if he had only good intentions. He had money as well.*[5] In her famous *Sermon on the Mound,*[6] she said that Christianity was about spiritual redemption, not social reform. She said, *We are told we must work and use our talents to create wealth,* and then went on to quote from *2 Thessalonians*: *If a man will not work he shall not eat.*

---

[1] Thatcher.

[2] *Independent*, 5 July 2010.

[3] *Inferno*, Canto XIX.

[4] Source: Mason. The top 1% is defined as those earning more than $341,000 per year in 2008.

[5] TV Interview for *Weekend World*, January 1980.

[6] Delivered to the Church of Scotland in the Edinburgh Assembly Rooms, address: *The Mound*.

The 'me' years

Thatcher publicly praised the virtues of hard work and saving but her actions centred mainly on the individual and the freedom to make money, unimpeded by social or legal constraints. A legacy of Thatcherism were the *me* years. Centred on *my* demands for what *I* want, *when* I want it, Britain became a society prizing money as a badge of success and a route to instant gratification.[1] Those with money spent it extravagantly,[2] and those without it borrowed on credit cards.

It should not be necessary to say that brotherly love may be about *us* or even *you*, but it is certainly not about *me*. Antony Beevor remarks that the 1980s saw:

> ... *the decline of collective or tribal loyalties – with both the trades union in Britain and the traditional officer class disintegrating at the same time.*[3]

The rise of managerialism

Early capitalism featured a capitalist risking his own money in a venture. That capitalist took a day-to-day interest in the affairs of the company and any business loss or fine for a misdemeanour affected him personally. This has changed and now investors may not be aware where their money has been invested. Companies are run by their managers and it is rare for management to suffer for losses or misdemeanours. Failures affect only the share price, often in odd ways.

> BP shares rose after a US judge capped the maximum fine it faced for the Gulf of Mexico disaster at £9 billion ($13.7bn), ruling that BP had released 3.2 million barrels of oil into the sea. The US government had estimated 4.2 million. The fine was the largest ever levied in the US for pollution. (3 July) BP announced a £12bn ($18.7bn) deal to settle all outstanding claims in the US. BP closed up 3.67%. The total cost to BP has been £34.4bn ($53.8bn). *Independent* January 2015

Morality is no longer central to business decision-making, a common view being that the only proper aim for management is profit maximisation. On such a view it would be wrong for a company to obey anything more than the letter of the law and then only if necessary, seeking to evade its impact if possible. Union Carbide's actions, post-Bhopal, may be a case in point. The question to be answered by the management, again on this view, is whether doing the 'right thing' would have been cheaper in the long run and thus whether Union Carbide's decision turned out to be simply mathematically wrong.

---

[1] It would seem that the surprise Conservative Party victory in the 2015 election will lead to the completion of the Thatcherist experiment.

[2] In 2002, at the Petrus restaurant in London, six bankers from Barclays Capital spent more than $62,700 mostly on wine. The owner was so impressed he did not charge for the food. *New York Times.*

[3] 'Will a continent turn its back on democracy?' *Prospect Magazine*, December 2012.

In 1984, an explosion at the Union Carbide plant in India released poison gases including hydrogen cyanide and carbon monoxide, allegedly causing 16,000 deaths. The company paid $470 million out-of-court, a settlement granting company officials immunity from prosecution. The victims' representatives claimed that much of the compensation was never paid out and that 120,000 survivors were still in need of medical help. In 1999 lawyers filed a class action lawsuit charging the corporation with violating the human rights of victims and survivors, and with fraud and civil contempt for their perceived failure to comply with orders of the courts of the United States and India. It was reported that in 2004 8,000 tonnes of toxic waste was still lying in the Union Carbide factory. The story came back to bite Dow Chemicals in 2011, by then the owners of Union Carbide. Associated Press reported that UK Member of Parliament Keith Vaz tabled a motion expressing reservations over Dow's ties to the 2012 London Olympics, which were expected to stir concern among Britain's Indian community. The Indian Olympic Association lodged a strong protest.

The 'undeserving' poor again

Thatcher spoke of what she thought of as a Victorian notion, the *undeserving poor*:

> ... *they distinguished between the 'deserving' and the 'undeserving poor'. Both groups should be given help : but it must be help of very different kinds if public spending is not just going to reinforce the dependency culture. The problem with our welfare state was that ... we had failed to remember that distinction and so we provided the same 'help' to those who had genuinely fallen into difficulties and needed some support till they could get out of them, as to those who had simply lost the will or habit of work and self-improvement.*

The notion of the undeserving poor pre-dates the Victorian era and was used to justify the workhouse, an institution so deliberately unpleasant that only the genuine poor would enter it. You may recall that, despite this, outdoor relief continued. Decency recognised that poverty had always threatened even the most deserving poor. Nevertheless, Thatcher claimed to have identified a large group of people who were too lazy to work, preferring to live on benefits. I shall show later that the cost of benefits and tax credit fraud amounts to the same costs as errors made by the administration and that unclaimed benefit is nearly four times benefits fraud. If the undeserving poor do exist, they form a very small percentage of the population.

More important are the undeserving rich. The gap[1] between tax owed and tax collected is in the UK is estimated to be about 600 times as much as benefits fraud. Richard Murphy writes that Italy has an external debt of €1.9 trillion and loses about €183 billion a year through tax evasion. Much the same ratio is true for Greece and Spain. Murphy argues that if tax evasion were taken seriously in these countries there would be no eurozone crisis.

---

[1] 'Collect the evaded tax, avoid the cuts,' *Guardian* 25 November 2011

The implications of phases 1 & 2

Before examining phase 3, we should examine some implications of the first two.

Denial

The period from 1850 to 1950 was a long time, even for Freemasonry, and we became so accustomed to a constant flow of candidates that today's problem grew, almost unseen, for another half century. Even as meetings without ritual increased, lodges were blithely confident that candidates would return; that membership was a cyclical matter; that we just needed a few younger brethren; that it was a matter of too many new lodges having been formed ... and so on. Whatever excuse was made, we were sure that the membership decline was purely temporary. Henderson and Belton point to New Zealand where although the ... 'Condition of the Craft' Committee, against a background of a 25% fall in membership between 1963 and 1982, was forecasting a further decrease of 30% by 2001, the view from the top was that all was well.

Busfield reports leaders of the Craft in New Zealand saying :

> 1981 – I can assert that there is growing evidence to show that we have arrested the decline ... the future now offers real hope of improvement.
>
> 1982 – The decline is showing signs of levelling off and we will, I am confident, show an increase in the near future.
>
> 1983 – With the co-operation and support of all members there will be an early return to increasing membership.
>
> 1984 – We have inherited a wonderful institution which I believe is in a healthy condition.

It is unfair to single out one Grand Lodge. Such statements have been common during the period of our decline. Even in 2014, a member of the UGLE Membership Focus Group said that we're getting lots of people wanting to join.[1] We must now avoid complacency and recognise that the problem won't go away on its own. Until we recognise that it is systemic, we cannot begin to solve it. As Will Murray puts it ... the ability to believe exactly what you want to believe to be true, even though you are miles off, is the last refuge of those in denial.

End of predictability

Victorian values included service and the satisfaction of doing a good job. Gunn and Bell instance a surgeon who, retiring in 2000, talked about vocation, dedication and a duty of care. They contrast this with the words of his son, an accountant:

---

[1] Open Forum, in Freemasonry Today, Autumn 2014.

If I'm brutally honest about why I'm at work I wouldn't say it's for pleasure. I'm trying to earn money to guarantee a sense of security for myself and for my family. Money is what drives me to be at work.

What certainly had gone away was the middle-class ideal of a career:

... the middle class notion of the career was a compact between the organisation and individual. The middle class employee promised loyalty to the organisation, personal probity, hard work and deference to the hierarchical order. In return, the organisation repaid this commitment by assuring job security, a salary that would increase progressively with age and the opportunity of promotion over time ...[1]

In an interview with Gunn and Bell, Richard Scase commented:

In the 1970s middle-class privileges are undermined in a fundamental way for the first time. The major factor that undermines them is the end of job security, jobs for life. Suddenly because organisations are restructuring and using computer technology in their management systems, managers find they are prone to redundancy ... From the 1970s onwards middle classes in Britain are never the same again.[2]

In *Funky Business*, Ridderstråle and Nordstrom argue that the day of predictability in work has passed. People today cannot expect to find a safe job in a safe company, work their way up the hierarchy and comfortably retire 40 or so years later.[3] In a very clear sense, everyone today is self-employed, needing to gain and maintain a set of skills which are in demand, ready to sell them to the next bidder, the next employer;[4] the CV (*curriculum vitae*) has replaced the career.[5]

> Penelope Trunk, in *Why Job Hoppers Make the Best Employees* for BNET, writes that only job hoppers have stable careers. *The corporation doesn't provide stability for its employees. The stability you get in your career comes from you.* Job hoppers are also higher performers. *If you know you are going to leave your job in the next year, you're going to be very conscious of your resume and how it gets improved.* Further, they are more emotionally mature. *It takes self-knowledge to know what you want to do next and to go get it rather than stay someplace that for the moment seems safe.*

It is increasingly true that brethren cannot make a commitment to attend every LOI, or even every lodge meeting. They will no doubt do their best but if we think the less of them for their absences, we will lose them. Freemasonry has had

---

[1] Gunn & Bell.

[2] See also Scase & Goffee.

[3] As early as 1990–1993, 75,000 jobs were lost in banking; BT reduced its number of employees by 80,000, and around 50,000 civil service jobs were put out to tender.

[4] West (2).

[5] Interview with Ray Pahl in Gunn & Bell.

difficulties with retention as well as recruitment, hence the introduction of the mentoring scheme.[1] The fact is that lodges have not been doing a very good job in looking after their new members, primarily because they have not recognised the different drummers that people march to today.[2] The often-heard Past Master's remark, *When I was initiated* ... has almost no relevance today. Things have changed.

Change in the source of candidates

In the past, almost all candidates were friends and family of existing members. The questions we ask candidates and the way our leadership makes recommendations on recruitment reflect this. We properly stress the importance of vetting a candidate's suitability but place the primary responsibility for this on the proposer and seconder, implying that the candidate has a proposer and seconder before being considered by the lodge. That is increasingly unlikely. 80% of candidates in my mother lodge come via its website.[3]

The average age of our members is increasing, and the men they meet are also ageing. As we age, we meet fewer new people and our social circle tightens. In all probability, if existing friends and family have ever indicated an interest in Freemasonry, they would have already been invited. As a source of candidates, our existing members are a declining if not a spent force.

Is the interview still relevant?

The questions we ask candidates make assumptions which no longer hold and describe a society which has largely ceased to exist. For example, we ask *Would your wife or partner be supportive if you joined our Lodge* and *Does she (or he) know that you have come for an interview this evening?* The idea that one's wife or partner needs to give approval or support is a hangover from the *loving domesticity* of the Victorian middle class. Some lodges ask the question, *Would your wife or partner be supportive of our social functions?* In days past, such a question might have been relevant, but today a wife or partner is very likely to have her own career and interests. While no doubt happy to attend when her diary allows, she would not see her husband's or partner's interests as in any way binding upon her. Feminism has changed relationships.

Some lodges still tell candidates that *Freemasonry is not a form of life assurance* and ask, *Have you made provision for your family?* Such a question carries the implication that

---

[1] With what one must admit is patchy success. The lodge Mentor must work hand in glove with the Secretary and Almoner and be in constant touch with all brethren.

[2] Members of one lodge complained to me that of the last six candidates they had initiated, five had left. To lose one initiate may be regarded as a misfortune, to lose five looks like carelessness.

[3] St Laurence Lodge No. 5511 initiates three or four candidates a year. See West (4).

the man is the breadwinner and takes responsibility for the finances of his wife/ partner and family. We really must recognise that the relationship between the sexes has changed. The candidate's wife or partner really isn't waiting at home, oven gloves in hand and the table laid, for when he returns from work.

The question, *Are you happy to drink the health of Her Majesty?* while not being in any way improper, also assumes a way of life that has passed. It is not that anyone might object to the loyal toast; it is more that neither monarchism nor republicanism occupy much of people's thinking today. Polls[1] show that fewer than one in five Britons support the idea of republic and 75% of them expect the Prince George, third in line to the throne, to become King; but when asked which Royal was their favourite, 35% of respondents have no opinion.

In a recent poll on the Duchess of Cambridge, 89% of women declared no interest in being her, even for a day.[2] On the day that her first pregnancy was announced, only 2% of respondents thought this the most important story of the day. (The lack of such news under Henry VIII caused the Church of England.)

> *What is going on? The short answer might be that the more childish registers of the public-royal relationship are fading – gone the envy, the hysteria, the adulation, the schadenfreude ... The British public seem more prepared to view their relationship with Kate, and therefore with the future of the monarchy, for what it is: a socio-political contract.*[3]

Freemasons will continue to drink the loyal toast, but monarchism is no longer significant enough to form the basis of an interview question.

The old man in the sky

We ask, *Do you believe in the existence of a supreme being?* Freemasonry deemed regular by UGLE demands that all candidates express such a belief, although the phrase that used to be added, *and his revealed will*, seems to have dropped out of fashion. The consolation of religion is less sought today than ever before. Callum Brown's description of the church's pre-1950 experience is uncannily similar to ours:

> *The 1950s was in fact a deeply old-fashioned era, so old that it has often been described as the last Victorian decade. Nearly 2 million people came to hear Billy Graham preach in London ... in 1954, and a further 1.2 million came in Glasgow in 1955, with 100,000 worshippers packing Hampden Park football stadium for a single religious service.*

---

[1] ComRes survey for *The Sunday Telegraph*, July 2013.

[2] *Newsweek*, September 2014, report by Ed Docx. A mere 6% of men wished they were married to Kate and or wished they were dating her.

[3] Docx, *Newsweek*.

By 1983 about a third of the UK population had no religion and by 2011 that third had become a half. [1] The decline has been most marked in the Church of England and in those aged 18 to 24, of whom 64% had no religion by 2014.

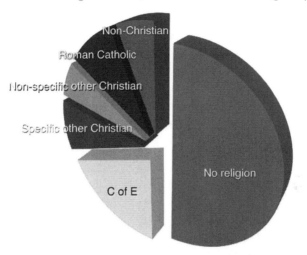

Britain is becoming less religious, with the numbers who affiliate with a religion or attend religious services experiencing a long-term decline. And this trend seems set to continue; not only as older, more religious generations are replaced by younger, less religious ones, but also as the younger generations increasingly opt not to bring up their children in a religion. [2]

Callum Brown shows that the 1948-1960 growth in membership of the Church of England was fuelled by young women. Female confirmations actually increased by 28% during that period while male confirmations remained in decline. However, from 1960, female confirmations also started to decline.

The sudden collapse of church recruitment, churchgoing and church membership in the early 1960s was triggered by the sudden appearance in 1960–62 of female defection from church recruitment, in addition to men's thirty-year-long continued decline.

In 1970s Ireland, more than 90% of the population attended Mass on a Sunday, but by 2013, following the paedophile scandals, attendance had fallen to 34%.

---

[1] The wording of the question affects the outcome. In a 2012 YouGov survey 76% claimed they were not very religious or not religious at all. The 2008 European Social Survey asked *Which religion or denomination do you belong to at present?* 52.68% said none. The 2009 British Social Attitudes survey asked *Do you regard yourself as belonging to any particular religion?* 50.67% said no. The 2010 Labour Force Survey asked *What is your religion even if you are not currently practising?* 22.4% said none. The 2011 census asked *What is your religion?* 25.1% said none.

[2] *British Social Attitudes*, 2011–2012.

Today, it is estimated to be 18% and many people in Ireland describe themselves as *post-Catholics*. The *Irish Catholic* newspaper calls them *functionally atheist*.[1] The period 1960 to 2000 has been described as *the slow death of Christian Britain*.[2]

> *It took several centuries ... to convert Britain to Christianity, but it has taken less than forty years for the country to forsake it ... Quite suddenly in 1963, something very profound ruptured the character of the nation and its people, sending organised Christianity on a downward spiral to the margins of social significance.*[3]

■ Baptisms per thousand live births

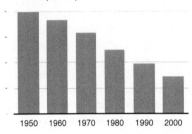

1950   1960   1970   1980   1990   2000

Based again on Callum Brown's data, this chart shows the decline in baptismal rate from 1950 to 2000. Freemasonry and the Church of England have shared much the same experience since 1850.

Religious beliefs of Freemasons

There is no data, that I am aware of, on the religiosity of Freemasons but my own straw poll indicates that only about 15% can be considered regular churchgoers, about the national average. The whole question of religious belief, if this is not too bad a pun, is up in the air. No theologian accepts the *old man in the sky*; 16% of practising C of E clergy do not accept a personal god.[4] Even many religions reject such a concept. The *great spirit* in indigenous North American beliefs is the name commonly given to a singular creator. Such a being:

> ... *probably existed in the ancient beliefs of some tribes, but is generally inconsistent with the spirit of egalitarianism and democracy that characterises most tribal groups.*[5]

Paul Tillich, one of the greatest of modern theologians, viewed god not as *a being* but as *being itself*, the ground of existence, and to demand of a candidate that he have a belief in *the old man in the sky* would prevent the initiation not only of atheists but also of theologians – and of Native Americans. I am not arguing for the removal of the VSL or prayers from lodge. I would, however, argue that the question on religious belief might be modified such that it reads more like the question on monarchy. On the pattern of *Are you happy to drink the health of Her Majesty?* we might ask, *Are you happy to participate in prayers in lodge?*

---

[1] Michael Kelly, appointed editor of the *Irish Catholic* newspaper in 2012.

[2] Among other faiths, attendance is greater: 80% of Muslims and 70% of Hindu believers identify themselves as practising members of their faiths, as opposed to 32% of Christians.

[3] Callum Brown.

[4] *Yougov* survey of 1499 clergy in 2014.

[5] Jones & Molyneaux.

An American view

Having reviewed a draft of this book, Kirk C. White, author of *Operative Freemasonry: a manual for restoring light and vitality to the fraternity*, was kind enough to observe:

> The preceding chapter makes reference to the young men who identify as 'none' on recent surveys of religious affiliation. As Dr West correctly points out, this is a growing demographic right in the middle of Freemasonry's recruitment pool and we would do well to find ways to include them. However, we should not be too ready to conflate them with atheists, especially in America. The general consensus within the American Academy of Religions is that such 'nones' are more likely to be spiritual seekers who have rejected affiliation with organized denominations and what they see as undesirably prescriptive, one-size-fits-all, ethical codes. Such men seek a close connection to divinity but don't want to be told what that divinity looks like, nor how it should be worshipped. They seek the doors to spiritual experience but wish to open those doors themselves and gain their own, unmediated experience, from which they can build their own moral code.
>
> Such men are religiously unaffiliated but they are not atheists. Many of them are the same men who are drawn to non-traditional, non-prescriptive religions such as those of the modern Paganisms (Wicca, Druidry, etc.), and here in the USA a significant percentage of new Masons are modern Pagans. There are entire lodges of men who identify as Pagan; enough that a past Grand Master of Florida tried to have them banned from membership in our Fraternity; an attempt that was rightfully rejected as a violation of our landmarks.
>
> To my mind, Freemasonry has much to offer such men. We do not tell them who or how to worship (although here in the US, many Grand Lodges still insist on monotheism) but rather give them the opportunity, resources and support to find the divine in their own way, helping them towards a dialogue about how to translate those experiences into personal moral and ethical codes for daily life.

Phase 3 – The end of decency: 2000–present

Rejection

Thatcher's rejection of anything resembling socialism was also a rejection of the idealism of brotherly love. As Beth Butler, a teacher aged 79, said:

> *What did we lose? A zest; a get-up-and-go; an optimism. People seemed to become gradually more passive under Thatcher, as though the colour had gone out of their lives. Possessions suddenly became far more important, too. Fashion, clothes and shoes – and the concomitant rise in fake goods. It was as though the zest for life had been replaced by self-centredness. People were interested in what they had for themselves, rather than doing things together.*[1]

Freemasonry has values far beyond self-interest, as the Royal Arch lectures on the *Robes and Sceptres* tell us. The first lecture could well emanate from the human relations movement in management:

> *Your sceptre bears a crown … Let it, however, remind you that to reign sovereign in the hearts and affections of men is far more gratifying to a generous and benevolent mind than to rule over their lives and fortunes …*

The second lecture talks of *union* and *harmony,* and of the *all-seeing eye* borne by the Second Principal's sceptre that instructs him *to stand as a watchman on a tower, to admonish the companions to fidelity and industry;* words that might have come straight from Dr Heaton, or indeed Samuel Smiles. The third speaks of *universal beneficence and charity* and the Third Principal's sceptre bears a mitre, *an emblem of dignity,* but there is no dignity in *Greed is all right, by the way. I want you to know that.* An objective for the renaissance of Freemasonry must be to restore such dignity.

> *Let me impress upon your minds, and may it be instilled into your hearts, that every human creature has a just claim on your kind offices. I therefore trust that you will be good to all. More particularly do I recommend to your care the household of the faithful, that diligence and fidelity in the duties of your respective vocations, liberal beneficence and diffusive charity, by constancy and sincerity in your friendships … [may] prove to the world the happy and beneficial effects of our ancient and honourable institution.*[2]

Nasty, grovelling and greedy

When the novelist Simon Raven died in 2001, Charles Spencer wrote of his …

> *… most cherished themes and obsessions – chiefly sex, betrayal, decay and death, as well as the possibility of maintaining some degree of honour in a fallen world.*[3]

---

[1] *The Guardian,* 13 April 2013

[2] *The Long Closing* in West (1).

[3] Charles Spencer, *Dangerously, deliciously addictive,* Telegraph, 19 May 2001.

In many ways Raven's views on behaviour echo those of Cardinal Newman. He wrote that up to the 1960s Englishmen held fast to the rule that *they should not irritate, nag, scold, embarrass or in any way incommode* other people, that they should *never interfere, pry or delate,* a wonderful Raven phrase. Even during the 1970s, he argued, the Englishman maintained a pride in his independence but in 1985 Raven described a generation that had become *shrill, demanding and hysterical, self pitying and unctuous; full of grievance at their own lot and envy of others' attainments.*[1]

Simon Raven was famously described as having *the mind of a cad but the pen of an angel,* but he took a moral, if caustic, view of the world, despite creating some of the most scurrilous characters in literature. Mrs Holbrook, in *The Rich Pay Late,* is an academic who explains why she does not leave her dreadful husband:

> '*I should miss him. You see ... he personifies the folly and meanness of the human race. Since I tend to live on a rather remote level of my own, it is salutary to be daily reminded of the sort of man by whom and for whom the world is mostly run. If I am ever in danger of thinking the truth lies there*' – she indicated the books around them – '*I can always take a look at your father. Nasty, grovelling, greedy – he is the truth about the world, Jude, and it does not do to forget it.*'[2]

Raven might have been amused, but more likely outraged, that his Mr Holbrook would become a quite normal figure in the years that followed his death. Mr Holbrook perfectly symbolises phase three of our account of social change since the 1950s. This phase has been bad enough to create the possibility of our resurgence. Many men find current society distasteful and are looking elsewhere for meaning and values. We can offer them a moral haven.

Reversal in management theory

A new theory of business occurred in about 2000. It was quite contrary to the principles laid down by Taylor and Fayol and their logical processes, and equally contrary to the conclusions of the OD movement. This new theory held that it was the CEO alone who created value in a company and companies set off in a search for that one magical person who would give all direction, make all decisions and create all innovations. A series of Mary Poppins-like figures came forward. Few succeeded. Most failed quite horribly but this has not reversed the philosophy, despite the predictable examples of system failures and customer dissatisfaction.

Bank leaders are now ... *suggesting that their organisations are too vast and their activities too convoluted and technical for them to understand.*[3] The implications of such a remark

---

[1] Raven (2).

[2] Raven (1).

[3] *Independent,* 17 November 2014.

are too painfully obvious to bear stating here. It is as if all the research undertaken on management since the 1930s never took place.

> UK banks and building societies have received a total of 19.7 million complaints, (almost 9,000 a day) since the middle of 2008. A spokesman for the Robin Hood Tax campaign, said: *Far from banks clearing up their act after causing the crisis, they've continued to treat the public they should be serving with contempt.*
>
> robinhoodtax.org.uk

The decline of employee morale

One result of this was the decline of employee engagement in almost all companies.[1] The aim of management changed from long-term success fuelled by interpersonal trust and creativity, to short-term profit through cost reduction and downsizing. Work lost much of its meaning and job satisfaction reached an all-time low. Those who have studied management will not be surprised that companies who remained true to earlier ideals proved to be far more successful than those who single-mindedly sought profit.[2]

> University of Pennsylvania research found that capital improvements increase productivity by 3.9%. Investing in engagement and loyalty increases it by 8.5%.

A 2008 Gallup survey found that only 13% of German employees were engaged with their workplace; 67% were not engaged and 20%, fully one-fifth of the workforce, were actively disengaged. This is an astounding result for a society like Germany, and even in the USA, the home of capitalism, similar results were obtained: 29% engaged, 54% not engaged, 17% actively disengaged.[3]

Part of the cause of this disengagement was redundancy. The UK Chartered Management Institute reported that 78% of managers had experienced redundancy by 2010 and that, perhaps as a result, only 33% of UK employees trusted their management, a figure which represented an all-time low.[4] The results of the 2009 Ipsos Loyalty Study indicated that only a quarter of US employees thought that their company deserved loyalty.[5]

In his book *Charging Back Up the Hill* on the subject of recovery after lay-offs, Mitchell Lee Marks quotes a survivor of downsizing saying:

---

[1] Although many pay lip service.

[2] Prime examples being John Lewis, Lincoln Electric, Southwest Airlines, the steel company Nucor, Iceland, voted best company to work for in 2012 and 2014, and the Brazilian firm Semco which grew its revenues from US$4 million in 1982 to US$212 million by 2003.

[3] Nink.

[4] Alfes et al.

[5] Keiningham & Aksoy.

There is no loyalty here; no one is going the extra mile after this. Two years ago, we worked sixty-five-hour weeks. People were willing to do it, because it was a great place to work and we were doing something that mattered . . . From here on in, it's just a job for me. I'll put in my forty hours and that's it.

> Research using the American Customer Satisfaction Index has found that firms that carried out substantial downsizing, experienced greater declines in customer satisfaction. The index of customer satisfaction has proved to be a good predictor of profitability. Downsizing usually has negative consequences for an organisation.

In 2004, UK research indicated that managers were working 9.24% longer than they were in 1984 and that stress was causing a loss of 13 million working days a year.[1] These figures will have got worse, not better. It seems that a majority of people were just going to work, not enjoying it nor finding satisfaction in a job well done. Many people, many of them our members, will have been tired, not exhilarated, at the end of the day – which has obvious implications for the LOI.

Worse, Patricia Harned, CEO of the US *Ethics & Compliance Initiative*, said:

While most US workers are currently 'doing the right thing' by following company standards and reporting wrongdoing when they see it, we see trouble ahead.

The number of US employees who had felt pressure to compromise ethical standards, or break the law at work almost doubled from 2009 to 2011 and:

... the percentage of employees who experienced some form of retaliation for blowing the whistle was 22 percent, an all-time high. This compares with 15 percent in 2009 and 12 percent in 2007. The proportion of respondents who felt they couldn't question management without fear of retaliation amounted to 19 percent of all employees.[2]

The undeserving rich

Loyalty is a two way street but rewards have largely become one way. Sean O'Grady reported that despite a ten year decline in share prices, since 2000, the remuneration of senior managers had quadrupled.[3] Smith and Kuntz, writing for *Bloomberg*, report that while in the 1950s the average US CEO received 20 times as much as the average worker in his or her company, by 2013 the multiple in the US had reached 204.[4] The highest multiple was in J.C. Penney & Co, known for its general merchandise stores. CEO Ronald Johnson's pay in 2012 was an amazing 1,795 times that of the average J.C. Penney worker.

---

[1] Will Murray.

[2] Verschoor.

[3] *Independent*, 5 July 2010.

[4] The average multiple in UK blue chip companies reached 130 in 2015, measured against their own company workers, but 183 against average pay of all workers.

To put this into some sort of perspective, if the average worker's pay were to be represented by a loaf of bread on end, Johnson's pay would be the height of the Empire State Building. Johnson was CEO for 18 months and left after a 25% drop in sales.[1]

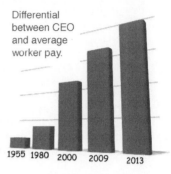

Differential between CEO and average worker pay.

1955 1980 2000 2009 2013

As the director of Corporate Governance and Pension Investment for the American Federation of State, County and Municipal Employees, Richard Ferlauto, said, *What does 'pay for performance' mean if you ignore performance?* [2]

As Freemasons, the issue of fairness should concern us, but the question of management credibility is also important. How can a senior manager understand the needs, fears, abilities and motivations of people when his/her life is so utterly and radically different from theirs – so different that it would take the average man or woman in the company nearly 2,000 years to earn what a CEO receives in just one?

In 2010, the *Independent* reported:

> *Staff at six UK airports owned by BAA have voted three to one in favour of striking in a dispute over pay ... Staff accepted a pay freeze in 2009 and their union, Unite, described the offer for this year – a 1% increase, with the possibility of an extra 0.5% if the union agrees to changes to the company's sickness agreement – as 'measly' and 'nothing short of confrontational'. The company has also said there will be no additional summer bonus this year, which is usually paid if BAA makes a profit, and is worth about £700.*

Contrast this with the report that in the middle of the recession Frank Chapman, CEO of the gas production firm BG, received a one year pay and pension package worth £28 million.[3] BG's share price performance during that period was unremarkable. BG was once known as British Gas[4] and *The Daily Mail* remarked that Chapman's pay award occurred when many poorer families:

> *... are being crippled by average gas bills of £750 and around four million households are in fuel poverty, spending more than 10 per cent of their income on heating their homes.*

---

[1] Elliot Blair Smith and Phil Kuntz, *Bloomberg*, April 30 2013

[2] Not speaking specifically of Johnson. He went on to say, *Executive pay is the ultimate shell game. Boards come up with all sorts of new ways to pay people whose performance shows they don't deserve it.*

[3] *The Daily Mail*, 4 April 2010. BG was one of the worst performing shares in 2014.

[4] The buying and selling of companies that arrived at BG from British Gas is somewhat tortuous.

In 1994 British Gas awarded its then CEO, Cedric Brown, a 75% pay increase. At the AGM, a pig named Cedric was paraded by shareholders. When Cedric (the man) retired he received (in 1996 money) a £240,000 annual pension, £120,000 in consultancy fees, a chauffeur-driven car and a staffed office, but his 700,000 share options were almost worthless because the British Gas share price was so low. Nigel Cope reported: *Shareholders were divided in their opinion of Cedric Brown's performance as chief executive. Most displayed anger or pity.* *Independent* May 1996

Some CEOs have seemed immune to the demands of normal decency. In the *Wall Street Journal* (November 2007), Kate Kelly described the behaviour of the CEO as Bear Stearns collapsed:

> *During 10 critical days of this crisis – one of the worst in the securities firm's 84-year history – Bear's chief executive wasn't near his Wall Street office. James Cayne was playing in a bridge tournament in Nashville, Tenn., without a cellphone or an email device … his team placed in the top third.*

CNBC described Cayne as one of the worst CEOs of all time but when Bear Stearns was sold at a knock-down price to JP Morgan Chase, he received $61 million for his stake. Now compare this with the story of Mr Alexander Shand, a man said to be of an unblemished 11-year record, who was fired for failing to clock out for a hospital appointment. Scottish Television (STV) reported that:

> *Mr Shand had clocked in for work as normal around 7.45 in the morning and told his manager he had a hospital appointment at 9 o'clock. Having been told there was no problem, Mr Shand left the plant at 10 minutes to 9 and was away for half an hour. In his hurry to get there and back, he forgot to clock off and so the company terminated his contract, arguing that Mr Shand's behaviour amounted to gross misconduct because by not clocking out he was effectively stealing money from the firm.*

Mr Shand won an action for unfair dismissal, and was awarded £8,000.

All in this together?

Sir Richard Lambert, then head of the Confederation of British Industry, said April 2010: *If leaders of big companies seem to occupy a different galaxy from the rest of the community, they risk being treated as aliens.*

The CEO of the International Airlines Group (IAG) was paid £6.4m in 2014, an increase of 30% on the previous year after IAG had reported after-tax profits of more than £730m. The company said the results were achieved by making 4,500 people redundant (about a quarter of the workforce) and reducing employment terms and conditions for crew at the airline Iberia.[1] I had recently visited the Falklands and I was struck by a contrast:

> *British soldiers were issued with the same rations regardless of rank; however the Argentinean officers had different rations to their men. The officers' ration pack was twice the size of the other ranks'. It also contained items such as writing paper and a miniature of whisky. This made them highly prized by British troops.*[2]

Did this have anything to do with the result? It is hard to think that it did not.

Memorial in Stanley, Falkland Islands

> *Without fanfare, the Company Commander, sited between 4 and 5 Platoons said, 'OK, let's go!' and stepped over the embankment. Swallowing hard, I croaked something similar and also climbed out to commence our advance. I took only a few paces and glanced to my left. From my position as right hand assault platoon commander, I could see the OC (very closely followed by his signaller), the 4 Platoon Commander and, barely in the gloom, the right hand assault platoon commander of A Company. And no-one else. For what must have been only the briefest of moments, but which seemed a lifetime, it appeared the officers and one signaller alone were advancing on the enemy. Then, with a muttering of barely audible curses, the men of A and B Companies spilled forward to assault Wireless Ridge.*[3]

Brotherly love may be partly defined by the phrase *all in it together*.

> *Following an inadequate meal of pemmican and pony meat on the night of January, 31, 1909, Shackleton ... privately forced upon [Frank Wild] one of his biscuits from the four that he, like others, was rationed daily. 'I do not suppose that anyone else in the world can ... realise how much generosity ... was shown by this,' Wild wrote, 'I DO by GOD. I shall*

---

[1] The CEO declined a 2% increase in his basic pay for 2015 which amounted to £17,000. The IAG annual report said: *Once again, the chief executive has continued to lead by example in proposing restraint in executive packages.*

[2] Royal Marines Museum.

[3] *A Platoon Commander's Perspective*, The Army, http://www.army.mod.uk

never forget it.' ... The mystique that Shackleton acquired as a leader may partly be attributed to the fact that he elicited from his men strength and endurance they never imagined they possessed; he ennobled them.[1]

Ennobled is quite a word to describe a leader's effect on his people.

Poverty and employment

The Trussell Trust runs over 400 UK food banks. The number of people helped in the first half of the 2014-15 financial year was 38% higher than numbers helped during the same period in the previous year. 492,641 people were given three days' food and support, including 176,565 children. While problems with the social security system were the most common trigger for food bank use, 22% of those helped were working people who needed support because of their inadequate income.[2]

The Joseph Rowntree Foundation reported (2014) that there were as many working families in poverty as non-working families. Two-thirds of people who gained work in 2014 were paid less than the living wage.[3] The Social Mobility and Child Poverty Commission[4] said:

Too many of the jobs ... created in the economic recovery offer low income and high insecurity. They are a dead end, not a road to social progress ... Poverty is set to rise, not fall.

In 2015, the Children's Commissioner for England,[5] Dr Maggie Atkinson, said that the UK was in breach of the UN *Convention on the Rights of the Child*.

The Office for National Statistics revealed that any rise in employment from 2008 to 2014 was not about jobs but largely about self-employment. In November 2014, there were 4.5 million self-employed (15% of the workforce), an increase of 280,000 in one year and more self-employed than at any time in the previous 40 years. The average income from self-employment had fallen by 22% since 2008 because the rise in self-employment was not altogether the re-birth of a nation of entrepreneurs but largely people trying to make ends meet[6] and companies seeking to reduce costs by changing the status of their employees. (Particularly by avoiding the payment of National Insurance, the burden of which fell upon the newly self-employed ex-employee. Apart from taxi drivers, the most common self-

---

[1] Alexander.

[2] The Trussell Trust, http://www.trusselltrust.org/mid-year-stats-2014-2015.

[3] McInnes et al.

[4] The SMCP Commission is an advisory non-departmental public body, sponsored by the Department for Education, the Cabinet Office and the Department for Work and Pensions.

[5] The Commission was established under the Children Act 2004.

[6] The number of over 65s who are self-employed more than doubled 2009–2015.

employed roles are in construction and management consultancy; the latter tending to mean office workers no longer on the regular payroll.)

With longer working hours, zero-hour contracts, increased shift work, forms of self-employment and worries about the future, many Freemasons no longer felt able to take time off to attend a meeting, even when holiday entitlement allowed. We need to recognise these changes and their impact on the private lodge. If a gulf opens between the worries of the ordinary Mason and the concerns of those wearing chains, we shall find it nigh on impossible to turn things around. Lodges, private and Grand, will have to recognise that the world has changed and that the rules and habits appropriate to the years from 1850 to 1950 must be re-evaluated.

Fraud and scroungers

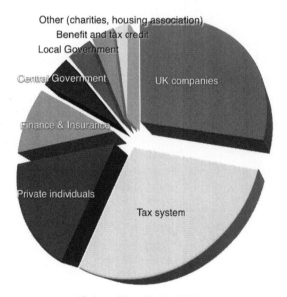

Victims of fraud in the UK 2013

The 2013 *Annual Fraud Indicator*[1] reported that the largest fraud losses were suffered by UK companies at just under £16.0 billion for the year, and 31% of total fraud. Tax fraud came in second at £14 billion (27% of total) although this official figure is widely regarded as an underestimate. Tax Research UK estimated the gap between tax owed and tax collected in 2012 to be £120 billion a year.[2]

---

[1] National Fraud Office, © Crown Copyright 2013.

[2] Richard Murphy, *Guardian*, 30 October 2012

A further £9.1 billion (17% of total) was lost by private individuals through identity theft, mass marketing and online ticket frauds. Next up at 10% was finance and insurance scams, including credit card, online banking and cheque fraud. Right at the bottom comes benefits fraud at £1.9 billion, a sizeable sum but merely 1% of the total and coincidentally 1% of the spend of the Department of Work and Pensions – and about the same cost as errors made by the department.

Put this 1% into perspective. The UK supermarkets keep a close eye on what is called *shrinkage*, that is to say theft in one form or another from their stores. In 2012-13, this amounted to 1.32% of sales.[1] Of course, the supermarkets make efforts to reduce this, but not at the cost of infuriating the great majority of their customers who are honest. It is no more true to say that benefits claimants are scroungers than it is to say that shoppers at Waitrose or Asda are dishonest.

There is ample evidence that benefits are underclaimed: that many people do not claim what is due to them. Underclaimed benefit in 2014 was just over £7.5 billion, about four times as much as fraud and, to be blunt, if one was seeking to reduce fraud, benefits fraud would not be the first place to direct one's efforts.

The political use of the word *scrounger* appeared during the banking crisis. It echoes both Mrs Thatcher's use of the word *workshy* and the 19th century complaints about the *dishonest poor*. The choice of words is designed to excuse a lack of compassion. If I can prove to myself that you are undeserving, I don't have to feel bad about ignoring you. *Scrounger* is a nasty, divisive and dishonest word, quite suitable to the end of decency, when you think about it.

---

[1] *Retail Crime in the UK*, Centre for Retail Research.

Reflections on phase 3

Let us pause for a moment to reflect on the implications for our order of this phase, *the end of decency*. When people at work have no trust in management; when they resent the lack of involvement and the absence of loyalty towards them; when they see senior management taking undeserved rewards (often as a result of reducing their own earnings and job security); when they notice incompetence being rewarded; indeed when they see management as aliens, they are unlikely to invest unthinking trust in any leadership of any kind, our order included.

We will have to demonstrate that our leadership is different; that it does understand the conditions of the ordinary men who form the bulk of our membership; that it genuinely does seek to hear their opinions and is ready to listen to what they say; that it does not hide itself away in executive bars and special dining rooms; that it is not a mutually congratulatory clique isolated from reality and that it does genuinely deserve the salutes and ovations that it demands.

When people see selfishness and immorality all around them,[1] we must demonstrate that morality matters and that in all our actions, we place moral considerations first. This goes not just for major crimes but also for the lesser sins of arrogance, pride and self-aggrandisement. I shall later seek to demonstrate how Freemasonry can play a major part in the rescue of society and how, in doing so, we can rescue ourselves. We can only do this from a position of moral security. Talk is not enough; the talk has to be walked.

> *Duty, honour, and gratitude now bind you to be faithful to every trust; to support with becoming dignity your new character and to enforce, by example and precept, the tenets of the system. Therefore let no motive cause you to swerve from your duty, violate your vows, or betray your trust; but be true and faithful, and imitate the example of that celebrated artist whom you have once represented. By this exemplary conduct, you will convince the world that merit has been your title to our privileges and that on you our favours have not been undeservedly bestowed.*[2]

The new audience

The middle class we once recruited from was largely defined by the nature of its employment. Generally speaking, we recruited white collar workers with careers in the professions, medium-sized firms, local government and the civil service with

---

[1] In a minor key but with forebodings about the future, a recent survey in the USA found that 33% of high school students and 16% of college students said they had stolen from a store in the past year. 33% said they would lie on a job application. 61% admitted to cheating in an examination in the past year. Source: Debra Viadero, *Education Week*, May 2015.

[2] West (1).

an admixture of self-employed men, commonly in building-related trades. Many of these men had followed their fathers, grandfathers and other family members into Freemasonry. Many needed to protect their careers and pensions and thus were not given to rocking the boat. They valued security and conformity.

The new audience is different. Less likely to be introduced by family members, they are making a conscious and personal decision to join us. They have ideals that they believe we will match and are deliberately seeking fellowship, meaning and purpose. They have researched Freemasonry via the web and know a lot more about us than the earlier audience. They tend to be more highly educated,[1] and to have good inter-personal skills. Some have full time jobs, but even then shift and weekend working is common. A greater number have less secure and even temporary employment in the form of part-time, agency or contracting work. Some have several jobs. Some are self-employed.

It is common to distinguish between a declining, traditional *core* workforce and a growing workforce *peripheral* to the core. Paul Mason writes:

> *The core workforce has been able to cling on to stable, permanent employment, with non-wage benefits attached to the job. The periphery must relate either as temporary agency workers, or via a network of contracting firms. But the core is shrunken: seven years into the post-2008 crisis, a permanent contract on a decent wage is an unattainable privilege for many people ... For both groups flexibility has become the key attribute.*

Paul Mason sees this as bad news for working people but there are many who adapt well to these peripheral jobs. They tend to be younger, more self-confident and flexible, able to do many types of work with a wide range of skills. Such men will form a good proportion of our new audience. Since they do not have careers or pensions to be protected, they place less value on security and conformity. They are open to change because change is central to the nature of their working lives. Their flexible minds make learning the ritual straightforward.

We must put in much greater efforts to make members of this new audience feel part of the lodge. In the past, such induction was carried out by the initiates' friends and relations. Now we have to consciously plan it. We must also remember that the new audience's free time is often unpredictable. We have to adapt to them, but the rewards are tremendous.

---

[1] The undergraduate population in the UK peaked at 1,928,140 in 2011/12.

A certain trumpet

In the first part of this book, I have laid out the cause of our modern decline, one similar enough to the 19th-century decline that understanding what happened then can help us understand what is happening today.

Values and purpose

Despite the damage caused to our order, then and now, both periods displayed a blossoming of values. During both, there were brief bursts of change and liberation; bursts quickly stamped on, I agree, but genuine enough. The 1960s, in particular, demonstrated values with which we might have allied ourselves had not the onset of nihilism and greed made that impossible. Nevertheless, such values still have some resonance. If we can amplify that resonance, we may be able to be of service to society and save ourselves.

There are two specific areas where we are needed; the first is of a lesser ambition but a step to the second, which I believe to be our true purpose. *The first* concerns the virtue and practice of trust; vital to society but now under threat. The complete loss of trust would mean the end of society. I shall describe its decline since 1980 and show how Freemasonry can become a guardian of trust and a reservoir of social capital. *The second* concerns the preservation of morality itself. I shall show how our order is one of the few communities able to sustain the moral life in what has become an amoral world. I shall contend that our greatest challenge and our greatest opportunity will lie in becoming a bastion for the virtues. It is our duty, and perhaps fate, to defend the moral life against the barbarians who would end it.

An uncertain trumpet

A problem for us is that the middle class was habit forming. We were hooked on it as a recruitment source. The fact that prior to the 1950s middle class candidates came along in a steady stream meant that we never had to question what we are, nor were there sufficient attacks on Freemasonry to act as a stimulus to make us analyse our values and decide what we offer to society. We have just taken it for granted that we have values and that we do matter to society – without ever having to articulate or justify either claim.

Now, when we need to be positive in the face of attacks on Freemasonry, we appear uncertain, incapable of articulating our values and our place in society. We are become defensive, seeking merely to placate our detractors. We respond to challenges by saying what we are **not**.

*Freemasonry does **not** teach universalism.*
*Freemasonry does **not** offer any path to salvation.*
*We have **no** dogma or theology.*
*Freemasonry today is **not** a whites only organisation.*
*We make **no** political statements.*

Our penalties are purely symbolic; they are **not** real. We do **not** use the name of the god Ba'al.[1] We **no longer** use the word *Jabulon*.[2] We add convoluted clauses to the ceremonies of initiation, passing and raising. We even translate our three grand principles into politically correct words. The website of the United Grand Lodge of England begins with negatives:

> *Freemasonry is one of the world's oldest and largest **non**-religious, **non**-political, fraternal and charitable organisations.*

It then tells us that Freemasonry teaches *self-knowledge through participation in a progression of ceremonies* and that our values are *integrity, kindness, honesty and fairness,* comments sufficiently anodyne as to be untrue. Such PR-driven language seeks to persuade the public to believe that Freemasonry is **not** really important; **not** really serious; **nothing** to worry about; **just** a hobby – as if we roll up our trouser legs for a laugh.[3] Rank-and-file Freemasons squirm uncomfortably in their seats when one of the rulers of the Craft tells them that Freemasonry is a hobby. They don't know what to think: either the speaker means what he says and has different values from theirs or he is just toeing a party line. Either way, embarrassment is the result. Frightened by unwise PR advice, we have avoided the 'big' statement.

A certain trumpet

This simply won't do. Father Theodore Hesburgh,[4] President of Notre Dame University, argued that leadership demands a clear vision. You cannot blow an uncertain trumpet, he said, referring to Paul's *Epistle to the Corinthians*:

---

[1] No one ever thought the penalties were real. As an aside, the word *Ba'al* means *master* and could be applied to any god or indeed boss. There were several gods who carried this title. There is a respected theory that there were three gods in early Israelitish religion: El, Ba'al and Yahweh.

[2] And so committed the Sojourners to discovering a word that did not exist until 1,700 years after their pick and shovel work. It is quite possible that *Jabulon* never had a meaning; that the mock-Hebrew explanation was *post facto*, as are the personifications of the 1st and 2nd degree words.

[3] The public would have difficulty in reconciling such a message with the presence of imposing buildings in the City of London (and elsewhere around the world) and the presence of a member of the royal family as an active leader. When PR is in conflict with evidence, suspicion is aroused.

[4] During the 35 years he was president, he increased the operating budget from $9.7 million to $176.6 million, endowments from $9 million to $350 million, and research funding from $735,000 to $15 million. Student numbers doubled to 10,000. Football matters at American universities: during his tenure, the *Fighting Irish* won 82% of their games.

73

For if the trumpet give an uncertain sound, who shall prepare himself to the battle? [1]

We need a clear trumpet call: one that says what Freemasonry **is** and shows the public (and the rank and file Mason) what we stand for. Given a clear statement, the public can agree or disagree with us but at least they will not rely on gossip, rumour or slander for information. A positive declaration of purpose will enable the ordinary Freemason to argue our corner. As things stand, the ordinary Mason is dissuaded from entering into discussion, being advised to leave such matters to those skilled in PR. That is just silly. The important discussions go on in the pub, at the golf club, in the gym or on the terraces.

The greed and near-criminal behaviour that we see reported in the press every day, the emptiness of almost all political statements and the continuing loss of religious belief, all combine to create a lack of meaning and purpose. As Andrew Hammer says of candidates:

> *We came for ideas, and the search for the meaning behind them. We came to discuss and explore those ideas in an environment of enlightenment which would not only be tolerant of them, but would also challenge us to see ourselves and the world around us in a different, or at the very least in an enhanced way.*

Since the value of Freemasonry is in large part the provision of meaning, we should make a positive statement of what we are and what we do. For example:

Freemasonry is a moral practice. We enable good men to live respected and die regretted.

There are periodic intervals in human experience when the moral life comes under attack. Now is such a time, and we must respond.

We will become a reservoir of social capital, enabling society to preserve the virtue of trust.

We will provide a bastion for the virtues in an amoral world, maintaining a community within which the moral life is lived.

In choosing to become a Freemason, a man accepts an obligation to live according to the virtues of the order. Such a choice cannot be made lightly.

There is no sense in which a man can say, 'I want to be a Freemason but not a good one.'

To be a good Freemason is to exhibit specific virtues. The most important of these are the three grand principles – brotherly love, relief and truth – and the four cardinal virtues – prudence, fortitude, temperance, and justice.

This is an ethical charter. It states that we are a moral order. It shows candidates what they should expect of us. It is an answer to the attacks of the insidious.

---

[1] 1 Corinthians 14:8

Social capital and the decline of trust

The World Health Organization expects road deaths and injuries to increase such that by 2020 road accidents will become the third greatest cause of death and disability worldwide,[1] following heart disease and depression. Statistics from the UK Department for Transport show that 45% of injuries and 22% of fatalities in UK car-related accidents take place at road junctions. 50% of people killed are pedestrians or occupants of other vehicles. In Britain, driving through red lights causes 10 casualties a day. This number is increasing.

A long-term study of the behaviour of car drivers at stop signs in suburban New York State reported in 1978 that a third of drivers came to a full stop as the law demanded, a third slowed right down in what is called a rolling stop, while a third drove right through. In 1996, the study showed that 98% of drivers drove right through.[2] A 2013 telephone survey by the American Automobile Association reported that 93% of drivers agreed that it is unacceptable to go through a red light but 35% said they had driven through one in the previous month.

Statistics from a Glasgow study[3] indicate that in 28% of red light infringements, the light had been red for between one and five seconds. Including reaction time, the average car driver can stop in 3.7 seconds from 40 mph. The amber traffic light means *stop if safe to do so* and lights are on amber for four seconds in a 40 mph zone.[4] Driving through a light that has been red for just one second in a 40 mph zone implies that the driver saw the lights change from green to amber, had time to stop before the red but refused to do so.

The response has been to invest in technology to catch drivers disobeying red lights. When cameras were installed in Strathclyde, Scotland, there was a 69% reduction in the number of red light infringements and a 62% reduction in accidents causing injuries – at junctions with cameras installed. There was little if any change at junctions without cameras. Reliance on people's respect for the law and on their desire to avoid injury to others is no longer sufficient. It is now only the likelihood of getting caught that results in a safer environment.

A police research study has indicated that the costs of installing and maintaining traffic light cameras is not inconsiderable. (As long ago as 1994, fixed costs were £9,200 and annual costs £5,600 per installation.[5]) However, the study showed

---

[1] The most common victim of road accidents is a man in the prime of life with family dependants.

[2] Putnam.

[3] Winn.

[4] Typically, lights are set for one second of amber for every 10 mph of the speed limit applying.

[5] Hooke et al.

that revenue from penalties quickly paid for the cost of installation and covered running costs. Somewhat disingenuously, the report said:

> *For traffic light cameras, all areas but three achieved a positive benefit within a year of the investment. Overall, the return was nearly twice the investment after one year and twelve times this by year five.*

The *positive benefit* referred to in this section of the report is not of a reduction in accidents but of ROI: return on (financial) investment. While red light cameras reduce infringements, the fines from the infringements that continue to occur are sufficient to cover costs and make a profit. In a like manner, speed cameras reduce speeding in the UK and save a thousand injuries and deaths a year but the fines from speed cameras are still sufficient to cover installation and running costs.[1] It seems that many drivers are willing to pay fines rather than be inconvenienced. In this, as in prostitution and banking, fines are treated as a cost of doing business.

Ten banks incurred £166.63 billion in fines and provisions between 2009 and 2013, an amount equivalent to the whole GDP of Belarus. The fines were for toxic mortgage products, Libor rigging, Forex rigging, violating sanctions, money laundering, electricity market manipulation, gold price fixing, assisting tax evasion, foreclosure abuses and payment protection fraud. (Roger McCormick of the CCP Research Foundation.)

The social contract

Thomas Hobbes (1588–1679) sought to explain the working of social life in terms of a *social contract*,[2] an agreement between members of a society that laws will govern them all for mutual benefit. Each person agrees not to do things they might otherwise want to do, in return for other people agreeing likewise.[3] Hobbes argues that without such an agreement, nothing good can be created:

> *... if one plant, sow, build or possess a convenient seat, others may ... be expected to come ... to dispossess and deprive him, not only of the fruits of his labour, but also his life ...*

Without a social contract, most good things would be impossible:

> *... there is no place for industry because the fruit thereof is uncertain and consequently no culture of the earth; no navigation ... no knowledge of the face of the earth; no account of time; no arts; no letters; no society; [but] continual fear and danger of violent death ...*

---

[1] Professor Richard Allsop said in his report: *Data for 2006-07 shows the cost of camera enforcement was being covered by penalties paid by detected offenders ... with only a modest surplus to the Exchequer of less than £4 out of each £60 penalty paid.*

[2] John Locke, Jean-Jaques Rousseau and Immanuel Kant also used the term.

[3] Hobbes does not see the contract as an historical event. He explains society *as if* the contract had been agreed by all.

and in Hobbes's ringing phrase, the life of man is:

> *... solitary, poor, nasty, brutish, and short.*

The social contract is enforced by a body Hobbes refers to as the *Commonwealth*, its name indicating its purpose: that by acting in common, we increase wealth for everyone. Today we would think of this contract as the rule of law, something central to the evolution of human society. Respect for the law is a social necessity and respect means obeying it, irrespective of the likelihood of being caught. The cost of enforcing the law depends upon the degree of respect. In a society with high respect, few people transgress and the cost of policing is low. With low respect, many transgress and the cost of policing is high.

> *The basis of all systems, social or political, rests upon the goodness of men. No nation is great or good because parliament enacts this or that, but that its men are great and good.*[1]

The need for trust

While it is necessary, the law is not sufficient. We cannot take every slight or injury to court. If a friend lets us down, a promise is broken, or a small service turns out not as expected, the law is of little help. The overwhelming majority of our relationships are governed by the principles of etiquette and decency. It is the moral life that fills in the gaps in the law, so to speak, and while it is the combination of the law and the moral life that makes social life possible, morality is the major partner.

Central to social life is the practice of trust. We need to trust a decorator when we have to pop out for a moment; a friend who promises to keep an important social engagement; a babysitter when we take an evening out; a delivery man who says he will arrive before noon, and so on. If we have to draw up a contract with a babysitter, if we have to pack away anything valuable when someone is working in our house and if friends are unreliable, social life becomes intolerable. We may be able to sue the dry cleaner who scorches a jacket or the delivery service when a wedding dress arrives late but a financial penalty yields no solace to a bride who cannot look her best.

We need to rely on people to do what they say they will do. Every failure of trust, every occasion on which our reliance on others is misplaced, makes social life that bit more difficult. Each of us becomes just a little more suspicious, cautious or cynical. At government level, extra steps have to be taken, extra safeguards put in place, more regulations adopted, and more laws enacted in an attempt to prevent failures of trust. At all levels, social life becomes more cautious, bureaucratic, expensive and ponderous.

---

[1] Kalam.

Tony Blair [was] *responsible for 54% more new laws per year in office than Margaret Thatcher ... it is estimated that an average of 2,663 new laws were added every year under Blair, compared to an average of just 1,724 under Thatcher. The statistics reveal that there has been a long term trend for each Government to legislate more aggressively than its predecessors.*[1]

Professor Sealy, Professor of Law at the University of Cambridge, said:

I think that a lot of the legislation is not so much originated by governments as part of their policy but is a reactive response ... fed from day to day by the media, which can make every bit of news into a crisis.[2]

The loss of trust

It is a sadness that trust is constantly being damaged, even where we would expect it to be most safe. In the stock market, my word seems no longer to be my bond. Banks have proved not only untrustworthy with their investors' money but capable of acting directly against the interests of their customers. Major accounting firms have acted contrary to their professional ethics, so seriously that one, Arthur Andersen, was shut down while another was prevented from taking new audits. Members of the House of Commons and the House of Lords have been found guilty of accepting bribes, as well as of fiddling their expenses. Newspapers have not only illegally invaded private lives but have told lies, knowing them to be so.[3] The leaders of many international sporting organisations act against their sports and players have thrown matches.[4] Celebrities have been found to be sexually predatory. Beef is not always beef and a lamb curry may not contain lamb. Advertising is often, if not usually, untrue and Public Relations little more than the skilled art of avoiding answers to questions.

An analysis carried out by the Youth Justice Board in 2008[5] suggests that one in six children in the UK experience serious abuse at some time in their childhood.[6]

---

[1] https://www.sweetandmaxwell.co.uk/about-us/press-releases/260607.pdf.

[2] Sweet and Maxwell.

[3] Fewer than 25% of the UK population trust government, fewer than 20% trust parliament and fewer than 15% have confidence in the press. Twice as many people take part in demonstrations compared to the 1970s. In 1983, 90% of the UK population trusted the banks; by 2009, the figure was 19%. The percentage expressing confidence in the police halved between 1981 and 2006.

[4] In recent years, 31 cricketers have been convicted of fixing international matches, 79% of Tour de France winners have been convicted of drug use, 40% of the top ten male 100 metre sprinters each year have been found guilty of doping.

[5] Day.

[6] Abused girls are more likely to suffer conditions such as depression, self-harm, suicidal tendencies, eating disorders, low self-esteem and psychological disorders. Abused boys are more likely to become aggressive, abusive, to offend or become involved in alcohol and substance misuse. *Child Abuse*: a fact sheet from the Department of Justice Canada.

> 1,400 children were abused in Rotherham over a sixteen year period. Victims as young as eleven were trafficked, beaten and raped. *Independent* August 2014

Perhaps worst of all are the revelations about torture, not just that it has occurred with such regularity, but that 53% of Americans[1] and 29% of the UK population[2] think it is sometimes or even often justified. In 1952, more than half of Americans thought people in general led honest and moral lives. Putnam reports that by 1998 fewer than one-third thought this. In 2001, only 41% of Swiss, 31% of Britons and 23% of the French said that most people could be trusted.[3]

Social capital

The term *social capital* is variously defined but essentially it results from interactions between people. Quite small acts can build social capital and the fact that Putnam's examples sound so old-fashioned is somewhat worrying:

> ... *raking your leaves before they blow onto your neighbour's yard, lending a dime to a stranger for a parking meter, buying a round of drinks the week you earn overtime, keeping an eye on a friend's house, taking turns bringing snacks to Sunday School, caring for the child of the crack-head one flight down.*

Trust is a social, not an individual virtue.

> *Social capital refers to connections among individuals – the social networks and the norms of reciprocity and trustworthiness that arise from them ... A society of many virtuous but isolated individuals is not necessarily rich in social capital.*[4]

The more that people know other people and the more frequently they engage with each other, the more social cohesion there is and the greater the social capital is said to be. The sociologist James Coleman has argued that social capital, like other forms of capital, enhances productivity; for example, when a transaction is made solely with a handshake such as in the wholesale diamond market, which to outsiders seems remarkable:

> ... *in the process of negotiating a sale, a merchant will hand over to another merchant a bag of stones for the latter to examine in private at his leisure ... The merchandise may be worth thousands, or hundreds of thousands, of dollars. Such free exchange of stones for inspection is important to the functioning of this market. In its absence, the market would operate in a much more cumbersome, much less efficient fashion.*[5]

---

[1] Pew Research Center, December 9, 2014. Associated Press/NORC found similar results.

[2] Poll carried out by Globe Scan for Amnesty International, May 2014.

[3] *The Well-being of Nations*, OECD, 2001. Highest Norway 65%. Lowest Turkey 6.5%.

[4] Putnam.

[5] Coleman.

The phrase *social capital* refers to the reservoir of trust in society. A society that is used to trust and trusting can be said to have a large reservoir of trust or high social capital. The activity of trust, trusting and being trusted, is also the result of social interaction. The less often we interact with people, the less we are likely to trust people and the less often we interact with people and so on. It becomes a vicious circle. When we tighten the circle of people we trust, we increase our fears of the world and the decline in trust creates fear and loneliness:

> *A survey by the Mental Health Foundation ... found that 48% of us believe people are getting lonelier in general. Loneliness affects many of us at one time or another. Only 22% of us never feel lonely and one in ten of us feels lonely often. More than a third of us have felt depressed because we felt alone ... The lonelier our society, the more likely we are to experience loneliness ...* [1]

Gated communities

One obvious symptom of the decline in trust is the growth of gated communities (GCs), where trust is restricted only to those within the gates and where the outside world becomes enemy-occupied territory. In 2014, there were 10 million homes in the USA within gates,[2] a 53% increase over 2001 and 10% of all homes. There is a correlation between the growth of GCs and the degree of disparity between rich and poor.

The choice to live in GCs has been called the *revolt of the elite*, a perception that affluent people seek *to exclude themselves from social bonds ... segregating themselves spatially as well as socially.* One of the most important implications of GCs is a tendency to opt out of local services and an increasing unwillingness to pay for them.[3] The rich argue against paying for social services and public medicine because they never use either. A short-term view, one may agree. After all, even the rich will suffer in a virus outbreak.

> There was no business case to make an Ebola vaccine for those who needed it most.
> *Independent* September 2014

Fear and safety

Homes in GCs are sold as *security enclaves*, in which people choose to live defended by gates and fences rather as the 14th-century moat defended the castle. Researchers speak of the creation of localised *cities of walls*, of urban development becoming *fortress-like* in character but a 1995 study of crime rates showed no

---

[1] Griffin.

[2] US 2009 Census data.

[3] Blandy et al.

difference between GCs and other high-income areas. As Richard Schneider, Professor of Urban Planning at the University of Florida, said,

> *You're just as likely to be burgled by your next-door neighbour, especially if there are teenagers. Criminals from outside are also quick to figure out how to get in. They learn the code from the pizza guy. The effects of gating decay over time.*[1]

Curiously, life in GCs actually *causes* a fear of people outside. People in them see crime rates as much higher than they really are. The only significant difference between high-income GCs and high-income non-GCs was that non-GCs had a greater sense of community.[2] The benefit of lower crime rates is illusory but the *erosion of the social fabric* is real. Social interaction matters.

The Retreat at Twin Lakes, Florida; the location of the shooting of Trayvon Martin in 2012.

The decline of interaction

Social interaction is declining in the UK. The UK *Social Trends* report for 2011 asked people what they do with their spare time.

Most common activities in the UK (percentage reporting each activity)			
	Age 25–34	35–44	45–64
Watching TV	85	88	89
Being with friends / families	85	85	83
Listening to music	78	76	74
Shopping	73	74	69
Eating out	71	70	72

---

[1] Blandy et al.

[2] 35% of people surveyed preferred to be part of a wider community and a similar number disliked the thought of living behind fences.

The most commonly reported activities are those which do not involve meeting new people, do not require commitment to others and can be taken up or dropped at will. Most people take their leisure opportunistically, as and when they have a moment.

Perhaps the biggest change involves the internet. In 2010, 80% of people aged between 16 and 54 accessed the internet every day. Social networking doubled between 2010 and 2014 by when 44% of respondents had their own networking profile. Social networking is not social. It makes no specific time demands and people can carry on their networking with or without the active involvement of any other individual. The audience of the social networker's postings exists primarily in the imagination and the social networker's own existence is as imaginary as his or her audience. There are few if any checks and the interactions require, and increasingly exhibit, no morality.

45% of the population went internet shopping in 2006; 90% in 2013. Men aged 35–44 were asked in 2012 what they would miss most if it were taken away. 52% said the TV, 19% the internet and only 3% their newspaper.

Civic engagement

The majority of people in the UK have lost interest in activities – be they political, religious or otherwise – which demand a time commitment. In the UK, it always has been the middle class that has been the most likely to join voluntary organisations and has been more likely to trust others as a result[1] but the middle class is in decline. Membership of political parties has plummeted. Low enough at 4% in 1980, it had dropped to under 1% by 2009.[2] The trend of trust in government has been downward for many years. *British Social Attitudes* again:

> *Britain's democracy has been a source of concern in recent years ... During the last 20 years, there have been numerous allegations of 'sleaze' and of financial irregularities ... the resignation of the Speaker of the House of Commons and ... three MPs being sent to prison. In response the public withdrew what little willingness to trust politicians they ... had.*[3]

Sport

Sport is not only an indicator of social capital but also of health.

---

[1] *British Social Attitudes*, Report 18.

[2] Membership of UKIP grew threefold between 2011 and 2014. UKIP may have been a protest party *(A plague o' both your houses!)*. This may have been the cause of the sudden spate of new members for the Liberal party after the UK 2015 election, for the Labour party with what seemed like the Corbyn leadership, and even the early success of Donald Trump in the Republican leadership battle. These events appear to show support for non-mainstream politics.

[3] *British Social Attitudes*, Report 28.

Public Health England estimates that the cost to the nation of physical inactivity is £7.4 billion a year. Its report, *Everybody Active, Every Day* says:

> *Physical inactivity is responsible for 1 in 6 deaths in the UK. This makes it as dangerous as smoking. Yet over a quarter of us are still inactive, failing to achieve a minimum of 30 minutes of activity a week … We are 24% less active than in 1961.*[1]

The average age of golfers who play at least once a week had risen to 63 by 2014, having been 49 just five years before; golf club membership in England fell by 20% from 2004 to 2014 and even in Scotland, the home of the game, it fell 14%. England Golf announced a strategic plan, claiming that a change of the game's image would reverse the decline. The manufacturer Acushnet, which owns the *Titleist* and *Footjoy* brands, predicted that the game will bounce back of its own accord. Neither sounds likely.[2]

During the period from 2004 to 2014, the number of people playing organised football declined by 20%, a loss of some 200,000 players. The decline was most obvious in park football where 2,360 teams disappeared. Somewhat more creatively than expecting the game to bounce back on its own or issuing a new logo, the Cambridgeshire Football Association launched an initiative known as *flexi-football*, the aim being to meet the problem of commitment head-on and to enable people to get a game when they could find the time. Glen Moore reported:

> *… every month the county will provide a decent pitch and a referee and organise matches, at various age groups and for both sexes, for anyone who turns up. Team sizes, pitch sizes, all can be decided on the day, with teams even tweaked mid-match if there is an imbalance, just like a kickabout in the park.*[3]

Bowling alone

The title of Robert Putnam's book, *Bowling Alone*, refers to the fact that while the number of tenpin bowlers in the US increased by about 10% between 1980 and 1993, participation in league bowling almost halved. Much in line with the other institutions I have mentioned, membership of the American Bowling Congress

---

[1] Varney.

[2] In the US, there were an estimated 30 million golfers in 2000. In August 2015, that number is 23 million. James Moore writes: *Golf's fans are ageing and a younger generation likes its sports faster, more fun, and less elitist. The flowering of interest that followed the emergence of the dynamic, multicultural Tiger Woods as the world's best player has faded along with his career.* Independent 7 August 2015.

[3] *Independent*, 25 October 2014.

peaked in 1955 and has declined 72% since. Putnam's book, of course, is not about bowling itself but about the decline of community life in general:

> ... *the numbers imply we now have sixteen million fewer participants in public meetings about local affairs, eight million fewer committee members, eight million fewer local organisation leaders and three million fewer men and women organised to work for better government, than ... in the mid 1970s.*

Putnam describes the change in terms of a Yiddish distinction: that people today are less like *machers* and more like *schmoozers*.

Machers are the doers, the involved people. They take the lead in clubs and associations, work on community projects and attend local community and political meetings. They are the source of lodge and temple management, the organisers of charity events, golf days and widows' lunches. They are the good citizens of their community, and above all they are reliable.

Schmoozers have just as active a social life but one less organised and purposeful. Their use of time is spontaneous and flexible, not planned ahead. They spend time with friends, visit relatives and attend events that interest them, but only when time and motivation coincide. They can readily change plans if something better comes along.

Machers are decreasing while *schmoozing* is on the increase and those organisations that require regular commitment of time have suffered as a result. A dramatic exemplification is Putnam's account of the US Parent–Teacher Associations (PTA). As a percentage of families with children of school age, membership reached 50% in the late 1950s, and the PTA was the largest secular organisation in the USA. Membership then declined so that by 1980 it was less than 20%.[1] Putnam also reports that the number of Red Cross volunteers peaked in 1956 in the USA but had reduced by 61% by 1980. (Note again the date of the peak.) Putnam sees such statistics as the end of the community:

> *Like casualties dryly reporting from someone else's distant war,* [the] *unadorned numbers scarcely convey the decimation of American community life they represent. In round numbers every single percentage-point drop represents two million fewer Americans involved in some aspect of community life every year.*

Putnam thinks of the *machers/schmoozers* distinction as psychological but it is just as likely that people become *schmoozers* with shift work, zero-hours contracts, sudden changes in work demands and top-down management.

---

[1] Membership of PTAs is low in the UK. Membership declined from 3% of the population in 1994 to 2% in 2000.

A lodge needs *machers*. Only by having a committed and energetic set of officers can a lodge survive and prosper and this is particularly true of those civil servants of the lodge: the Secretary, DC and Treasurer. Once succession to these offices fails, the lodge's fate is sealed. The decline of our membership is part and parcel of a much more significant decline, a great danger to our society.

Virtuous and vicious circles

Trust and social interaction go together, as *British Social Attitudes* reports:

> *Our findings suggest that those more organisationally-active tend also to be more trusting of others. They also suggest that it is the fact of affiliation rather than type or extent of activity, that is generally the most decisive factor … the connection between social trust and social participation is … a reciprocal link: so the more trusting people are, the more likely they are to be joiners and vice versa.* [1]

There is a *virtuous* circle in which high social interaction leads to more moral behaviour, which leads to greater trust, which leads to higher social interaction, as the wheel goes around. This virtuous circle drives a smaller involvement of the law and life is easier, less bureaucratic, less expensive and more safe. The circle becomes *vicious* when the opposite is true and the law cannot cope. We are perilously close to such a state today.

---

[1] *British Social Attitudes*, Report 18.

Building social capital

Part of our role in society must be that of maintaining and increasing social capital, enabling more good men to work together in greater love and unity. The decline of social capital and the loss of trust are dangerous to our way of life. It is clear that both are declining in our society at an alarming rate but the maintenance and indeed growth of social capital is a duty for which we are well suited. Social capital is created by social interaction and since our meetings are interaction, just by being, we create a reservoir of trust. Every meeting creates social capital when brethren gather together, get to know each other, exchange views and life stories, make and receive invitations to visit, and give and receive support and fellowship. We create social capital by loving as brethren.

Why us in particular? Other organisations and activities, from the Lions and the Round Table to five-a-side football, cycling and darts, create interaction but they, like all organisations which require commitment from their members are in decline. If they could turn their membership decline around, they would indeed make a tremendous contribution to social interaction, social capital and the virtue of trust. However, there is little sign that they can.

Can we turn our decline around? I believe we can, because we offer what few other organisations do.[1] In the past, the church provided a sense of meaning and purpose, and for many people it still does. However, religious commitment is declining and the church no longer plays the part that it did.[2] We can offer much that the church used to, but to all men, not just the religious. It is our offer of meaning and purpose which distinguishes us from the Lions for example. Unlike them, we are not primarily about raising money for charity. We give to charity (philanthropy) because it is part of love, but love comes first. As Hammer writes:

> We engage in philanthropy only because of the philosophical teachings of our order which compels us do so ... Without philanthropy, we are merely doing less in the world than our philosophy teaches. But without our philosophy we lose our meaning and when we lose our meaning we lose our reason to exist.

It is because of our offer of meaning and purpose, that we can be one of the few organisations in the social capital manufacturing business and so in all we do, we should have the aim of creating social capital in mind. We should go along to lodge meetings not just to enjoy ourselves but to help other brethren do so. We must improve the quality of our interaction as well as its extent.

---

[1] Oliver Kram, in reviewing Jonathan Sacks' book *Not in God's Name*, in *The Times* June 20, 2015, spoke of *youngsters searching for a sense of religious identity in a moral vacuum.*

[2] Archbishop Robert Runcie gave the Anglican Church twenty-five years. (He died in 2000.)

Visiting

Visiting is not just pleasant, it is a duty; part of our social capital manufacturing business. We must ensure that our visit adds to our host lodge's social capital. We must show our appreciation, enjoy the variations in the ritual, join in conversation with all our neighbours at the festive board and thank our host when we leave. If invited to speak, we must put effort into it and deliver something worth saying in a manner worth listening to. We must ensure that any visitor to our own lodge is made welcome; that no visiting brother is ever left standing on his own, that all visiting brethren are brought into our circle and made to feel one of us. Conversation at the festive board is not just a skill but a loving duty.

The table plan

Table planning is a minor art form. As I wrote in my book on recruitment,[1] a good table plan will facilitate conversation. Conversation will flow across the table more easily than sideways but both should be planned, taking into account common interests, mutual acquaintances or recent experiences. A brother must be sat with his guests but a guest may share interests with another brother besides his host. Newer brethren should be sat with different brethren at each meeting, helping them to get to know everyone. Grand officers are often exiled to top table when they could be dispersed among those brethren interested in their 'grand' lives. In a private lodge, conversation matters more than rank and precedence.

Honours

We should never seek advancement. When brethren are honoured we are pleased for them, but the advancement itself is not important, nor are the salutes that go with it. What is important is that brethren are honoured because they exhibit brotherly love, that they are brethren around whom trust pivots.

Brethren and time

It is often assumed that the decline in participation in sport, politics or Freemasonry is a matter of cost and that if costs are reduced, more people will become involved. Of course, cost is a factor. Gunn and Bell quote an accountant on his decision not to join a golf club:

> I could lose my job ... quickly if I don't deliver. We're all very insecure ... I won't join an expensive club with high [joining] fees because I may have to move in a couple of years.

This comment is more about the stability necessary to plan. Cost is significant but the issue of time management is central to the retention of new members.

---

[1] West (4)

The lodge of instruction

There can be no doubt that a strong LOI is important in building fellowship and brotherly love. The major weakness of the London lodge is its difficulty in organising regular meetings of its LOI. It used to be true that members worked in London and could attend LOI before going home. As lodges have aged, the greater proportion of the membership is retired and living away from London. Creativity is required. For example, a way around the problem might be to find lodges of instruction that operate in or near clusters of the brethren. The Preceptor, DC and ADC can share visits to see how brethren are getting on and everyone can be gathered together once or twice just before a lodge meeting in final preparation.

Involvement in the ritual

More voices make the ritual more interesting and if, instead of being passive observers, the brethren share in the event, they feel more strongly that they are part of things. Most of the ceremonies can be broken into parts and delegated by the Master. The working tools, charges, traditional history and tracing boards are obvious examples but many other parts can be shared out as well. Imagination can find many ways to involve brethren. The ceremony of installation can be carried out by several Past Masters working together, an opportunity for the Master Elect's proposer and seconder and even a representative from the mother lodge to participate. The lodge Mentor will want to ensure that newer brethren who are ready, and Past Masters still capable, are given opportunities to perform.

The ritual

Our daily advancement in Masonic knowledge is not a matter of learning the ritual by rote. Being able to repeat the words in the right order is necessary but far from sufficient. Ritual excellence is a matter of letting the meaning shine through. When memory, pronunciation, intonation, phrasing and timing are perfect, and when it is clear that the speaker is savouring the words as he delivers them, then the ritual inspires contemplation and meditation. That is its purpose.

Allegory and symbols

We learn about the virtues both by learning the ritual but also by discussing it. Today, we spend insufficient time in discussing the allegory and symbols of the ritual. Symbolism is often a matter of personal interpretation of what is presented. Rarely is there just one interpretation and that is what makes symbolism interesting. Do the rough and perfect ashlars represent a life of learning, an eternal striving towards perfection or an example of what the skilled craftsman can attain? Does the black and white pavement represent the joys and sorrows of our chequered existence, night and day, or the logic of the chessboard?

Is the lewis an example of human creativity, problem solving or working together? Do white gloves mean purity, honest working hands or protection from the dangers of the world? In his *Symbolism in Craft Masonry*, Colin Dyer wisely avoids providing definitive explanations. He says:

> *All I seek to do in this book is to take some of the more common symbols found in the Craft and to endeavour to trace what our forebears intended to teach us by including them and why those particular symbols may have been chosen: and also to consider and appreciate some of the immense amount of speculative writing over the years.*[1]

What makes his book so useful is that it offers *possible* meanings which can lead our speculation. We need to explore what our forebears have said about the Craft and ritual not only because we may have forgotten important lessons but also because in learning their reasons for what they said, we can gain a new perspective on the meaning of the ritual. It is a great pity that few of the authors of the earlier speculative school of Masonic writing are read today. There is much in George Oliver, A.S. McBride and Francis de Paula Castells worth meditating on. A recent example of speculative work is Craig Weightman's *A Journey in Stone*.

It is a pity also that it is not common in England to read the extensive American literature on our order and it is true that there are significant differences either side of the Atlantic. Nevertheless, I have quoted several times from Andrew Hammer's *Observing the Craft*, a book I cannot praise too highly. John Bizzack's *For the Good of the Order* and Kirk C. White's *Operative Freemasonry: a manual for restoring light and vitality to the fraternity* are rewarding. White has a nice comment on the place of ritual in life:

> *Ritual causes mental change and that is its purpose. How ritual accomplishes that change is by bracketing the time spent as 'special' and unlike our ordinary mundane lives … Our opening and closing rituals mark the time in lodge as different from our daily lives.*

Recruitment

Finally, let us look at recruitment. Part of our social capital manufacturing process is welcoming new brethren into our order. I dedicated an earlier book[2] to an explanation of how a lodge can attract candidates. This is not a theoretical account but a real life story of how my mother lodge initiates three or four candidates a year and, more importantly, how your lodge can do the same. Here is an extract:

> **St Laurence Lodge, No. 5511** is a perfectly normal, private lodge which meets in Upminster in Essex and initiates four candidates each year. Our regular meetings and our annual emergency meeting are insufficient to handle our work, so we take most of

---

[1] Dyer (1).

[2] West (4).

our seconds and thirds out to other lodges in other temples on what we call 'away days'. These are very popular. We take a fair number of our own brethren with us which makes a nice addition to the attendance at our host lodge. We have so far carried out two triple initiations, using a version of the rubric we invented ourselves – minimising repetition but keeping things personal to each candidate. (The method is described in the book and we are planning to use it for double initiations as well.)

We are often asked how we achieved this and so we produced a book entitled: *Things to do when you have nothing to do* which is about *how to find those candidates who have been looking for you all this time.* The illustrations in the book feature the brethren of St Laurence and one reviewer said, *The affection the brethren of the author's lodge feel for each other and their lodge is profoundly evident.* I do hope so.

Central to what we do is the *Law of Paradoxical Intent*. I'll explain this later but let me start with saying that the better a lodge feels about itself, the more likely it is to attract candidates. The unfortunate truth is that many lodges have ceased to feel good about themselves; numbers are low; visitors are few; ritual is poor and the festive board a quiet affair which finishes early. When a lodge has no work to do, all too often it launches a desperate search to find someone, anyone, willing to entertain the brethren. When *All we had at our last meeting was a talk*, the brethren feel bad and brethren are unlikely to invite friends into a lodge they feel bad about.

Pushing at the world

I have had a mixed career. After graduation, I spent a couple of years as a buyer at Fords and then went back to University for my doctorate. I taught at university for a while before returning to industry. I became General Manager of Scotland and Northern Ireland and head of International Personnel and Public Relations for Xerox, then a partner in an accounting firm and finally founded *The Working Manager Ltd* from which I am now retired. The point of this is to show that in much of my career, I have had to sell my services and it has been my constant belief that if I put in the effort, work will result – but *rarely from the direction for which my efforts had been intended.*

I might meet potential clients, speak at conferences, network and attend conventions. I might create marketing literature for a sales drive and so on but the contracts I won were almost never from companies I targeted. However, I always found that if I didn't put in the effort, no work at all came in. You see, it was the effort that mattered. I succeeded because I was *pushing at the world* and the world responded – and it is the same in our lodges; we need to be pushing at the world. It should be obvious that candidates will come to energetic lodges; ones that are involved, active and ready for something new – and thus feel good about themselves.

Law of paradoxical intent

When faced with a problem, we usually try to solve it on the basis of our experience. That's fine, but when past experience repeatedly lets us down, we have to do something different. We must challenge the assumptions behind our experience. If we don't, we repeat the same failures.

We assume – don't we? – that candidates will come via existing members and so call upon brethren to find them. When this fails, we don't question our assumption, and so repeat the failure. The constant pleading and repeated failure to find new candidates, just makes the brethren feel worse, and gradually they stop attending.

The law of paradoxical intent holds that by doing the *opposite* of what past experience tells us to do, we will be more likely to succeed; that busily *not* seeking candidates, causes them to appear. We must change our assumptions. After all, doing the *same old, same old* hasn't achieved anything. So stop complaining about the absence of candidates; stop nagging the brethren; stop wasting meetings on talks; ban rehearsals of ceremonies in lodge meetings and focus on enthusing and exciting the brethren.

Every dull talk, every dull rehearsal in lodge, is a step backward. People will rarely talk about dull, grey lodges but they will talk about lodges that are busy, vibrant and exciting – and excitement is infectious. As the title indicates, our book offers lots of *things to do when you have nothing to do*; things that will make the brethren feel good. Follow what's in the book or use your ideas but whatever you do, make it new, exciting and a real advance in Masonic knowledge. Help the brethren feel good.

Look, I am not saying that this is easy but I am saying it works.

The progressive ceremonies are letting us down. The idea that a real Masonic meeting is a performance of the progressive ritual, the Masonic waltz and the installation, is quite recent. In the 18th century, lodges were small. There were only two degrees and the ritual was brief: an initiation taking possibly fifteen minutes and a second about ten, and what is more, they probably took place outside the lodge meeting proper. There was no installation of the Master and no limit on tenure of the chair. Those lodges met ten times a year, so it cannot have been the progressive ceremonies that occupied our 18th century brethren. They must have done something different.

With their pretence to be all that Masonry is, the progressive ceremonies make a meeting without them seem a failure. But it needn't be – and it shouldn't be! We can do many exciting things that offer a genuine advancement in Masonic knowledge. Our book contains four plays *wot I wrote* to involve the brethren – entertainments we call them – about the Lectures,[1] which are what our 18th century brethren actually used; the Antient Charges and the Old Charges; the change of the words of recognition; Jack the Ripper and the Seddon murder; and the exposures of Freemasonry. We know they work because we have performed them all. Use the contents of the book as they stand or as starters for your own imagination, but whatever you do, obey the law of paradoxical intent and become a lodge that is always busy, always doing exciting and interesting things.

Websites

The old saying that if you invent a better mousetrap, the world will beat a path to your door, is false. You have to go out and tell the world. Today, a website is a cost effective vehicle but I know of two lodges who paid for a custom website and were still waiting two years later. Do it yourself. Many hosting sites offer easy tools and with these I have created a site in an afternoon. But do please remember, a website alone is not enough. There are many boring lodge websites which achieve nothing.

Our own site gets 15,000 hits a month. To put that into context, the website of the United Grand Lodge gets 30,000. Why do we get those hits? It is because our site is lively, updated at least once a week, and carries lots of photographs.

---

[1] Not a lecture or talk!

It reports our meetings, our visits to other lodges, our social and sporting events. It features our meetings, away days, the St Laurence Grand Prix (racing in go-karts), our attempts at ten-pin bowling and clay pigeon shooting, the new constellation temple at Upminster, the Upminster Fun Day with a great video of our dinner ladies dancing, the Stisted Garden Party, the Pride of Essex award, our e-Bay purchase of a 1963 St Laurence Lodge Past Master's jewel, the TLC skydive and a board in Rochford Hundred Golf Club celebrating its winning the Thornton Cup in 1977. Why? One of our current brethren was a member of that team.

We look for news to report. One of our members travelled around Cape Horn and the Antarctic and sent back photos which we featured – daily. Our site shows Freemasonry to be exciting and interesting, and it is.

So remember, only the website of an active and interesting lodge will attract candidates but your website should be more than just an advert. It should carry our message, combat the silly accusations made about us and state our values. The more lodges who do that, the louder our message. Perhaps the most successful ad ever was *Persil washes whiter*. It was said over and over again. Frequency of message matters – and we have a great message.

Getting to know candidates

Contacts via the web are strangers and you have to put in the effort to get to know them. We arrange visits to Freemasons Hall, tours of the British Museum, pizza evenings, an hour or two at a pub and dinner at an Indian restaurant – and of course we invite contacts to our social events. Our rule is that each candidate must attend at least four such events and wait a year between first meeting and initiation.

By the way, names of towns and counties are repeated around the world. One contact said he lived in Essex and so we invited him to a pizza evening in Upminster. Two days beforehand, he asked us for directions. Alarm bells rang. He did indeed live in Essex – the one just outside Baltimore in the USA. Our website says we are men only but twice ladies have contacted us. We pass them on to the Order of Women Freemasons.

Do be careful

We are very careful with contacts. Initial meeting is always in a public place. There are no addresses on our website and we use email, not telephone, until we are sure the contact is genuine. A stranger may not wish us well so our first email is carefully worded. There is an example in the book. Occasionally, a contact is not appropriate and we have to say this. Sometimes, the contact is looking for more than we can offer, perhaps even psychological help.

Mentoring

We start mentoring immediately. We ensure that contacts meet members of the lodge and other candidates. We watch the flow of conversation to ensure that everyone is involved. We play 'general post', moving senior brethren around the group to talk to all contacts and ask them what they want to know about Masonry.

Our mentoring does not stop with initiation. We work hard to get candidates, and we work just as hard to keep them. We take new brethren to visit other lodges and to see other forms of the ritual. Our table plans are designed so new brethren get to know different members and visitors at each meeting. We give new members a job at LOI right away. We find small passages of ritual for them to work in lodge. After one year, they are expected to do the first degree working tools and after 18 months the charge after initiation – and they do. We are always delighted with the refreshing quality of the response. Our web contacts have been really good candidates. They have researched us, thought about the fraternity and really know why they want to join. They have proved active and involved Masons, ready to share in the leadership of the lodge, organising events and performing excellent ritual.

So in conclusion let me restate the theme:

- Doing nothing will result in nothing.[1]
- Remember the law of paradoxical intent.
- Doing something completely different, makes us more likely to succeed.
- Lodges who are energetic and ready for something new feel good about themselves.
- The brethren talk about energetic lodges and thus *push at the world*.
- The more that a lodge feels good about itself, the more likely it is to attract candidates.
- The more it attracts candidates, the better the story it has to tell.
- A great website tells that story.
- Retention has to be worked at – every day.

Remember that the most common reason for NOT becoming a Mason is that *It is not for people like me*.[2] We have to go out and tell people that *it is*.

---

[1] As W. Bro. Barry Patchett, a member of one of our sister lodges, said to me: *Waiting for the phone to ring never brings in business but have you noticed how often the phone rings when you are already talking to a customer?*

[2] *The Future of Freemasonry*, The Social Issues Research Centre, 2012.

A purpose to life

I spoke earlier of two purposes for Freemasonry. The first, which I have just described, is about the preservation of trust. The second and greater role is the preservation of the moral life itself, becoming a bastion for the defence of the virtues. This will be our greatest challenge.

To describe it, I need to take you through some moral philosophy. I will do my best to restrict the use of technical jargon but I cannot avoid it altogether. Thus some parts of the following chapters may be somewhat heavy going. It will help to have read two of my previous books, *The Goat, the Devil and the Freemason* and *Deism,* which I wrote partly to form a foundation for this book. The following overview may also help. I hope it will entice you to go through the chapters in as much detail as you feel comfortable with. In the overview, I shall just state the points. The argument is in the text.

Overview

Philosophers have shown that we cannot derive a moral statement (an *ought*) from a factual statement (an *is*.) I sometimes refer to this as the ought/is distinction and it dates from as early as David Hume (1711–1776). If not from facts, how are moral statements derived? Some writers have sought the justification of morality in religion; that certain actions are wrong or right because a god has said they are. There are philosophical arguments against such a theory but, in any case, people who have no religion can and do make moral judgements and so religion cannot be the (only) basis of morality.

Some philosophers, and many ordinary people, say that moral statements are just expressions of feelings. In philosophy, this theory is known as *emotivism.* However, we justify our moral judgements by argument, using examples and appeals to precedent, not something we normally do with feelings. What is more, without the prior existence of morality, we could not refer to those many emotions which are described in moral terms, such as pride, indignation, patriotism and contrition.

Jean-Paul Sartre (1905–1980) argued that what we must *not* do is accept morality as merely tradition or habit: doing certain things because they are socially acceptable or avoiding certain actions simply because our parents told us that they were wrong. To be *authentic,* a moral judgement must be rational and made by ourselves. Sartre says that in deciding whether an action is right or wrong, we define ourselves.[1] In accepting *thus and such* an action, we become the person who thinks *thus and such* is acceptable. Sartre seems to offer no objective criteria upon

---

[1] This is part of what is known as *existentialism.*

94

which to make such judgements and with no criteria, any decision can only be random, which is not what we mean by morality. What is more, we simply do not have the time to make a unique moral judgement in every new situation. Nevertheless, Sartre's view of *authenticity* is helpful. Morality is more than habit.

The tradition of the virtues that stems from Aristotle does not start from facts. That tradition assumes a purpose-to-life, the description of which is in itself a moral statement. *Life is all about ...* is not a factual statement but a value judgement. It is tantamount to stating what is *important* in life, and this depends upon the social context. What the warrior hero might see as important in life is different from what the religious hermit might think. If we can ascertain and describe a purpose-to-life, we can generate the moral life from it. The form of such an argument is: *Life is all about ... therefore we must ...*

We cannot decide anew what to do in every situation but we might be able to *choose* to adopt a purpose-to-life and the morality that derives from it. If carried out rationally and after due consideration, such a choice may still be *authentic* in Sartre's terms. We define ourselves as a person who accepts that form of moral life. For example, the *Rule of St Benedict* implies a purpose-to-life and those who choose to live by the rule define themselves as Benedictines, which is much more than just a name. To be a (proper) Benedictine is to live by the rule.

The use of the words *purpose-to-life* is dangerous. I should like you to think of it as a technical term and for that reason I have added the hyphens. Its use does not imply that there is only one purpose-to-life.

The moral life is in danger because it is almost impossible to find a context, a purpose-to-life, which can support it today. With no context, the moral life must wither and decay, hence the time I have described as the end of decency. On a parallel to St Benedict and his rule, I argue that Freemasonry offers a purpose-to-life from which a moral life can be derived. I shall go further than this and argue that safeguarding the moral life itself is the function of our order.

I will argue that Freemasonry is one of very few institutions today which can achieve this. Safeguarding the moral life becomes our function and duty and it is also the way that we will save ourselves. Many men are seeking some meaning to life which they find in perilously few other orders and institutions. The search for meaning is a search for a context in which the moral life finds traction.

I argue this in the chapters *Values and relativity, Morality and context* and *A bastion for the moral life*. In the following *The virtues of Freemasonry*, I set out the virtues that define us. To offer a moral life, we must be very clear about our values.

Values and relativity

November 2014

In one of the darkest days in the histories of the City and Wall Street, six major banks were fined a total of £2.6 billion ($4.10bn) by regulators. A seventh, Barclays, is still in talks over the size of its penalty. The punishments came after an inquiry by watchdogs in Britain, the US and Switzerland into rigging of the foreign-exchange market. Over £3 trillion ($4.75trn) is traded daily on the international currency market, and the banks' traders were found to have manipulated prices.

What was shocking, even by the standards of the scandals of the past few years, was what regulators portrayed as the arrogance of the bank employees. They formed groups and gave themselves nicknames such as 'The A-Team', or 'The Three Musketeers'. They communicated with each other via chatrooms. One HSBC trader complained in an email to another team member who had not given him the information he needed: 'You are useless ... how can I make free money with no fcking heads up.'

The report, by Britain's Financial Conduct Authority, laid bare the contempt in which some bank employees hold their banks, colleagues and clients. But what is especially shaming was that the manipulation occurred recently – after a series of scandals which resulted in banks paying enormous fines and employees losing their jobs. This gives the lie to the claim by the banking community they were reforming their ways and were doing everything they could to prevent misdemeanours.[1]

Update May 2015

Citi, JPMorgan, Barclays, RBS, Bank of America and UBS will pay almost $6 billion to authorities, bringing the total fines over the FX scandal to $9 billion. In a particularly embarrassing twist, the forex charges come right on the heels of the Libor interest rate scandal, where banks were found to be rigging the rates banks use to lend to each other to their advantage. One Barclays trader wrote in a chatroom in November 2010: If you ain't cheating, you ain't trying. [2]

Near-criminal behaviour

It has been said that Ivan Boesky (of *greed is good* fame) wore a T-shirt emblazoned with the words, *He who has the most when he dies, wins.* If true, it partly explains the City of London's near criminal behaviour. The money the traders made was a measure of success, a badge of victory, a scoreline; nothing real or of enduring value. They lived in a nonsense world. Simon English writes:

The unofficial offer from the bank that employs the traders is this: here are a series of rules we take very seriously. Try to get around them without getting caught. If you make a bundle,

---

[1] Chris Blackhurst, City Editor, *The Independent*, 13 November 2014.

[2] *Independent*, May 21 2015.

we'll give you a slice. If you lose it, well, that's unauthorised dealing. Best of luck.[1]

I was once told by the UK head of Moët Hennessy–Louis Vuitton that less than half of their champagne was ever drunk; the rest was poured over people in celebrations. The world of the trader is as artificial as the champagne.

Greed (avarice, covetousness or cupidity) is, of course, one of the seven deadly sins. In Dante's *The Divine Comedy*, the souls suffering torment in the fourth circle of hell learn that *not all the gold that is beneath the moon* can purchase rest for them.[2] St Thomas Aquinas wrote that greed is:

> … *a sin directly against one's neighbour, since one man cannot over-abound in external riches without another man lacking them, for temporal goods cannot be possessed by many at the same time … It is a sin against God, just as are all mortal sins, inasmuch as man views things eternal with contempt, preferring temporal things.*[3]

Would Boesky, or for that matter the *A-Team* and the *Three Musketeers*, be brought up short by what the saint said? None of them would give a damn, to use an appropriately religious pun. For Boesky, the fact that *temporal goods cannot be possessed by many at the same time* was just the point. The CEO of a broking firm said:

> *Blaming traders for being greedy and manipulative in these circumstances, where you put temptation in their way, is like putting a fox in charge of a hen coop and then expressing surprise about the outcome.*[4]

The trading took place and, if commentators are to be believed, still takes place in a moral vacuum. While there may be a distorted echo of ethics in the question, *How can I make free money with no fcking heads up?* (the implication being that the other trader *ought* to have given him illegal information) any genuine moral judgement on their actions would have meant little to them. Their world builds a wall around itself and becomes a morality-free zone. There is no point in accusing a fox of greed or cruelty.

> *The culture of the trading floor is worse than any media commentator, author or film can depict and nothing, absolutely nothing has changed since the banking crisis. These guys think they are untouchable. It's a pervasive culture where if your face fits, you're in and it's tolerated by the guys at the top because the traders bring in such vast commissions and profits.*[5]

---

[1] Simon English, *Evening Standard*, 13 November 2014. His description of a trader is fascinating: *He was brilliant at knowing why* [the bonds] *would move and when. He made clients and himself oodles of money. After a while something became clear. He didn't know much about anything other than German bonds. He had never been to Germany and hadn't the slightest interest in going. He thought the capital of Germany was Frankfurt.*

[2] *Inferno*, Canto VII.

[3] Aquinas (1), II, Section 118.

[4] Terry Smith, CEO of Tullett Prebon.

[5] English, *Evening Standard*

Psychopaths

The behaviour of traders is similar to that of psychopaths. Often thought of as the most dangerous of human beings, a psychopath[1] has no conscience and is incapable of experiencing gratitude, guilt, remorse or shame. They have no genuine connection with others and are psychologically incapable of living the moral life. They have no compunction about cheating and lying. When found out, they will express surprise and regret, make apologies and then repeat the crime.

> [They] *will commit theft, forgery, adultery, fraud, and other deeds for astonishingly small stakes and under much greater risks of being discovered than will the ordinary scoundrel.*[2]

They can mimic normal behaviour and can be very convincing. They can charm others into thinking they are decent and reliable. They use people. The criminologist, David Wilson, describes psychopaths as *hiding in plain sight*. Around 1% of the UK population are psychopaths and they can and do function in organisations. Being charming to those above them but abusive to those below, they are more commonly found at higher levels of the hierarchy and figures of three to four percent have been suggested for more senior positions in business.[3] They will exist at higher levels in Freemasonry.[4]

> Psychopaths are quite different from people with autism. An autistic person may have difficulty in understanding that others have emotions and may appear uncaring. Unlike psychopaths, they do value others and can learn to respond appropriately.

Traders and psychopaths

Similarity in behaviour does not necessarily indicate a similarity in cause of behaviour. A study carried out by Thomas Noll et al. indicates that competition motivates traders more than financial gain. In pursuit of competitive advantage, they are ruthless and willing to harm others. Using a version of the *Prisoners Dilemma* on a sample of traders, Noll et al. discovered that:

> ... *the traders used an even more uncooperative strategy than the psychopaths,*[5] *maximizing their relative gain only by harming the game partner. This result ... is surprising in view of the fact that traders are supposed to maximize the total gain for their businesses. By*

---

[1] The word *psychopath* was replaced by *sociopath* and then by *people with Antisocial Personality Disorder.* I have kept the original word because it is used in the works I have I have quoted from.

[2] Cleckley.

[3] Hare.

[4] Psychopaths have average intelligence with no delusions, nervousness or neurotic signs. They are unreliable, untruthful, insincere with no sense of remorse or shame. They indulge in antisocial behaviour without compunction but display poor judgement and a failure to learn from experience. They lack insight and are pathologically egocentric. (From Cleckly.)

[5] They used a computer simulation of psychopaths.

jeopardizing their total gain only to improve the relative gain, the traders seem to be motivated more by competition than by lucrative pragmatism.

The *Prisoners' Dilemma* was developed by Merrill Flood and Melvin Dresher. The police have arrested two suspects who they think worked together to commit a crime. If both remain silent under interrogation, the police cannot hold them for lack of evidence. If only one talks, the silent one will receive a stiffer sentence while the one who turns state's evidence will receive a lighter sentence. If both confess neither gain any advantage.

The psychopath cannot appreciate other people's needs and the trader simply wants to win. Traders may be isolated from the moral life, while psychopaths are incapable of living it. In neither case would persuasion have any effect in getting them to change their ways. If someone does not live the moral life, there is no way that we can prove to him or her that they ought to.

Ought and is

I have presented this as a matter of psychology but it is also a matter of logic. Wittgenstein wrote:

> *In the world everything is as it is and happens as it does happen. In it there is no value – and if there were, it would be of no value.*[1]

That is to say, values are not objects in the world but ways in which we view such objects. I have rehearsed this argument in my monograph *Deism* but briefly the continuum that starts with Descartes and reaches a conclusion in Logical Positivism, leaves us with a recognition that no statement of value can be deduced from a statement of fact. Hume wrote:

> *In every system of morality, which I have hitherto met with, I have always remark'd, that the author proceeds for some time in the ordinary way of reasoning, and establishes the being of a God, or makes observations concerning human affairs; when of a sudden I am surpriz'd to find, that instead of the usual copulations of propositions, is, and is not, I meet with no proposition that is not connected with an* ought, *or an* ought not.

The moral agent

Take four statements, similar in content but differing in their overtones.

A. *That act will in all probability result in the death of a human being.*
B. *You will kill someone with that car.*
C. *You were drunk and you ran him over.*
D. *You murdered him.*

---

[1] Wittgenstein (1)

Statement A is, on the surface, a statement of fact. The speaker seems to be simply informing the listener that an act being considered carries dangers. Nevertheless, the wording is stilted, as if seeking to suppress overtones.

Statement B seems similar but the overtones are now obvious. They are carried by the personalisation to the driver, the use of the word *kill* as opposed to *result in the death of*, and the phrase *that car*, the implication being that the car is improperly maintained or capable of speeds beyond the skill of the driver.

Statement C is tantamount to a moral accusation. The overtones are so loud that the statement might be that of a judge giving sentence.

Statement D is a moral judgement. The word *murder* means *wrongful killing* and so the evaluation is contained in the meaning. The question in a court of law is not whether murder is wrong (which is a tautology) but whether the act of the accused counts as murder.

> Sir Edward Coke (d. 1634), the greatest of early jurists, wrote: *Murder is when a man of sound memory and of the age of discretion, unlawfully killeth ... any reasonable creature in rerum natura under the King's peace, with malice aforethought ...*

The overtones show our moral sense at work. Most of us would say that if an action *is likely* to result in the death of a human being, it *ought not to* be carried out. However, as Hume says, there is no logical connection between the statement:

That act will in all probability cause the death of a human being

and a moral conclusion such as:

If you can prevent that act, you ought to do so.

Another step is required:

Statement A	*That act will in all probability cause the death of a human being.*
Add Premise	*Causing the death of a human being is wrong.*
Conclusion	*If you can prevent that act, you ought to do so.*

It is a mark of a moral agent that he or she consciously or unconsciously adds that extra step. Psychopaths would hear no overtones. The added premise would not register with them although they are capable of logical reasoning.

> *The presence or absence of conscience is a deep human division ... What distinguishes* (psychopaths) *from the rest of us is an utterly empty hole in the psyche, where there should be the most evolved of all humanizing functions.*[1]

The psychopath has no conscience while the trader's has been suppressed.

---

[1] Stout.

Emotivism

Since it seems impossible to convince anyone to lead the moral life if they do not do so already, some philosophers and ordinary people have taken moral statements to be no more than an expression of feelings. It is after all common enough for someone asked for justification of a moral position to reply, *I don't know. I just feel that …*

In philosophical terms, a corollary to the *no-ought-from-is* argument is that the truth or falsity of a moral statement cannot be tested by reference to facts. As I showed in my previous book, *Deism*, Logical Positivism holds that only statements about the world (*contingent*) or about logic (*tautologous*) can have meaning and thus moral utterances are strictly speaking meaningless. Nevertheless, since moral statements and judgements form a major part of human discourse, philosophers who have held Positivist views have had to recognise they serve a function; hence the theory of *Emotivism*. According to this theory, the statement *Causing people unnecessary pain is wrong*, expresses a negative feeling, something like *Boo! to causing people unnecessary pain*. The statement *It is a duty to help others in distress*, expresses a positive feeling, something like *Hooray! for helping others in distress* and the statement *You ought to help people in distress* is a matter of encouragement to share the feeling, something like *Shout hooray! for helping others in distress.*[1]

Moral persuasion

Charles Stevenson's treatment of the theory contains many valuable insights, particularly in his treatment of moral persuasion. It is often true that:

> *A redirection of the hearer's attitudes is sought not by the mediating step of altering his beliefs, but by exhortation, whether obvious or subtle, crude or refined.*

Redirection of feelings is accomplished by creating emotional impact through:

> *… emotive meaning, rhetorical cadence, apt metaphor, stentorian, stimulating, or pleading tones of voice, dramatic gestures, … establishing rapport with the hearer or audience …*[2]

Great speech makers from Cicero[3] to Martin Luther King[4] have aroused emotions in this way but a problem for Stevenson is that the emotions aroused are described in moral terms. (The words that follow in italics carry the moral force.) Cicero sought to arouse feelings of *shame* in Lucius Sergius Catilina (Catiline) and *righteous anger* in the Senate at Catiline's attempt to *overthrow democracy* in Rome.

---

[1] The exclamation mark acts a logical marker, showing the statement is an expression of emotion.

[2] Stevenson.

[3] *When, O Catiline, do you mean to cease abusing our patience? How long is that madness of yours still to mock us?*

[4] *I have a dream that one day this nation will rise up and live out the true meaning of its creed. 'We hold these truths to be self-evident, that all men are created equal.'*

Martin Luther King sought both to arouse *shame* in the American population at their *selective memory* of Abraham Lincoln's 1863 executive order on *emancipation* and to *stiffen the resolve* of black Americans in their *fight for equality*. Winston Churchill successfully aroused the *patriotism* of the British people and motivated them to make the *necessary sacrifices* in preparation for the *Nazi invasion* that every Briton in June 1940 believed to be imminent.

> *Even though large tracts of Europe and many old and famous States have fallen or may fall into the grip of the Gestapo and all the odious apparatus of Nazi rule, we shall not flag or fail. We shall go on to the end. We shall fight in France. We shall fight on the seas and oceans. We shall fight with growing confidence and growing strength in the air. We shall defend our Island, whatever the cost may be. We shall fight on the beaches. We shall fight on the landing grounds. We shall fight in the fields and in the streets. We shall fight in the hills. We shall never surrender.*

A redirection of the hearer's moral attitudes can often be achieved by exhortation but the emotions that are being redirected are moral emotions: *shame, righteous anger, stiffening of resolve, patriotism, necessary sacrifices* and so on. To describe the emotions aroused, we need to use the moral terms first. (A philosopher would say the moral terms are *logically anterior* to the emotion.)

The logic of emotion

No doubt feelings are (often) associated with shame (hot flushes, perhaps) but the feelings are not the emotion itself. There are logical and grammatical requirements for the use of the word. To experience shame, one or someone close to one has to have done something wrong, just as to feel pride, one or someone close to one has to have done something well. It would not be just psychologically odd, but logically odd to feel shame at having done something praiseworthy.

Suppose the traditional *Poor Old Lady* (*POL*) is taken ill, requiring help which a friend of ours does not give. If our friend were to say, *I am feeling really bad about not helping said POL*, we might well reply, *Well, so you ought*. Suppose the *POL* dies and the friend says, *I feel such pain that I did not help that POL*; we would not recommend an aspirin but rather suggest some act of penitence. The pain of remorse is logically different from the pain of a headache. The latter is a sensation, the former a confession. When talking about shame, we are talking about morals, quite separate from any expression of feelings.

Living the moral life is about attributing value to the world. Valuing is something we do. Emotion comes in because we have feelings about what we value. A proof that someone genuinely holds values is that they are upset if such values are transgressed. Values are not part of the world – not objects to be touched alongside railway trains, tall buildings or waves on the sea, nor events like coronations, tennis matches or traffic jams, nor indeed actions such as doing a job

102

of work, giving a kiss or picking something up from the floor. Values are how we view objects, events and actions. While adjectives such as *blue, soft, shiny* or *transparent* refer to qualities of an object, words such as *dignified, proper, handsome, impressive, beautiful, ugly, good, bad, right* or *wrong* show the way in which we evaluate it. Aesthetic judgements operate in the same way as moral judgements. In the description of a sunset, the word *beautiful* does not further the description so much as evaluate the sight.

Arbitrariness

The fact that it may be impossible to convince someone of a moral judgement, does not mean that discussion of moral issues is irrational. In fact, it is common that opposing views in a moral debate are supported by evidence. (The somewhat silly, *I just feel that …* is not the only support given to moral arguments.) Alasdair MacIntyre provides[1] several examples of contemporary moral debate, showing that each opposing position is supported by evidence. Take the example of war.

Some people argue that local wars in foreign countries are none of our business; that intervention makes things worse. Others hold that developed democracies are morally required to minimise bloodshed in less developed countries. Still others hold that no war can ever be right because holy books say that killing people is wrong but others hold that there are religious justifications for war. Jonathan Riley-Smith writes of the Crusades:

> *All Christian justifications of positive violence are based partly on the belief that a particular religious or political system or course of political events is one in which Christ is intimately involved. His intentions for mankind are therefore bound up with its success or failure … If the only way to preserve the integrity of his intentions from those who stand in their way is to use force, then this is in accordance with his desires.*

Utilitarianism argues that there can be just wars where the good to be gained outweighs the evil done. The use of atomic bombs on Japan in 1945 might be justified by the reduction in the number of deaths of Allied soldiers[2] but, then again, John Donne wrote:

> *Who bends not his ear to any bell which upon occasion rings? … No man is an island, entire*

---

[1] MacIntyre (4).

[2] One of the most powerful statements about Hiroshima and Nagasaki comes from George Macdonald Fraser's *Quartered Safe Out Here*, his memoir of the Burma campaign. While personally convinced that the bombing was justified, he believed that the men under his command, had they known what results the bombs had, would have gathered their gear *with moaning and foul language and ill-tempered harking back to the long dirty bloody miles from the Imphal boxes to the Sittang Bend and the iniquity of having to go again, slinging their rifles and bickering about who was to go on point, and 'Ah's aboot 'ed it, me!' and 'You, ye bugger, ye're knackered afower ye start, you!' and 'We'll a' get killed!',* and then would have moved south to continue the 'normal' war. 2015 was the 70th anniversary of the use of atomic bombs on Japan.

of itself; every man is a piece of the continent, a part of the main … any man's death diminishes me, because I am involved in mankind, and therefore never send to know for whom the bells tolls; it tolls for thee.

The best way to ensure peace, we are told, is to prepare for war. Not only should our nation arm itself, it must show that it is prepared to use its armaments. *Mutually Assured Destruction* ensures nuclear peace. On the other hand, the Campaign for Nuclear Disarmament argues:

Nuclear weapons have no legitimate purpose; nor would their use be legal due to civilian casualties being unavoidable … Not only do nuclear weapons kill indiscriminately but the radioactive fallout … means that their effects know no geographical boundaries.[1]

The arguments are presented in a reasoned way, but since there are no independent criteria for deciding which premises are correct, disagreement too easily becomes, as MacIntyre says, a matter of assertion and counter-assertion. In his view, moral argument is *disquietingly arbitrary.*

Antigone

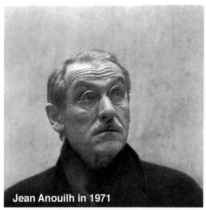

Jean Anouilh in 1971

MacIntyre directs us to Sophocles' play, *Antigone.* I know the Jean Anouilh version better and will refer to that. The background to the play is of two Theban brothers who have fought each other in a civil war. Both have died. Créon, the new ruler of Thebes, decides that to regain peace, the populace need to see that good has triumphed and evil has been punished.

He decides that one of the dead brothers will be treated as a hero and the other as a traitor:

I had the prettier of the two carcasses brought in and gave it a state funeral; and I left the other to rot. I don't know which was which. And I assure you, I don't care.

Contrary to Créon's edict, the eponymous Antigone, a sister of the two dead brothers, creeps out at night to bury the remaining corpse, and is arrested. Complicating matters is Antigone's betrothal to Créon's son. The dramatic centre of the play is the face-to-face debate between Créon and Antigone, the former arguing that what he has done is necessary for peace, while the latter insists that

---

[1] Quote from CND website.

familial and religious duties require her to bury the body. Créon is the pragmatist. He sees himself as an embodiment of the law. He does not like many of the things that a leader has to do and never wanted to be king. He was landed with the job after the civil war. Chorus says at the start of the play:

> *I'll tell you something about Créon. Now and then, when he goes to bed weary with the day's work, he wonders whether this business of being a leader of men is worth the trouble.*

He doesn't see kingship as romantic:

> *It is my trade; a trade a man has to work at every day; and like every other trade, it isn't all beer and skittles. But since it is my trade, I take it seriously.*

Antigone is often seen as the idealist, someone for whom any compromise in her ethical and religious ideals is anathema. She is ready-made martyr material. Chorus says of her at the beginning of the play:

> *All that she knows is that Créon won't allow her dead brother to be buried; and that despite Créon, she must bury him ... Antigone doesn't think, she acts; she doesn't reason, she feels, and from the moment the curtain went up, she began to feel that inhuman forces were whirling her out of this world.*

The stand-off between Créon and Antigone is a perfect example of two contexts with no contact.

Créon:	*Why did you try to bury your brother?*
Antigone:	*I owed it to him.*
Créon:	*I had forbidden it.*
Antigone:	*I owed it to him. Those who are not buried wander eternally and find no rest. Everybody knows that. If my brother were alive and he came home weary after a long day's hunting, I should fetch him food and drink and see that his bed was ready for him. Polynices is home from the hunt. I owe it to him to unlock the house of the dead in which my father and my mother are waiting to welcome him. Polynices has earned his rest.*
Créon:	*Polynices was a rebel and a traitor, and you know it.*
Antigone:	*He was my brother.*
Créon:	*You heard my edict. It was proclaimed throughout Thebes. You read my edict. It was posted up on the city walls.*
Antigone:	*Yes. Of course I did.*
Créon:	*You knew the punishment I decreed for any person who attempted to give him burial.*
Antigone:	*Yes, I knew the punishment.*

Créon's argument that both brothers were a bad lot and both deserved to be executed for treason, does not move Antigone, but he makes a last appeal:

105

Don't think that I am not just as offended as you are by the thought of that meat rotting in the sun. In the evening, when the breeze comes in off the sea, you can smell it in the palace, and it nauseates me. … It's vile; and I can tell you what I wouldn't tell anybody else: it's stupid, monstrously stupid. But the people of Thebes have got to have their noses rubbed into it a little longer.

Antigone refuses to compromise and tells Créon that if he leaves her alive, she will bury her brother again. Who wins? No one, of course. Antigone's sister, Ismène, declares that she too will attempt to bury her brother and Antigone crows:

Antigone: *You hear that, Créon? The thing is catching! Who knows but that lots of people will catch the disease from me! What are you waiting for? Call in your guards! Come on, Créon! Show a little courage! It only hurts for a minute!*

It is not a fun ending. Antigone is walled up alive and Créon's son, Haemon, goes with her. Realising this, Créon calls for the wall to be knocked down but Antigone has already hung herself and Haemon kills himself with his sword. Créon then receives the news that his wife has cut her throat:

Créon: *She, too? They are all asleep. It must be good to sleep.* [To Page.] *My lad.*

Page: *Sir?*

Créon: *Listen to me. They don't know it but the truth is the work is there to be done and a man can't fold his arms and refuse to do it. They say it's dirty work but if we didn't do it, who would?*

Page.   *I don't know, sir.*

Créon: *Of course you don't. You'll be lucky if you never find out. In a hurry to grow up aren't you?*

Page: *Oh yes, sir.*

Créon: *I shouldn't be if I were you. Never grow up if you can help it. What time is it?*

Page: *Five o'clock, sir.*

Créon: *What do we have on today at five o'clock?*

Page: *Cabinet meeting, sir.*

Créon: *Cabinet meeting. Then we had better go along to it.*

Who was right?

You may think that Antigone's resistance to compromise is admirable, that she is right to stick to her ideals of familial and religious duty. You may think that what Créon did was necessary, a matter of politics, the art of the possible. You may also think that Créon was an *apparatchik*, willing to compromise moral demands for the needs of the situation. You may also think that Antigone was a spoilt brat. I suppose that all these views are true and that is the power of the play.

It is said that when Anouilh's version was first produced in Paris in 1944,[1] the Nazi authorities sided with Créon and the French saw Antigone as a heroine of the resistance. That view was certainly denied by *Le Populaire*, in its review by Guy Desson on 30 September 1944: *Antigone n'est pas davantage le symbole de la Résistance que Créon l'apologie de la dictature.* (Antigone is no more the symbol of the Resistance than Créon the apologist for the dictatorship.) Most commentators agree that Créon and Antigone are equally balanced and that is the point. Anouilh shows us how two opposing moral positions lead to tragedy.

Morality and interpretation

It is often said that all we need to do is to *teach children the difference between right and wrong*; that everyone knows that murder is wrong and so is stealing, lying and swearing. Such statements are tautologies: the truth is contained in their meaning. Like murder, stealing is defined as wrong. The *Theft Act* 1968 starts:

A person is guilty of theft if he dishonestly appropriates property belonging to another with the intention of permanently depriving the other of it.

While we might tell a child *Lying is wrong*, such a form of moral statement is rare in normal discourse. Moral issues often arise as matters of interpretation:

Doesn't everyone occasionally pay cash to avoid VAT? Surely it doesn't matter if I exceed the speed limit a bit when I'm in a hurry. There's such a thing as a white lie, you know. Finders, keepers. If someone said that to my wife, I'd give him a good hiding. People who stop on every amber just hold up traffic. I'd vote for hanging.

It is the interpretation that matters. Is hanging a form of murder? When is a lie a white lie? Can you really keep money you find in the street – and does the amount make a difference? Personally, I find it objectionable to be offered a cash price to avoid VAT but a close friend thinks I am far too picky. Another friend likes fast cars and drives them fast. Can we really take the law into our own hands? While someone might never cheat a family member, he or she may have fewer reservations about cheating a stranger, perhaps seeking to recover a loss on a transaction in a shop, adding a bit on for the next customer. While people may avoid lying to their friends, they may well be ready to lie when employed to sell or advertise products, even seeing it as their job to do so.

No list of commandments could even begin to approach the resolution of such moral issues – although effective sermons might be preached on them. The reference to *The A-Team*, psychopaths, emotivism, *Antigone* and the apparent arbitrariness of moral judgements shows not only that discussion about them

---

[1] In fact there were two opening nights for the play: the first under the Nazi occupation in February 1944, and the second after the liberation in September. (Barsacq.)

cannot take place unless both disputants admit of the moral life, but that, even then, finding any agreement is very difficult. To be a participant in the moral life is to have decided that some things matter. The question is what things? On what can we base our moral decisions? To what criteria can we appeal?

Holy books and moral decisions

50% of UK citizens have no religion; only 9% attend church (almost) every week.[1] Even in the USA, 16% (25% under 30) have no religious belief.[2] A Canadian 2005 survey found 22% had no religion, double the figure of 1985. 1 in 3 Canadians never attends church.[3] Younger people are less likely to have religious belief, and attendance has declined even among those with a religious affiliation.[4] 71% of East Germans born after 1975 have never believed in a god.[5]

When nearly everyone had a religious belief, discussions about ethics were, in theory at least, resolved by reference to a holy book. We say in the ritual:

> As a Freemason, I would first recommend to your most serious contemplation the Volume of the Sacred Law, charging you to consider it the unerring standard of truth and justice and to regulate your actions by the Divine precepts it contains.

In fact, it is never that simple. In Judaism, it is not too far from the truth to say that the Torah contains the laws while the Talmud contains the arguments.[6] It is not often that an appeal to a holy book resolves important moral or even religious questions. Consider failures to resolve questions about contraception, abortion, assisted dying, stem cells, blood transfusions, women bishops or lesbian, gay and transgender issues, even within one religion and using one book. It is much the same with our own *Book of Constitutions (BoC)*. We say that there is *scarcely a case of difficulty can occur in the lodge but what reference to that book will not set you right*, but the BoC makes no reference to any of the important questions facing a lodge: how to recruit candidates, how to manage finances, how to resolve personal disagreements, how to train brethren for future roles or how to teach the ritual.

Reference to a holy book is even less useful today, both because many different books are in use and because an increasing number of people, and a majority in some countries, have no religious belief. People increasingly hold religion to be distinct from morality. In countries as widespread as Argentina, Australia,

---

[1] 2011 census.

[2] 2014 Pew, *Global Attitudes Survey*

[3] Canadian General Social Survey (GSS) 2005.

[4] WIN/Gallup poll, 2014.

[5] Callum Smith.

[6] They are both about the same length, although the Talmud with commentary (a commentary on a commentary) is twice as long.

Canada, Chile, Israel and Japan, as well as most European countries, a majority of people reject the claim that belief in a god is necessary to ethics. Younger, university-educated people are more likely to be of this opinion[1] but if religion is not the default arbiter of morality, what is?

Various criteria have been suggested, perhaps the most famous being the utilitarian principle, the *greatest good for the greatest number*,[2] but none are completely satisfactory. We lack any rational foundation on which to build a system of morals.

Psychology and morality

It is characteristic of moral demands to be self-justifying.

> *I have to do this because it is right.*
> *I cannot do that because it is wrong.*

The reasoning is circular and the demand uncompromising. It is in the nature of ethics that conflicts are between absolutes. If I have promised to give a book to someone, I have to fulfil the promise, even when the book actually belongs to someone else. I should not have made the promise but, having done so, I am now caught between two opposing demands, neither of which admits of compromise.

How is this? We see and do many things during the day, only a few of which are new to us. Most of the time we operate on what one might call *automatic pilot*. From tying a shoelace to eating a sandwich, we are operating in an automatic mode. Even driving the car can be automatic. (How many times have you driven home from work or a visit to a relation and had no recollection of what happened en route?) Most of the time, we do not consciously decide how to react to events or people. There is insufficient time to give each and every event individual attention and so our minds store experiences away in a sort of filing system, together with a package of suitable reactions of words, opinions, actions and emotions. Normally lying dormant, the relevant package is triggered by the appropriate stimulus. This explains stereotypes.[3]

We are unconscious of the existence of these packages, which psychologists call *schema*, but much of what we think, do, say and feel is caused by them.[4] The schema are laid down by our upbringing, education and social norms. Our ethical stances and beliefs are very much part of this. Such a process is not necessarily orderly. Philip Larkin wrote:

---

[1] Pew.

[2] Others include the golden rule: *Do as you would be done by,* the Kantian, *Do what you would will would become a universal rule* and every mother's argument, *Suppose everyone did that?*

[3] For an explanation of schema and single and double loop learning, see West (2).

[4] Fine.

They fuck you up, your mum and dad.
They may not mean to, but they do.

Our ethical system is not logically consistent because our moral decisions carry baggage from our upbringing, our education and traditions – and these are often contradictory. It is the baggage that makes moral decision-making so hard; because moral demands are uncompromising and because we carry incompatible moral schema, we frequently find ourselves facing insoluble moral dilemmas.

Existentialism

Existentialism effectively holds that bringing such schema to our consciousness and preventing them from making decisions, is the groundwork of an authentic moral life. For Jean-Paul Sartre, an authentic decision is one made independently of our past: of our upbringing, schooling, and experience. Sartre argues that to make such comments as *That's just the way I am*, or *That's just the way I was brought up* is to allow the past to define us, to refuse to take command of our lives. To be authentic demands that we ignore the unconscious promptings of *what we are* and use our conscious reason to choose *what we will become*, what will define us for the future. This is the existentialist response to the apparent arbitrariness of moral decision-making. When faced with two contradictory demands, we accept neither but rationally analyse the possible courses of action and choose, thus becoming the person who made that specific choice.

It is difficult to see what criteria one could use in making such a decision. If we are to ignore any promptings of the past, there is a risk that our decisions have to be random, like those in *The Dice Man*, whose life decisions are made on the throw of dice.[1] Still, Sartrean authenticity makes it plain that moral decision-making requires a conscious exercise of the will to resist the often unconscious promptings of schema, by bringing them into conscious view. We must not rely on the unexamined promptings of past assumptions and traditions.

> Sartre's socialism follows from his views on authenticity. Capitalism, colonialism, sexism, racism etc. define people and prevent them from becoming what they would choose to become.

Interim summary

I have argued that we cannot prove to anyone that they ought to live the moral life. This is almost a tautology. The *ought to* comes from the moral life and if someone is not part of that life then the words *ought to* have no meaning. This argument is related to Hume's insight that no statement of value can be deduced from a statement of fact: the *no-ought-from-is* argument. This has led some thinkers

---

[1] Cockcroft.

to the view that moral statements are no more than expressions of emotion, the relativistic theory of emotivism. I showed that while this theory provides insight into moral persuasion, it has logical faults at its centre and has to be rejected.

Nevertheless, since there appear to be no independent criteria for deciding moral questions, disagreement too easily becomes a matter of assertion and counter-assertion. In MacIntyre's view, moral argument is disquietingly arbitrary. Following MacIntyre, I took the example of the play *Antigone* to show how two opposing moral positions can lead to tragedy. To be a participant in the moral life is to have decided that some things matter but what things? On what can we base our moral decisions? To what criteria can we appeal?

I have shown that it is in the nature of ethics that conflicts are between absolutes and explained this from the psychological point of view, in terms of *schema*. Our moral decisions carry inconsistent baggage from our upbringing, our education and traditions and so we frequently find ourselves facing insoluble moral dilemmas. Moral decision-making requires a conscious exercise of the will. We must not rely on the unexamined promptings of past assumptions and traditions.

In what follows, I will explore the idea that there is no one set of virtues admired in all societies at all times. I shall suggest that the answer to the problem of relativity of morals lies in the use of a difficult and dangerous phrase: *the purpose-to-life*. This will take some explanation and I start with a discussion of Alasdair MacIntyre's views on *virtues*. At the end of my book *Deism*, I wrote:

> *There may be no threats of hell or promises of heaven to make us good. There may be no set of laws or commandments laid down for everyone. That means we have to decide for ourselves where values lie. I cannot decide for you and you cannot decide for me, but we may both decide to share a form of life; if so, we become brothers. Explanation of this requires another book but as an introduction to it, I am in fact happy with Newton's remark that such talk is for the sake of dreams and … fictions of our own devising, but you will note that three dots now replace the word vain.*

I hope now to explain what I mean by this.

Morality and context[1]

Eudaimonia

Plato and Aristotle viewed ethics as the attainment of well-being or happiness (*eudaimonia*). This is not a simple concept and the usual translation of the word *eudaimonia* as happiness is misleading. Neither Aristotle nor Plato viewed *eudaimonia* as a pleasure principle, for example. To get the drift, try to combine rationality, well-being, control and success with an absence of guilt or stress. Not easy, I agree. To make it easier, I will adopt a Masonic phrase which I think comes near to what Plato and Aristotle mean. During the installation of the Master, he is advised that by *rising to eminence by merit* [he] *may live respected and die regretted,* and I will take the attainment of the state of *living respected and dying regretted* to be similar to Aristotle's attainment of *eudaimonia.* Someone who lives respected and dies regretted is someone who has achieved admirable ends in an admirable way.

Aristotle's list of virtues included:	
Courage	Experiencing fear & being sensibly cautious but neither cowardly nor rash. Facing death in a dignified & resolute manner.
Liberality	Knowing the right way to use money, being neither mean nor profligate; generous with a sense of style.
Magnificence	Being able to afford magnificent actions and substantial expenditure, perhaps endowing a new warship or temple.
High-mindedness	Sacrificing personal ease for noble purposes; neither brash nor humble, disparaging oneself being as bad as boasting.
Wittiness	Having charm, wit and tact for good conversation, enabling people to enjoy being together. Neither a bore nor a clown.
Amiability	Neither sycophantic nor ingratiating, neither presumptuous nor self-abasing, enjoying company, even at some personal expense.

Aristotle lived 384–322 BCE[2] in Athens, a place and time very different from our own when *to be a good man was on every Greek view at least closely allied to being a good citizen.* Aristotle's virtues describe a man who *lives respected &c.* at that time and in that place, but not necessarily in any other time and place.

Excellences

In the ritual, the word *virtue* often appears in the singular, as in ... *to the just and virtuous man, death hath no terrors equal to the stains of falsehood and dishonour.*[3] Here the

---

[1] This chapter relies heavily on the insights of Alasdair MacIntyre.

[2] BCE = Before Common Era. CE = Common Era. CE more or less = AD.

[3] This statement might well fit with Aristotle's virtue of courage.

word means *morally good* with the implication that there is only one form of virtue. The idea that different virtues matter in different times and in different social contexts may be initially surprising. However, the ritual also uses the word *excellences* as a synonym of *virtues:*

> ... *as a Freemason, there are other excellences of character to which your attention may be particularly and forcibly directed.*[1]

Using the word *excellence* in place of the word *virtue* may help in understanding what Aristotle means. It is easier to accept that certain excellences of character were required to *live respected &c.* in the context of Athens and that other excellences would be admired in other contexts.

The purpose to life

Please note the word *context*. It is very important to recognise that the excellences change with the context. A context is, to use a dangerous phrase, a matter of *the purpose-to-life*, and by context I mean *a certain set of beliefs about the purpose-to-life in a certain place and at a certain time.* It is important to recognise that what is thought of as *the purpose-to-life* may vary according to time or place.

It is also important to recognise that a statement of the purpose-to-life is a moral statement which already contains an *ought*. It is usually of the form:

> *The reason we are here is to ... and therefore we ought to do ...*

The reason we are here is not a statement of fact but a moral statement.

> *The reason we are here is to help others and therefore we ought to assist that poor old lady.*
> *The reason we are here is to create beauty, therefore we should ensure that statue is preserved.*
> *The reason we are here is to praise god, therefore we should keep Sunday holy.*

In these statements, the second clause, *and therefore we ought* or *therefore we should*, is entailed by the first. Thus there must be an unstated *ought* internal to the first clause, since no *ought* can be derived from an *is*. The phrase *the purpose-to-life* may be helpful only for as long as we remember that any such *purpose-to-life* has meaning only within a context which will not be permanent. It is in this way that we overcome relativity: we accept that there can be other purposes to life but only one for our own context – and we can live only in our own context. The phrase is dangerous because it seems to imply that there is a *purpose-to-life* external to human existence: that someone *put us here* to achieve some purpose.[2]

---

[1] From the first degree charge.

[2] See West (5). Some people do believe that someone caused life on this planet (and perhaps others) and there was a time when such a belief was held by the majority and so could form the context of the moral life. However, as we have seen in the statistics, the idea of a creator god with purpose(s) for our lives has largely fallen into disuse and is no longer helpful in moral discourse.

Of course, if someone deliberately caused life in this universe, then whatever purpose that someone had in doing so would be his or her purpose, and not ours.

Excellences in heroic societies

Alasdair MacIntyre

MacIntyre discusses the excellences of what he calls *heroic societies* as described in Homer's poetry, which dates from perhaps 1000 BCE, and Norse sagas, which date from around 1200 CE. It is perhaps helpful to note these societies are a long way apart in time and that many societies with a very different notion of the purpose-to-life existed between these dates. From the comfort of a seat in lodge, it is not easy to put oneself in the position of a Norse *beserker* facing a shield wall but as MacIntyre writes:

… one central theme of heroic societies is also that death waits for [all]. *Life is fragile, men are vulnerable and it is of the essence of the human situation that they are such … The man therefore who does what he ought moves steadily towards his fate and his death. It is defeat and not victory that lies at the end. Understanding this is itself a virtue; indeed it is a necessary part of courage to understand this.*[1]

The purpose-to-life in a heroic context may well have been to live it as if it were a story, a *saga* if you like, that the man who *lives respected and dies regretted* in such context is one whose life can become a tale told around future camp fires.

Honour is conferred by one's peers and without honour a man is without worth.[2]

The courage of the heroic warrior is not simply bravery but the stillness of heart with which the courageous man faces the inevitability of death when it comes – in battle, by drowning, illness (the action of some god), or even treachery – thus making a good end, often a song.

This is exemplified in the saga, *The Life and Death of Cormac the Skald*.[3] Cormac dies in battle with a giant Scot who crushes Cormac's ribs in his death embrace. Caught under the weight of the giant's dead body, Cormac is unable to move. At last he is found and carried aboard his ship. Then he makes this song:

---

[1] MacIntyre (4).

[2] MacIntyre (4).

[3] Edited Jane Smiley. The word *skald* means *singer* or *poet*.

Of yore never once did I ween it,
When I wielded the cleaver of targets,
That sickness was fated to foil me,
A fighter so hardy as I.
But I shrink not, for others must share it,
Stout shafts of the spear though they deem them,
O hard at my heart is the death pang,
Thus hopeless the bravest may die.

One can see that within such a context, certain other features would have been admired in addition to courage, including perhaps strength of arm, fleetness of foot, cleverness and tactical cunning. They would have added lustre to the story and while we might have difficulty in thinking of these as virtues, we can perhaps understand them as excellences. Such a context still has some resonance for us, for example in the battle cry of Théoden, King of Rohan:[1]

Arise, arise, Riders of Théoden!
Fell deeds awake, fire and slaughter!
spear shall be shaken, shield be splintered,
a sword-day, a red day, ere the sun rises!
Ride now, ride now! Ride to Gondor!

And then all the host of Rohan burst into song, and they sang as they slew, for the joy of battle was on them, and the sound of their singing that was fair and terrible came even to the City.

We can imagine life within that context and how its moral system might have worked but as the context changes, the excellences change. That a context has resonance for us does not mean that it is relevant to our own decisions.

Incompatible contexts

The purpose-to-life in Aristotle's Athens was not the same as that of Théoden or Cormac but there are structural similarities. Some of the excellences that would have led an Athenian citizen to *live respected &c.* are, like fleet of foot and strong in the arm, not available to everyone. In Athens, to *live respected &c.* required intelligence, personal charm and indeed wealth. The Athenian excellences are incompatible with Christianity:

It is easier for a camel to go through the eye of a needle, than for a rich man to enter into the kingdom of God.   Mark 10:25

The Christian virtue of humility would have been a vice for Aristotle. Humility is opposed to magnificence. Paul spoke of the nine fruits of the spirit:

---

[1] Tolkien.

But the fruit of the Spirit is love, joy, peace, longsuffering, gentleness, goodness, faith, meekness, [and] *temperance: against such there is no law.*[1]

These sit uneasily alongside liberality, magnificence, high-mindedness, wit and amiability, and MacIntyre writes:

> *Aristotle would certainly not have admired Jesus Christ and he would have been horrified by St Paul.*[2] *... the notion of a final redemption of an almost unregenerate life has no place in Aristotle's scheme. The story of the thief on the cross is unintelligible in Aristotelian terms.*[3]

Re-cap

The excellences are what enables one to fulfil the (socially agreed) purpose-to-life. They are what enables a man to live well and be admired in a certain time and place, within a certain view in common of what matters in life. Note that there is no sense to the question of what excellences a man or woman ought to exhibit *in any context*. All excellences are context-specific.

Unconscious embers

We live with the embers of a number of incompatible contexts. As a literate society with easy access to books, films, TV documentaries and historical dramas, we are aware of many contexts in a way that no earlier society has been. We can be affected by elements drawn from different and often competing contexts.

- from Christianity: *chastity, forgiveness, poverty, the reward of heaven.*
- from philosophical rationalism: *the greatest good for the greatest number, do as you would be done by* or Kant's dictum *Do what you can will to be a universal law.*
- from the context of manliness: *stand up for yourself, walk tall, stick out your chest, hold your head up, take responsibility.*
- from traditions of independence: *a man's gotta do what a man's gotta do,*[4] *never apologise and never explain, winning isn't everything but it sure beats coming second.*
- from so-called feminine virtues: *stand by your man, gentleness, nurturing and feeling.*
- perhaps from Jane Austen's time: *It is a truth universally acknowledged that a single man in possession of a good fortune must be in want of a wife* and *There is nothing like staying at home for real comfort.*
- from courtly behaviour: *ladies first, the gentler sex, not in front of the ladies.*

---

[1] Galatians 5:22-23. The context is Paul on the difference between Christianity and the Mosaic Law.

[2] MacIntyre (4).

[3] MacIntyre (4).

[4] As far as I can tell, there is no film in which anyone actually said this but John Wayne and Charlton Heston came close.

There are more modern elements: telling a man to *get in touch with his feminine side* and the saying *A woman without a man is like a fish without a bicycle*. We still have the remains of the ideals of social democracy: *equality, decency, giving someone a leg up, positive discrimination, do your own thing,* and *make love, not war,* even if they are all under attack now.[1]

Contradictory demands

All these elements are capable of making demands upon us and since it is the nature of moral demands to brook no disagreement, we frequently find ourselves faced with contradictory moral imperatives. We cannot resolve the contradictions because we have no context in common, no one common purpose-to-life.

To use a metaphor, a wait in the doctor's surgery leafing through the magazines on offer, tells us that we are inadequate unless our garden is perfect, our house decorated in the latest fashion, our furnishings selected from the best stores and local artists, our record collection including only the most talked about composers and musicians, our reading list featuring only prize-winning novels, our clothes reflecting the latest trends (and in the best materials) and our cuisine consisting of the most imaginative dishes prepared from ingredients bought fresh every day.

This is silly. No one can be perfect at everything any more than we can be at the same time a brave and dominant warrior, a high-minded Athenian citizen, a holy person destined for heaven, a pioneer, a businessman, an excellent wife of a loving husband, a man in touch with his feminine side, an independent career woman, a dedicated mother, a well set up and philanthropic Victorian paterfamilias, a respectable professional person or Clint Eastwood as the Preacher. Not only would there never be enough time but many of the virtues contradict each other.

Pale Rider

Clint Eastwood's Preacher in *Pale Rider* has six bullet wounds in his back and shoots down a dozen or so men in the finale. The only response that Megan receives to her shouted love for him are the echoes of her voice in the canyon. The Preacher demonstrates no virtues of forgiveness, domesticity, philanthropy, respectability, high-mindedness or entrepreneurial behaviour. Why indeed should he? The context of the film is the lawlessness of a no doubt largely mythical[2] Wild West in which the weak must be protected by someone whose values are almost the exact opposite of theirs.

---

[1] In an interview with Trevor Phillips, Nigel Farage said that concern about race discrimination 'would probably have been valid' 40 years ago but that is no longer the case. *Guardian*, March 2015.

[2] See West (3). Dodge City was a railhead for the cattle business from 1876. With gunfighters, brothels, saloons and even bullfights, the city flourished for just ten hard-living years until the cattle business ceased.

A context for today

Now we come to the nub of the matter. To decide what excellences are important today requires that we identify what will enable us to *live respected and die regretted;* that we can identify the *purpose-to-life* for today. The apparent arbitrariness of moral decision-making, the way in which we cannot resolve moral disagreements, and the fact that we have so many contradictory elements drawn from different contexts implies that there is no dominant view in our society and hence no list of excellences that we can all share. Unlike in many earlier societies, we have no way of establishing common rules for *living respected &c.*

As a result, moral relativity arises and we have come to live in an amoral, even an immoral world, a view that our analysis of *the end of decency* may be taken to support. Jonathan Sacks expresses something similar when he writes:

> It is often assumed that we have moved beyond morality, that instead of thinking in terms of shared, objective values we now make choices on the basis of subjective inclination. The decisions we make have, and are meant to have, validity for us alone. We would not seek to impose them on others, and we resent it if others try to share their values with us. The old ideas, that there are moral rules and moral knowledge, that there are virtues we need to learn, have gone, never to return. That, at any rate, is the prevailing orthodoxy, reiterated daily in the media.

The failure of moral traditions

Sacks seeks an answer in the Judaic-Christian tradition but such a tradition can provide a *purpose-to-life* only to the increasingly few people who accept a Judaic-Christian deity. As a context in common, that tradition is exhausted. It is MacIntyre's view that all other available contexts within our culture have also been exhausted. The (moral) assumptions made by the Judaic-Christian tradition, liberalism, capitalism and Marxism/socialism, no longer hold.

For our purposes, **Liberalism** may be represented by the views of Thomas Hobbes who sought to explain and justify the rule of law by reference to a social contract, whereby everyone agrees to avoid those behaviours which would damage society. The contract would be silent on all other behaviours, which is why I take Hobbes to be a liberal for now. Such a contract implies the virtue of trust. If I abide by the rules of the social contract, I have to trust that you will not seek an advantage and will abide by them too. If you do not, then the contract breaks down. So many people now abuse the trust of others that the excellences of liberalism – *open-mindedness, respect for the law, personal responsibility* and *consideration for others* – can no longer provide a common moral basis. In place of open-mindedness we find fundamentalism and in place of consideration we find greed.

As Mikhail Gorbachev wrote:

A serious threat is hovering over European Culture ... one can only wonder that a deep, profoundly intelligent and inherently humane ... culture is retreating to the background before the primitive revelry of violence and pornography and the flood of cheap feelings and low thoughts.

For **Capitalism** to work requires fair competition within the rules, including the rules of decency,[1] otherwise there is a race to the bottom. The successive crises in capitalism indicate that the race is now on. Competition now requires constant and expensive policing to prevent illegal practices and even then immorality and illegality too often win out. We have seen that the audit process for identifying and reporting failures of governance is itself under stress and that those charged with oversight have frequently proved themselves unworthy. Rather than welcoming the stimulus of competition, business now pursues monopoly.

Richard Freeman contends that *the economic interests of small groups of 'crony capitalists' ... dominate government responses to the financial crisis and ensuing recession. The danger is not an ever-expanding socialist state ... but of a move to economic feudalism, in which a small set of wealthy masters ... subvert or outsmart efforts to regulate their behaviour or rein them in.* Given such weaknesses, the virtues demanded in the capitalist system – *fair competition, risk and reward, thrift, hard work, entrepreneurship, creativity* – have become unusable.

Marxism was a reaction to the conditions of the poor in the 19th century and was essentially optimistic, as was its close relative, **Socialism** (which one might think of as Marxism without the theory.) Socialism has had its successes. In the UK, governments from Churchill to Callaghan agreed on many socialist essentials; Cuba has a splendid health system; Chile has recovered from the CIA-inspired dictatorship of Pinochet to become a stable liberal democracy, and the co-determination process of industrial management in modern Germany has strong socialist roots. Sweden has long been a successful social democracy.

However, socialism was severely damaged in the monetarist years. Its virtues – *social welfare, fraternity, sharing, help for the underdog, fairness* – have lost resonance in the primacy of cost, the false arguments of low taxation and trickle down, the rise of populism and the attacks on the welfare system. The argument of the undeserving poor has once again raised its ugly head.

---

[1] *... if, on entering the butchers shop as a habitual customer I find him collapsing from a heart attack, and I merely remark, 'Ah! Not in a position to sell me meat today, I see,' and proceed immediately to his competitor's store to complete my purchase, I will have obviously and grossly damaged my whole relationship to him, including my economic relationship, although have done nothing contrary to the norms of the market ... Market relationships can only be sustained by being embedded in certain types of local non-market relationship, relationships of uncalculated giving and receiving ...* MacIntyre (3).

Sacks writes:

> *Relationships, whether at work or in private life, become a choice between manipulating and being manipulated, exploiting or being exploited. The idea that one might value another person or an institution sufficiently to make a long-term binding commitment ... begins to seem old-fashioned and naive ... there is no relationship so intimate, no secret so private, that it cannot be confessed in front of television cameras or sold for money to the press. It would be hard today to find a code of honour that cannot be broken for profit ...*

And it is MacIntyre's conclusion that:

> *The tradition of the virtues is at variance with central features of the modern economic order and more especially its individualism, its acquisitiveness and its elevation of the values of the market to a central social place[1] ... it now becomes clear that* [the tradition of the virtues] *also involves a rejection of the modern political order.[2]*

The incompatibility of virtue and success

If MacIntyre is right, as a society we can no longer agree on the purpose-to-life, and so have no common values and no moral life. As a thought experiment, try putting the following into a rank order:

1. *The film star who marries a prince.*
2. *The cleaning lady who gives everyone a smile.*
3. *The undercover agent who fools the enemy.*
4. *The man who gives all his money away and becomes a monk.*
5. *The female chieftain who successfully defies the invader.*
6. *The soldier who creates an empire.*
7. *The religious man who dies for his faith.*
8. *The uneducated man who retires rich at 40.*
9. *The pearly king who collects for charity, rain or shine.*
10. *The wealthy woman known for her support of the arts and her great parties.*

Homer, Skallagrimsson, Aristotle and Ignatius would each have used different criteria and reached a different rank order, but their list would be the same whether they used *success* or *virtue* as a criterion. For them, the successful life would have exemplified the virtues, and the virtuous life would have been successful. I doubt whether there would be any consensus today on a rank order for this list. We have no common understanding of what counts as success or virtue, and for many people success and virtue would be opposite poles of a continuum: the more successful, the less virtuous and vice versa.

---

[1] MacIntyre (4).

[2] MacIntyre (4).

A new dark age

Society is increasingly psychopathic with no ability or indeed desire to live the moral life and MacIntyre declares that a new dark age is upon us. He compares our current situation with the end of the Roman Empire when the barbarians gathered and Roman life became impossible. As Lyman Andrews wrote:

> In ninth century Britain the
> Saxons built wooden towns, refused
> To enter the crumbling Roman city,
> Drafty and full of spirits, because
> The Saxons could not understand
> How to make the Roman heating work: so
> They shivered under the ruined gaze of marble.

As society fell apart, the only hope lay in groups of people seeking to maintain principled ways of living together. MacIntyre says optimistically of today:

> ... if the tradition of the virtues was able to survive the horrors of the last dark ages, we are not entirely without grounds for hope.

But he then cuts the ground from under such optimism by saying:

> This time however the Barbarians are not waiting beyond the frontiers; they have already been governing us for some time.[1]

This may sound pessimistic and it is. Politics has ceased to deal in ideals. Cynicism reigns. Moral behaviour is today seen as weakness. There is little support for honesty; little applause for correct behaviour; and little inducement to live the moral life. It is as if morality is counter-cultural.

Local forms of community

MacIntyre concludes that:

> What matters at this stage is the construction of local forms of community within which civility and the intellectual and moral life can be sustained through the new dark ages which are already upon us.[2]

There is no context in common within our society, no commonly agreed *purpose-to-life* from which agreed moral *oughts* can be derived. Morality is retreating within society as a whole. Thus, if morality is to be preserved it can only be within a community of people of a common mind who agree on specific ideals, and who will work together in fraternity and concord. Such a community will coalesce around an agreed *purpose-to-life* from which it will derive a moral system. Members

---

[1] MacIntyre (4).

[2] MacIntyre (4).

will support each other in their intention to live the moral life just as in Alcoholics Anonymous members help each other remain sober.

Our challenge and opportunity

Here then is our greatest challenge and opportunity: to take on the duty of sustaining civility and the moral life through the new dark ages. Our order must become one of MacIntyre's *local forms of community* in which the moral life can be continued, combatting *the horrors of the modern dark age* — and as such it is supremely important. I contend that our order is a context within which virtues find traction. Sustaining *civility and the intellectual and moral life* must become our reason for existence. In achieving it, we shall save ourselves.

A bastion for the moral life

St Benedict

Alasdair MacIntyre writes that society is waiting not for some new *Godot* – not for an external and probably mythical agency to come to our aid – but *for another, doubtless very different, St Benedict*. The reference to the saint is significant for us. First set down in about 530 CE, the *Rule of St Benedict* was written to govern monastic communities voluntarily bound to live together, adopting specific virtues and, so to speak, agreeing to a series of *oughts*. Parts of the rule bear close similarity with Freemasonry.

> *Distinctions between the brethren may be made only on merit.*
> *A council of all brethren will discuss and decide on matters of importance.*
> *Decisions of the council and Abbot* (WM?) *should be cheerfully obeyed.*
> *Precedence is decided by date of admission, merit or decision by the Abbot.*
> *Moderation is necessary in all behaviour and speech.*
> *The importance of divine offices* (the ritual?) *is emphasised.*
> *Brethren are exhorted to zeal and fraternal charity.*
> *Guests are to be received with courtesy.*
> *Clothing is to be plain and suited to the climate.*

And one that should be in Freemasonry but has been driven out by PR:

> *A wayward brother who has left the monastery must be received again.*

Hammer reminds us that:

> *Masonry is and was always intended to be an initiatory organisation that an individual must seek to join. He does so not out of necessity or hope of material benefits, but out of an inner calling to greater wisdom, i.e., intellectual and spiritual light. Then after he makes that choice, he must in turn be chosen by others who agree to admit him into their assemblies.*

Like candidates for St Benedict's rule, every potential initiate for Freemasonry must understand that he will be called upon to seek the attainment of the excellences and virtues of our order. To become a Freemason is to agree to attain those excellences. All of them.

Choosing to be

Choosing to adopt a set of criteria, such as the set that St Benedict offered, is still *choosing to be*. A choice of a rule seems to be a validly authentic decision in a Sartrean sense, as long as the implications of that choice are carefully examined. The monks who, willingly and after long consideration and examination, adopted the Rule of St Benedict, *chose to be* governed by a set of rules and, in doing so, committed themselves to the observance of some behaviours and the rejection of others. The rule provided the basis on which they made their decisions; they did not have to make a decision *ab initio* in every case.

On a parallel with the Rule of St Benedict, a man may *choose to be* a Freemason and in doing so commit himself to a set of excellences by which to live a life. Since to make that choice is to choose *a purpose-to-life* (in the technical sense that we have used this phrase), Freemasonry becomes a context in which specific virtues/excellences make sense. Brethren must exhibit these excellences to be good Freemasons. Central to these are *brotherly love, relief* and *truth*. As MacIntyre says, membership:

> ... *involves standards of excellence and obedience to rules as well as achievement of goods.*

Choosing to be a Freemason

I have insisted that we can only understand virtues, excellences and moral decisions with reference to their philosophical, religious, social or historical context. I have done this in order to help us understand that the moral life is not independent of human life but changes with the context in which we live.[1] It is only as conscious, evaluative beings that we give life meaning and attribute value and there is no meaning to the phrase *purpose-to-life* outside this. I argue that Freemasonry can sustain a view of the purpose-to-life in exactly the same way as Aristotle's context of Athens or indeed St Ignatius's context of early Christianity. As Freemasons, our study should be to tease out and describe that *purpose-to-life* within the context of Freemasonry.

To be clear at this point, I am not saying that everyone (in the world) ought to exhibit the excellences of brotherly love, relief and truth. Indeed, it should be obvious by now that there is no clear sense in which such a statement can be made. We, as Freemasons, might be of the opinion that global society would be better if everyone did exemplify brotherly love, relief and truth, but this is a contingent statement (which may be true or false) and not a moral one.

What I *am* saying is that *if* a man *chooses* to be a Freemason, *then* he *ought* to exhibit certain excellences of character. (I have emphasised the words carrying the ethical message.) Please understand that the *ought* is derived from the *choice*. To be a *good* Freemason is (at least) to exemplify brotherly love, relief and truth and, most importantly, there is no sense in which a man can say *I want to be a Freemason but not*

---

[1] Wittgenstein said that *sprachspiele* exist within *forms of life*. What is said and done can only be understood by reference to a form of life and a form of life is always an interpersonal or societal affair. The argument here is similar to Wittgenstein's argument against a private language so I will not go into them now. Suffice to say that the veracity of any moral judgement, which itself can only exist within a form of life, requires that it can be checked by another member of that form of life. In this way, moral judgements obey something like the verification principle in Logical Positivism.

a good one because Freemasonry is a moral practice. (It might be worth your while to read the preceding paragraph again.)

The point I am making is taken from Wittgenstein:

> *Supposing that I could play tennis and one of you saw me playing and said, 'Well, you play pretty badly,' and suppose I answered, 'I know, I'm playing badly but I don't want to play any better,' all the other man could say would be, 'Ah then that's all right.' But suppose I had told one of you a preposterous lie and he came up to me and said, 'You're behaving like a beast,' and then I were to say, 'I know I behave badly, but then I don't want to behave any better,' could he then say, 'Ah, then that's all right'? Certainly not; he would say, 'Well, you ought to want to behave better.'* [1]

There is no obligation on any man to choose our *peculiar system of morality veiled in allegory and illustrated by symbols.* It is a choice that must be made properly because it is a choice to accept the whole of Freemasonry: to become a Freemason. As the Royal Arch ritual says of the candidate, *may he not enter our Order lightly, nor recede from it hastily, but pursue it steadfastly.* In making the choice to become a Freemason, one accepts the obligation to adopt our rules and principles – and this is the point in becoming a Freemason. To adopt the ethical structure of Freemasonry is to become a Freemason, and to become a Freemason is to adopt that structure. There is no meaning to the statement that one can be a Freemason and not adopt our ethical structure. It would be like saying *I am a democrat but do not believe in voting.*

Being a candidate

It is supremely important that a candidate for Freemasonry should be told that his decision to join us is not a decision to join a club, even a fraternity, but a decision *to choose to be governed by our principles.* A candidate should never be in any doubt about the commitment to our principles or the specific virtues and excellences required to be a good Freemason, and indeed that the intention to become a good Freemason is the only acceptable reason for joining. This should be explained to the candidate before he joins and continually reinforced during the period leading up to his being raised to the sublime degree of a Master Mason.

No man will understand the whole body of Masonic excellences right away. That demands study and it is for that reason that the Masonic life is to be lived, not just learned by rote. As a man learns about the excellences of our order, he is able to accept or reject them, to decide whether to adopt the ethical structure that Freemasonry offers. Once he makes that choice, he becomes a Freemason but he cannot truly make that choice until he understands the excellences demanded of him. Thus, the period of Entered Apprentice and Fellow Craft should really be

---

[1] Wittgenstein (2).

seen as a time of reflection and qualification.[1] Chapter 58 of the Rule of St Benedict is far more strict and precise than any rule for candidates to Freemasonry but the essence of it is worth examining. It shows many similarities to our practice, or what our practice ought to be:

> [If] *someone comes … knocking at the door, and if at the end of four or five days he has shown himself patient … and has persisted in his request, then he should be allowed to enter and stay in the guest quarters for a few days. After that, he should live … where the novices study, eat and sleep. A senior chosen for his skill* [Mentor?] *should be appointed to look after them … The novice should be clearly told all the hardships and difficulties … If he promises perseverance … then after two months have elapsed let this rule be read straight through to him, and let him be told: 'This is the law under which you are choosing to serve. If you can keep it, come in. If not, feel free to leave.' If he still stands firm, he is to be taken back … and again thoroughly tested in all patience. After six months have passed, the rule is to be read to him, so that he may know what he is entering. If once more he stands firm, let four months go by, and then read this rule to him again. If after due reflection he promises to observe everything and to obey every command … let him then be received into the community. But he must be well aware that … from this day he is no longer free to leave the monastery, nor to shake from his neck the yoke of the rule …*

Our purpose

Our purpose, then, is to be a community in which the moral life can be continued, even as the virtues and virtue are lost elsewhere. Central to our work of preservation is the maintenance of the ability to trust and to be trustworthy, to be a reservoir of social capital. Beyond this, we are to be a moral stronghold, combatting MacIntyre's *horrors of the modern dark age*, a context within which virtues find traction. Sustaining *civility* with *the intellectual and moral life* must become our reason for existence. In the absence of any agreed social or political context (an absence that neither Plato nor Aristotle would have understood) or of any widespread religious belief (an absence that St Ignatius would have found incomprehensible), Freemasonry becomes, almost uniquely, a vital *form of community within which civility and the intellectual and moral life can be sustained.*

It is easy to view such a task as beyond us but it may be of some comfort to recognise that the task has fallen on others before. The attacks on values happen in cycles, like economic recessions. There are periodic intervals in human experience when scientific, religious and economic events demand new ways of understanding our relationships with others and during such upheavals moral

---

[1] One might well argue that no joining fee should be payable until a brother has taken his third degree, for only then will he be fully able to make a decision to join us, abide by our principles and live his life according to the virtues of the order.

relativity seeks to take over.[1] One of those periods occurred in the 1800s, a period that saw Freemasonry's near terminal decline. I quoted from Thomas Carlyle earlier. He railed against the damage to the spiritual value of human life caused by mechanisation: the destruction of the virtues of expertise, imagination and devotion to the task, as skilled handcraft was overtaken by the production line.

> *Were we required to characterise this age of ours by any single epithet, we should be tempted to call it, not an Heroical, Devotional, Philosophical, or Moral Age, but, above all others, the Mechanical Age ... On every hand, the living artisan is driven from his workshop, to make room for a speedier, inanimate one ... The truth is, men have lost their belief in the Invisible, and believe, and hope, and work only in the Visible ... Only the material, the immediately practical, not the divine and spiritual, is important to us... Our true Deity is Mechanism.[2]*

The Victorian middle class that followed managed to create a virtuous capitalism, in which decency combined with creativity and energy to bring about Britain's economic leadership in the known world. Virtuous capitalism has now been destroyed and with it the values which the middle class sustained. The barbarian attacks on decency must be resisted once again. Now it is our turn.[3]

---

[1] Examples of periods of moral uncertainty other than today and the end of the Roman Empire include: (1) The so-called *Crisis of the Late Middle Ages* in 14th and 15th centuries which saw uprisings all over Europe caused by a widening gap between rich and poor, increased poverty and the Little Ice Age which resulted in the great famine of 1315-17. The 100 Years War began in 1337 and the Black Death, which halved the population, ten years later. The effect was religious upheaval in which Master Eckhart argued that men and women could reach god simply by meditating on the spirituality of Christ and John Wyclif and the Lollards argued that god had already chosen those to be saved and that the Church was therefore unnecessary. (2) The *Enlightenment*, whose effect on religious belief I discussed in my book, *Deism*. Before Bacon, Locke and Descartes, the discussion was about which religion was best. After them, it was about the need for religious belief at all.

[2] 'A Mechanical Age' in the *Edinburgh Review*, 1829.

[3] Byung-Chul Han writes *Given the atomization of society and the erosion of the social, all that remains is the body of the ego, which is to be kept healthy at all costs. The loss of ideal values leaves ... only the health value behind.* Given the absence of any values, the only purpose of life is to keep living. Life, *stripped of all transcendent value, has been reduced to the immanency of vital functions ...*

The virtues of Freemasonry

... a community whose shared aim is the realisation of the human good presupposes of course a wide range of agreement in that community on goods and virtues, and it is this agreement which makes possible the kind of bond between citizens which, on Aristotle's view, constitutes a 'polis'.[1]

The three grand principles

The three grand principles, we might assume, have been in the forefront of the minds of Masons from time immemorial but the phrase, *brotherly love, relief and truth*, as far as I can see, seems not to occur until Preston's *Illustrations of Masonry*, published progressively after 1772. The phrase seems to be Preston's invention, even if it has a genesis in earlier words and phrases and it is to Preston's raw materials we need to turn for the original meaning and force of the words. It helps that those materials are from a more simple and direct time. Here is a lovely charge from the *Dumfries No. 4* MS of 1710:

> *every man yt is a massone or enters y' inters y' interest to aggrandise & satisfie his curiositie looke to y' following charge if any of ye be guilty of y' following Immoralitys see yt you Repent & amend speedily for you will find it a hard thing to fall into ye hands [of] our angry god and more especialy you yt are under the voues take hee[d] yt you keep y' ath and promise you made in the presence of allmighty god think not yt a mental Reservation or Equivocation will serve for to be sure eury word you speak the whole time of your Admission is ane oath and god will examin you according to the purness of your heart and cleaness of your hands it is ane sharp edged tool yt you are playing with beware you cut not your fingers we intreat you that y' forfit not your Saluation for any other seeming content.*

My transliteration of this runs:

> *Every Mason, or anyone who enters the order to satisfy his curiosity, should take notice of the following charge. If any of you are guilty of these sins, see to it that you repent and make good without delay, for you will find it hard to fall into the hands of an angry God. You are still under your vows, so be careful to maintain the oath and promise you made in the presence of that God. Do not think that mental reservation or equivocation will serve because every word you spoke during the whole of your admission into Freemasonry constitutes an oath and God will examine you according to the purity of your heart and cleanliness of your hands. It is a sharp-edged tool that you are playing with, so beware of cutting your fingers. We entreat you not to forfeit your salvation for any apparent pleasure.*

In the following pages, I have generally modernised spelling and grammar of passages I quote.

---

[1] MacIntyre (4).

Understanding brotherly love

The phrase *brotherly love* makes its first appearance in Anderson's 1723 *Constitutions*, described as *the foundation and capstone, the cement and glory of this ancient Fraternity.* Three years later, the *Graham* MS has the phrase *truth and justice and brotherly love* but the sentiments appear much earlier. Around 1390 the *Regius Poem* reads:

> ... *each one shall teach the other, and love together as sister and brother* ... *Masons should never one another call, within the craft amongst them all, neither subject nor servant, my dear brother, though he be not so perfect as is another, each shall call other fellows by friendship* ...

This charge appears in other documents including the *Cooke* MS of about 1450:

> ... *that ye love together as ye were brethren, and hold together truly; and he that hath most cunning teach it to his fellow.*

and the *Dowland* MS of about 1500:

> *That they should be true each of them to other, and that they should love truly together, and that they should serve their lord truly for their pay; so that the master may have worship and all that* [be]*long to him.*

The answers *the more the merrier* and *the fewer the better cheer,* appear in many catechisms including the *Chetwode Crawley* and *Sloane 3329* MS (both around 1700) and in 1714 the *Kevan* MS introduces a greeting we are all used to, *Brother John, greet you well* with a reply, *God's good greeting to you, dear brother,* but that is about it.

The five points of fellowship

While the phrase *brotherly love* is not common before Preston, the five points of fellowship are very common indeed and seem to have been more important in earlier times than today. Because there was initially just one degree, the five points were not tucked away, as they are today, in the third degree. They were therefore more prominent, doing the work of the phrase *brotherly love*. They are not explained in any extant documents until 1760 (which is not to say that explanations never existed) but they are listed in just about all exposures, with slight variations. To choose just one example, the *Chetwode Crawley* MS runs:

> *How many points of fellowship are there?*
> *Five: foot to foot, knee to knee, heart to heart, hand to hand, ear to ear.*

As in the *Chetwode Crawley,* the five points are followed by both the (modern) first and second degree words and it could be argued that the points really belong in our first degree. They are among the oldest examples of moral teaching that we have. To live by the undertakings of the five points of fellowship is to be trustworthy; to act upon them is to trust. Thus, the five points are an important part of Freemasonry's role as a reservoir of social capital. The first explanation is provided in the 1760 *Three Distinct Knocks* (TDK):

Hand to hand	*I always will put forth my hand to serve a brother as far as lies in my power.*
Foot to Foot	*I will never be afraid to go a foot out of my way to serve a brother.*
Knee to knee	*When I kneel down to prayers I will never forget to pray for my brother as well as myself.*
Breast to Breast	*I will keep my brother's secrets as my own.*
Left-hand supporting the back	*I will always be willing to support a brother as far as lies in my power.*

Note the use of the phrase *as far as lies in my power.* A 1725 version similarly states *as far as your ability will allow you.*[1] The more mealy-mouthed addition *without being detrimental to myself or family* occurs elsewhere in TDK and may be original to it.

A more personal relationship

In discussion, Glyn Jarrett pointed me towards C.S. Lewis on love, and in particular to Lewis's comments on the Greek φιλία (*philia*), true friendship. Lewis writes that to the Greeks, such friendship seemed *the happiest and most fully human of all loves; the crown of life and the school of virtue.* The tragedy of the modern world, Lewis writes, is that it seems to ignore *philia.* It is this form of love which is central to Masonry and the five points of fellowship indicate a personal relationship between Masonic brothers. The *Long Closing* reads in part:

> *Let me impress upon your minds, and may it be instilled into your hearts, that every human creature has a just claim on your kind offices. I therefore trust that you will be good to all. More particularly do I recommend to your care the household of the faithful ...*

The *household of the faithful* refers to Freemasons, those who have taken and live by their obligations and it is *more particularly* their care which is recommended. The word *household* indicates a community, and essential to any community is a shared recognition of moral values. *Be good to everyone but love your brother* is the original statement of virtue in Freemasonry, a meaning that has progressively weakened over time. Preston's 1772 wording and the 1908 *Taylor's Lectures* are almost identical. The latter reads:

> *... we are taught to regard the whole human species as one family ... sent into the world for the mutual aid, support and protection of each other.*

---

[1] *Institutions of Freemasonry,* 1725.

An honourable sentiment no doubt, but a generalised version of the original meaning. The distinction between the modern, more generalised virtue and the original and more intimate one is seen again in the principle of *relief*.

Understanding relief

Here is a thought for you:

> *Though I speak with the tongues of men and of angels, and have not charity, I am become as sounding brass, or a tinkling cymbal. And though I have the gift of prophecy, and understand all mysteries, and all knowledge; and though I have all faith, so that I could remove mountains, and have not charity, I am nothing. And though I bestow all my goods to feed the poor, and though I give my body to be burned, and have not charity, it profiteth me nothing.*

Compare this with:

> *If I speak in the tongues of men or of angels, but do not have love, I am only a resounding gong or a clanging cymbal. If I have the gift of prophecy and can fathom all mysteries and all knowledge, and if I have a faith that can move mountains, but do not have love, I am nothing. If I give all I possess to the poor and give over my body to hardship ... but do not have love, I gain nothing.*

This is *1 Corinthians 13*. The first passage is taken from the King James version while the second is from the New International. The difference appears in their translation of the Greek word αγαπη (*agape*): in the King James as *charity*, and in the New International as *love*.[1] How is it that charity and love are the same? The *Catholic Encyclopaedia*, my regular resource on such matters, reads:

> ... *charity is that habit or power which disposes us to love God above all creatures for Himself, and to love ourselves and our neighbours for the sake of God.*

It is the motivation that provides the meaning. The encyclopaedia again:

> ... *when a person with the virtue of charity in his soul assists a needy neighbour on account of the words of Christ, 'as long as you did it to one of these my least brethren, you did it to me,' or simply because his Christian training tells him that the one in need is a child of God, the act is one of supernatural charity. It is likewise meritorious of eternal life.*

Charity is thus an act of love and only an act carried out for love is considered an act of charity. That love may be motivated by a love of god but acts of natural charity are also acceptable, again provided the motivation is correct:

---

[1] There were four words in ancient Greece with meanings based on love. *Agape* was described by C.S. Lewis as a selflessness, committed to the well-being of another person. We might think of this as married love or love of one's children. In Christianity it is about the love of god. *Philia* (φιλία) is what we mean by brotherly love. Eros (ἔρως) is sexual love. The fourth word *storge* (στοργή) is more like our word *affection* and is used in the context of an extended family.

... it is not necessary that acts of brotherly love should rest upon this high motive in order to deserve a place under the head of charity. It is enough that they be prompted by consideration of the individual's dignity, qualities, or needs.

Relief of an individual

In the beautiful 17th century English of the King James Bible, the word *charity* actually means something close to giving love, itself very close to the meaning of the word *relief* that we find in the older rituals. The word *charity* has today come to mean little more than giving money to an impersonal if worthy cause, but it is important to stress that this is not the meaning of the word *relief.* The target of relief is specific, not impersonal. Relief is of a person, an individual, and while relief may be about money, it is more about behaviour. Earlier documents, including the *Harleian* MS (c1660), demand that a Mason:

... set strangers at work, having employment for them, at least a fortnight and truly pay them their wages; and if you want (lack) work for them, you shall relieve them with money to defray their reasonable charges to the next Lodge.

Whenever it is used in these earlier documents, the word *relief* is always used in connection with improvident Masons. The *Dumfries No 4* (c.1710) may seem to demand that a Mason help the general poor:

... make it your business to relieve the poor according to your abilities; let not prudence overcome your charity by thinking one person or the other unworthy or not in need but let no opportunity slip by. It is for god's sake you give it and in obedience to his command.

However, the poor referred to are the local poor, those eligible for local outdoor relief under the Poor Law. The wording of *Dumfries No 4* implies that the recipient is known to the Mason:

Visit the sick; comfort and pray for them and let them not be in any distress that is in your power to prevent. If god calls them hence, attend their funeral. [Be] affable and kind to everyone but more especially to widows and the fatherless. Stand stoutly on their behalf, defend their interests and relieve their necessities ...[1]

Smith's *Pocket Companion* of 1735 speaks of the Mason not *sitting down contented while his fellow creatures but much more his brethren are in want* and even Preston, in differentiating it from charity, writes of relief:

By this principle we are prompted to kind and friendly offices, which strengthen our connections, and preserve our attachment. We not only feel for the misfortunes of our brethren but never desert them in the hour of distress, till the wounds of their hearts are healed, and peace is restored to their disturbed minds.

---

[1] The *Dumfries* MS argues that the Mason should especially concern himself with widows and orphans even though, in a curious phrase, *this bread be thrown upon uncertain waters.*

Relief is not just about money but also about action and emotion: visiting people when sick, comforting them and acting from the feelings of the heart. The lodge box, found particularly in early Scottish lodges, is evidence of this as is Anderson's *Constitutions* which reads:

> *Every new brother at his making is … to deposit something for the relief of indigent and decay'd Brethren, as the Candidate shall think fit to bestow …*[1]

The motivation of giving

In lodge we collect *alms*, another word associated with relief. The word *alms*[2] derives from the Greek ἔλεος *(eleos)* which means mercy, compassion, having pity. Its early meaning is of relief of the poor as a religious duty and again it is the motivation that makes the difference. Donating money without the motivation of mercy, compassion, or pity is not giving alms. It follows that attempts to use charitable donations for PR purposes is not giving alms and is as improper in Freemasonry as donating or collecting for charity in the hope of grand rank.

Relief and alms are different from philanthropy, which is about giving money to impersonal but good causes, and if we see philanthropy as the primary purpose of our order, then our ritual, *a peculiar system of morality veiled in allegory and illustrated by symbols*, becomes secondary. This cannot make sense. I think it is fair to say that the modern importance in Freemasonry of philanthropy is an innovation, perhaps commencing around the time when the Duke of Suffolk instituted charity jewels.

Modern ritual does indeed make reference to charity (philanthropy) which *should know no bounds save those of prudence*, as the explanation of the first Tracing Board says. The *Address to the Brethren* tells us that we should lessen *the aggregate of human misery and vice by extending the bounties of charity to every deserving object under heaven.*

Nevertheless, the meaning of relief as love is still there. The ritual still talks of the need to *relieve and befriend with unhesitating cordiality every brother who might need your assistance*. The initiate is still told that concealed among the many under our banner there are those *who from circumstances of unforeseen calamity and misfortune are reduced to the lowest ebb of poverty and distress;* that it is on their behalf that *we awaken the feelings of every newly made brother by making such an appeal to his charity* (this time as relief) *as his circumstances in life may fairly warrant.*

Dr George Oliver adds much that is useful here:

> *Wherever a Mason may stray … he will always find a home; he will always meet with some kind friend and Brother to give him welcome, to greet him with the right hand of fellowship, to promote his interests, and to give him comfort and consolation in his distress.*

---

[1] *Indigent* means *poor* and *decayed* means something like *handicapped by age.*

[2] The word *alimony* is connected.

A new focus

Geo Oliver D D

For many reasons, some worthy and some less so, we have begun to focus more on philanthropy than on relief of our brethren. I think that it is fair to say that we have been scared off the practice of relief by accusations that *Freemasons just look after their own*. Our response to such accusations has been to stress, and even advertise, how much we donate to non-Masonic causes. Patrick Byrne, for one, longs for a return to the old ways of charitable giving:

I am one of those traditional Masons who miss the old days, when we did our bit for charity and basked in the knowledge that no one else knew what we had done.

I know that we began to publicise our charitable work as a response to those who wished to denigrate our order, but I'm not sure that in making our charitable works public, we have accrued any benefit.

While there is nothing wrong with philanthropy, the original virtue of relief of brethren and the local needy, has been lost in translation. Given the issues that society faces today, relief is more important than ever and lodges ought perhaps to be encouraged to put more money aside to provide immediate help to their own brethren, widows in distress and their local community.

Understanding truth

Of the grand principles, truth is the most difficult to describe. In my book *The Goat, the Devil and the Freemason* I wrote, all too hastily, that truth concerns honesty in word and deed. A reviewer took me to task about that, clearly wanting the word *truth* to have some spiritual or religious meaning. I really do not think it does, but I do agree that it means more than honesty in word and deed. I have said that the phrase *brotherly love, relief and truth* does not occur until Preston's *Illustrations of Masonry* and it is difficult to find a capital-T use of the word *truth* before Preston.

I am not even sure that Preston knew what he was talking about when he invented the triad, because his own description of *truth* is not good.

Explain Truth: By this principle we are taught to secure the favourable opinions of the world by the sincerity of our conduct. It is a divine attribute and the foundation of every virtue; while to the former principles it adds energy and effect. How is this principle applied in masonry? In masonry this principle has peculiar influence, for swayed by it in the Lodge, hypocrisy and deceit are unknown, sincerity and plain dealing mark our conduct, and heart and tongue combine to promote the welfare, and rejoice at the prosperity of our brethren.

… much of which sounds suspiciously like waffle. If I stand accused of describing Masonic truth as nothing more than a matter of honesty in word and deed (for which error I apologise) I am at least in good company. Preston describes it as no more than sincerity and plain dealing … and perhaps a lack of envy.

True in early rituals

Apart from a use in the *Regius* poem that has little to do with the virtues:

Gemetré the seventh syens hyt ysse,
That con deperte falshed from trewthe y-wys[1]

… the virtue of *truth* (in the form of an abstract noun) makes a brief appearance in the *Graham* MS of 1726, more significantly, after the five points of fellowship have been given in the 1696 *Edinburgh Register House* MS. where the instruction appears to *shake hands and you will be acknowledged a true Mason.* A similar use of the word appears in the 1700 *Chetwode Crawley* and the c.1714 *Kevan* MS. The exposure *Shibboleth* uses a phrase not so very far from this in describing Masons as *true to each other.*

In the English language, the word *true* takes on a range of meanings: from loyal, genuine and legitimate to accurate. We speak of a true friend, a true emotion, the true path, the true heir and true north. We speak of a mechanical fitting being true, an archer aiming true, of the need to remain true to one's beliefs and of a portrait being a true likeness. These are the uses of the word *true* that occur in the early rituals. A true Mason is unfeigning and genuine. He is one who is true to our principles, a true and constant friend whose love of his brethren is truly demonstrated and here, I think we have the meaning of *truth* in the three grand principles. I do agree with Preston when he says that truth *adds energy and effect* to brotherly love and relief because if our brotherly love is truly shown to be unfeigned and if our relief is truly offered with genuine concern for others, it will be seen as sincere and all the more welcome and appreciated.

Brotherly love: relief and truth

Earlier I said that I would show that brotherly love, relief and truth amount to the same thing and that the three grand principles might be better punctuated as

---

[1] *Geometry is the seventh science, that is a discipline that distinguishes truth from falsehood.*

brotherly love: relief and truth (note colon). Perhaps it is now clear that relief and truth are nothing more, and nothing less, than ways of showing love. We show our love in helping a brother and in being faithful and true to him at all times. This is the meaning of the three grand principles in the light of the five points of fellowship.

The four cardinal virtues

In our ritual today, the quartet appears in the Charge after Initiation, *Let prudence direct you, temperance chasten you, fortitude support you and justice be the guide of all your actions.* Dr Roy Murray argues that the four cardinal virtues have been connected with Masonry since time immemorial and while they adorn the four corners of the Grand Temple in Freemasons' Hall in London,[1] I have not found them in rituals before Preston. They do appear in the apocryphal *Wisdom of Solomon*:

> *And if a man love righteousness her labours are virtues: for she teacheth temperance and prudence, justice and fortitude: which are such things as men can have nothing more profitable in their life.*[2]

In the 2005 *Compendium of the Catechism of the Catholic Church*, the cardinal virtues are described as *the hinges* of a virtuous life. (The word *cardinal* is from the Latin *cardo*, a hinge, as in the hinge of a door.)

> *Prudence disposes reason to discern in every circumstance our true good and to choose the right means for achieving it.*
>
> *Justice consists in the firm and constant will to give to others their due.*
>
> *Fortitude assures firmness in difficulties and constancy in the pursuit of the good. It reaches even to the ability of possibly sacrificing one's own life for a just cause.*
>
> *Temperance moderates the attraction of pleasures, assures the mastery of the will over instincts and provides balance in the use of created goods.*[3]

Prudence

Today prudence is a matter of looking before you leap but Aristotle and following him, Aquinas, thought of it more as the ability to identify right from wrong. Aristotle's word is *phronesis*, related to knowledge but more about its acquisition and dispensation, requiring the ability to consult others and seek advice as well as the skill of speaking well without giving offence. It is sometimes thought of as practical wisdom involving the use of reason to consider ends and means. In a similar vein, Preston writes:

---

[1] So do the signs of the zodiac and they have nothing at all to do with Freemasonry.

[2] *King James* version 1611.

[3] Part three, questions 380 to 383. I have slightly edited the explanations.

By prudence we are taught to regulate our conduct by the rules of right reason; judge and determine with propriety, in every measure, with respect to the general good ...

So when the ritual says *Let prudence direct you*, it is not telling us to avoid risk but to use reason and logic, to think about questions, particularly moral questions, to be open to advice and to express ourselves with others in mind.

Fortitude

Plato thought of this as the soldier's virtue of courage but for Aquinas fortitude is what gives us the strength to do what should be done; an excellence that enables us to overcome fear and to remain steady in pursuit of the good. In *Lecture 15* of Aquinas' commentary on Aristotle's *Nicomachean Ethics*, he discusses Aristotle's view that fortitude is a matter of reason:

... fortitude is principally concerned not only with fear of death but also with boldness in danger ... brave men ... act manfully by meeting dangers in those circumstances where fortitude is praiseworthy and where it is noble to die, as in battle. It is good that a man endanger his life for the common welfare. [Fortitude] endures and fears the right things, for the right motive, in the right manner. Likewise the brave man acts daringly, for he endures and acts in conformity with what is worthy and according to reason.

The *beserkers*, those Norse warriors so admired in the sagas, who fought in an enraged and probably drug-induced trance would not have been considered courageous by Aristotle. Fortitude is facing known odds rationally and accepting death only as necessary to the defence of what is right. For Aquinas too, courage has a moral dimension:

Fortitude denotes a firmness of soul by which it remains unmoved by the fear of dangers.

For us, fortitude is about maintaining our principles in the face *the attacks of the insidious* as the ritual says, those temptations and persuasions that stealthily, deceitfully and treacherously beguile us into unworthy actions.

Temperance

Plato sees temperance as a matter of harmony, the avoidance of the excess that disturbs life. Aquinas, a Christian following St Paul, sees it as restraint, avoiding over-indulgence of the animal appetites. (Not specifically alcohol.[1])

In his commentary on Aristotle, Aquinas says:

The temperate man desires whatever pleasures are useful to the health and well-being of the body, and he wants them according to right measure and as he ought. He desires other pleasures only if they are not a hindrance to health, nor opposed to what is honourable, nor

---

[1] *... use a little wine for thy stomach's sake and thine often infirmities.* 1 Timothy 5:23.

beyond his means. One who is otherwise disposed takes more enjoyment than is reasonable. The temperate man is not of this nature but he acts according to right reason.[1]

Temperance for Aquinas is about the nature of desire, of simply *not wanting*. St Paul would have preferred that sex just did not happen: that *it is good for a man not to touch a woman*. He wished that *all men were even as I myself* but recognised the reality of desire and therefore as matter *of permission, and not of commandment*, said that people should marry *to avoid fornication*. The distinction is therefore between the virtue of controlling desire (Paul) and the virtue of not having desire (Aquinas). Aristotle distinguishes between the *temperate* man and the *continent* man:

> *Whereas the temperate man is equable by nature so that he does not experience strong desires, the continent man is of a more energetic nature and therefore does experience such desires, yet governs them according to the dictates of reason … The continent man thus possesses a more ardent and positive nature … he is subject to strong impulses and aspirations, and holds himself in control only by making reason a guide of his life.*

The *temperate* man has no desire while the *continent* man has desires but seeks to control them. It is in the sense of *continence* that the common gavel:

> *… denotes the force of conscience which should keep down all vain and unbecoming thoughts.*

It is continence rather than temperance that one might think is descriptive of the Masonic life, a life managed by reason, *avoiding fear on the one hand and rashness on the other*, while experiencing human desires and feelings. As the 1730 pamphlet *A Defence of Masonry* says, the design of Freemasonry is *to subdue our passions, not to do our own will*.[2] Nevertheless, in the Long Working Tools of the Second Degree we are instructed to make our *passions and prejudices coincide with the strict line of* [our] *duty*. This is more like Aristotle's concept of temperance, achieving a state of having no desire that conflicts with our moral values. Perhaps we may see this as another journey from the rough to the smooth ashlar, one from continence to temperance, a journey doubtless assisted by age, as the blood of youth cools.

Justice

Isaiah 28:17 makes justice sound peculiarly Masonic in saying *I will make justice the measuring line and righteousness the plumb line*. For Plato, the just person is one who is guided by a vision of the good. Aristotle argued that justice requires that everyone receives what is due to them according to merit, including moral merit – their *just desserts* as we might say. The vice of *pleonexia* (greed or avarice) meant seeking to gain more than one deserves, and Ivan Boesky, as we have seen, celebrated this

---

[1] Aquinas (2), Lecture 21.

[2] It goes on: *to make a daily progress in a laudable art; to promote morality, charity, good fellowship, good nature and humanity.* Knoop et al.

vice. The problem we face in our society is that with no view of the good in common, we have no commonly held criterion for what constitutes just desserts; no common view of fairness or equity. The power of Michael Sandel's book *Justice* lies in the examples he mounts to demonstrate this. He writes:

> *To ask whether a society is just is to ask how it distributes the things we prize – income and wealth, duties and rights, powers and opportunities, offices and honours. A just society distributes these goods in the right way; it gives each person his or her due ... The hard questions begin when we are asked what people are due and why.*

The free market capitalist would argue that his skills, knowledge and risk-taking justify a greater share of the world's goods, that it is the duty of the state to ensure that a market is free so that his efforts are rewarded. Liberal democracies would temper capitalism by concern for the disadvantaged, through a welfare system or positive discrimination. Communism requires state control over all goods and services and distributes them solely according to perceived need. Sandel writes:

> *Justice is inescapably judgemental. Whether we're arguing about financial bailouts or Purple Hearts, surrogate motherhood or same-sex marriage, affirmative action or military service, [or] CEO pay ... questions of justice are bound up with the competing notions of honour and virtue, pride and recognition. Justice is not only about the right way to distribute things. It is also about the right way to value things.*

Negative and positive justice

However, in the negative sense, it is clear that justice is about impartiality; making decisions without fear or favour; not being swayed by popular opinion; not taking bribes; consulting with others to see all sides of the issue.[1] In making a decision, we should always ask ourselves whether we are being *influenced by mercenary and other unworthy motives.*[2] Motivation matters as much as content.

However, for Freemasons, impartiality is only part of what we mean by justice. There is also a positive side: ensuring that certain values are protected and even enhanced. As Freemasons, we have a moral core,[3] definitive moral values held in common which provide a basis on which we apply justice. Isaiah 1:17 reads, *Learn to do well; seek judgment, relieve the oppressed, judge the fatherless, plead for the widow.* For us, justice calls us to take the side of the unhappy and the downtrodden, to protect our brethren in distress, to help the needy, especially the orphan and the widow.

---

[1] *Do not follow the crowd in doing wrong. When you give testimony in a lawsuit, do not pervert justice by siding with the crowd.* Exodus 23:2. *Do not accept a bribe, for a bribe blinds the eyes of the wise and twists the words of the innocent.* Deuteronomy 16:19. [It] *was customary for the king to consult experts in matters of law and justice, he spoke with the wise men who understood the times.* Esther 1:13.

[2] The great OD practitioner Bill Reddin often used to ask *Whose needs?* That is, *Whose needs would be satisfied by the action you are thinking of taking?*

[3] Note that the word here is *core* and not *code*.

You swore with generous gifts to care
For those to sorrow bidden;
The brother on the darkened square;
The widow full of grief and care;
The sorrowed orphan doomed to stray
Along life's cold and cheerless way,
While tears pour forth unhidden.[1]

The *Long Closing* reminds us of our fallibility:

> *Remember that at this pedestal … you have promised to remind him in the most gentle manner of his failings and to aid and vindicate his character whenever wrongfully traduced; to suggest the most candid, the most palliating and the most favourable circumstances, even when his conduct is justly liable to reprehension and blame.*[2]

In other words, justice starts with the *household of the faithful*. We are to take our brother's part, be on his side, do our best to help him out of his troubles, even when his conduct is *justly liable to reprehension and blame*. Being brothers, we cannot pick and choose when to take sides. As Dr George Oliver wrote:

> *As we are none of us free from faults, it is the duty of every brother to bear with the infirmities, to pardon the errors, and to be kind and considerate towards those with whom he is so intimately connected … we must not expect to meet with all we could wish in every brother who is linked to us in the indissoluble chain of Masonry.*

Regret, apology and amends would no doubt be required, but to return to the *Walking Charge*:

You swore to deal in honesty
With each true heart around you;
That honour bright should ever be
T'unbroken bond twixt him and thee;
Nor wrong, nor guile, nor cruel fraud
Should loose or break that holy cord
With which these vows have bound you.

For a Freemason, a just decision is one which we have tested for impartiality by consulting others, that is made without fear of popular opinion; is not motivated by hope of personal reward; and is in tune with our principles, mindful of our vows concerning brotherly love and mercy, the *unbroken bond*.

---

[1] *Walking Charge*, West (1).

[2] *Long Closing*, West (1).

A little amusement

It is amusing to think that our forebears thought it also necessary to remind brethren not to argue in lodge, not *to drink drunk*, not to play cards for money, and not to swear or use obscene gestures. The expression of our principles has naturally changed over time. A lovely early phrase is *taciturnity and concord*. In the 18th century, *taciturnity* meant *being habitually silent*, while the word *concord* is derived from the Latin and means *of the same mind*, or more literally *hearts together*. We are told to remain free from *pollution*, a word which once meant *desecration* or *defilement*.

King and country

Some excellences or virtues have undergone change and the virtue of patriotism is described in progressively less strong terms as time goes by. For example, the *Dumfries No. 4* MS, dated c.1710, reads:

> *You shall be true to the lawful King of the Realm and pray for his safety … be no partaker of any treasonable designs against his person and government.*

James II landing at Kinsale in 1685

This statement positions the person of the king as the focus of patriotism and *Dumfries No. 4* was written during the period of the dangerous Jacobite rebellions, when a putative king sought to replace an incumbent: James II landing at Kinsale in 1685, Bonnie Dundee (1689), the Battle of the Boyne (1690) and the Old Pretender, James Francis Edward Stuart (1715).

Dumfries was concerned in a very personal way. Being a city in the Borders, it would have suffered in any full-scale war between the English crown and the Jacobite forces, who were mainly Scottish Catholics. In the event, the Old Pretender's landing at Peterhead, admittedly a long way from Dumfries, was rendered irrelevant by the incompetence of the Earl of Mar[1] and by 1723, the statement had softened and the focus of patriotism changed from King to nation. Anderson's 1723 *Old Charges* read:

> *A Mason is a peaceable Subject to the Civil Powers ... and is never to be concern'd in Plots and Conspiracies against the Peace and Welfare of the Nation ... So that if a brother should be a Rebel against the State, he is not to be countenanced ... however he may be pitied as an unhappy Man.*[2]

In the same year, *A Mason's Examination* says, more pithily, that Masons should be no *perjured Plotters or Conspirators against the establish'd Government*,[3] while in the *Institution of Free Masons* of 1725, this has been further reduced to *Be a true liege man to the King*.[4] By 1735, Smith's *Pocket Companion* merely says a Mason should be *a peaceable subject, conforming cheerfully to the government under which he lives*.[5]

The changes reflect historical events. The passion with which the charge is worded declines as the likelihood of any genuine rebellion recedes. The Jacobite cause was effectively brought to an end in 1760 with the defeat by Sir Edward Hawkes of a French fleet in Quiberon Bay, but it had been a declining threat for some time before that. It is true that Bonnie Prince Charlie attempted a rising in 1745,[6] taking Carlisle and getting briefly as far south as Derbyshire. However, with no English support, his voluntary decision to retreat and his subsequent defeat at Culloden were of little surprise.

As romantic as Charlie is today, the attention of the English government at the time was directed more towards the war of Austrian Succession, having been forced into that conflict after years of peace. As Trevelyan describes Charlie's *astonishing adventure*:

> *He found an island almost denuded of troops, utterly unaccustomed to war or self-defence and so selfishly indifferent to the issue between Stuart and Hanoverian that the inhabitants let 5,000 Highlanders with targe and broadsword march from Edinburgh to Derby, gaped at but equally unassisted and unopposed.*

---

[1] Leader of the Jacobite forces at the battle of Sheriffmuir in 1715.

[2] *The Constitutions of the Free-Masons*, 1723.

[3] Knoop et al.

[4] Knoop et al.

[5] Knoop et al.

[6] He spent three days in Dumfries until given news of the approach of the Duke of Cumberland.

Targe

In 1765, *Shibboleth* provides modern phrasing:

A Mason is obliged to conform to the laws of the place in which he resides, to avoid all combination against the peace and order of governments ...[1]

Reflecting upon brotherly love in 1772, Preston took in the whole brotherhood of Masons throughout the British Empire:

We are taught to regard the whole human species as one family ... By this principle of Masonry men of the most distant countries and most discordant settlements are in the lodge united on one bond of union.[2]

It is a pity that we have no ritual stemming from the time of the French Revolution, Bonaparte and the *Unlawful Societies Act*, a time which might have produced stronger wording. Our current ritual has been watered down.

As a citizen of the world, I enjoin you to be exemplary in the discharge of your civil duties: by never proposing or at all countenancing any act which may have a tendency to subvert the peace and good order of society; by paying a due obedience to the laws of any state which may for a time become the place of your residence or afford you its protection; and above all by never losing sight of the allegiance due to the Sovereign of your native land ...[3]

Peaceable subjects

The instruction never to countenance the subversion of society is reflected in the *Ancient Charges* read during the installation of the new master, directing him to be:

... a peaceable subject, and cheerfully to conform to the laws of the country in which you reside ... [and] promise not to be concerned in plots and conspiracies against government, but patiently to submit to the decisions of the supreme legislature.

These words appear to count out the British citizens' inalienable right to grumble! More seriously, this charge cannot mean that we are to remain peaceable even when a government has lost the right to govern. Despite the instruction *not to be concerned in plots and conspiracies against government,* many brethren have admired the struggles for independence and have celebrated those brethren involved. The romantics among us have even wanted to believe that the French, American and South American revolutions were all initiated and led by Freemasons.

[1] Jackson.

[2] Dyer (2).

[3] West (1).

Mitch Horowitz argues that Freemasonry was at least instrumental in the American revolution and that ... *early American Freemasons rejected a European past in which one overarching authority regulated the exchange of ideas.*[1] He says of our order that:

> As a radical thought movement that emerged from the Reformation, Freemasonry was the first widespread and well-connected organisation to espouse religious toleration and liberty – principles that the fraternity helped spread through the American colonies ...

George Washington, Benjamin Franklin, John Hancock and others in America were Masons but 18th-century French Freemasonry was an aristocratic affair, repressed during the revolution. The Masonic membership of the *libertadores* of South America, apart from Simón Bolívar, is unlikely. Bolívar was initiated around 1805, but neither José de San Martin nor Bernardo O'Higgins were regular Masons, neither was *El Precursor*, Francisco de Miranda. The *Lautaro* lodges, which claim them, were almost certainly no more than quasi-Masonic.[2]

Civil magistrate

The fourth charge uses the term *civil magistrate*, who is distinguished from *ecclesiastical* authority. The two can be, and often have been in opposition. The 19th-century Presbyterian Robert Lewis Dabney, conservative to a fault,[3] wrote:

> ... few governments are strictly just; and the inquiry therefore arises how shall the Christian citizen act, under an oppressive command of the civil magistrate? I reply, if the act which he requires is not positively a sin per se, it must be obeyed ... If the thing commanded by the civil magistrate is positively sinful, then the Christian citizen must refuse obedience, but yield submission to the penalty therefor ... It is God's will that such a government ... should be obeyed by individuals, rather than have anarchy.

This is Antigone's situation in the face of Créon's edict.

> Who is to be the judge when the act required of the citizen ... is morally wrong? I reply, the citizen himself ... Every intelligent being lies under moral relations to God.[4]

Keith Doney writes of the heroism of such brethren as Pierre Brossolette, Martial Brigouleix, Rolf l'Hermite, Serge l'Hermite and Georges Lapierre during the Nazi occupation of France. It is worth dwelling on their names for a moment or two. Both Bro. Rolf and Bro. Serge seem to have survived the war but Bro. Pierre threw himself from a high window to his death, fearing he would reveal information about other members of the Resistance under further torture.

---

[1] *Masons and the Making of America*, USNews, September 14, 2009.

[2] See Mitre, Reynolds and Zeldis.

[3] He argued in favour of slavery right into the 1880s.

[4] Dabney

Pierre Brossolette

Bro. Martial was shot among a group of hostages. Bro. Georges died in Dachau concentration camp.[1] They were not, to their eternal credit, *peaceable subjects* but were outlaws bravely *concerned in plots and conspiracies against* a government that they did not see as legitimate: the invader forces and their French collaborators.

True godliness

At the beginning of the first degree, the Chaplain expresses the hope that the candidate *may be the better enabled to unfold the beauties of true godliness* and just as the instruction regarding patriotism has declined in strength, so similar changes occur in the wording concerning religious belief. The *Dumfries* No. 4 MS, in the middle of Protestant and Catholic conflict, talks of the need to serve the true god, keep his *ten words* (the commandments), to be true and steadfast to the *holy catholic*[2] church, to shun heresy and schism, and observe the sabbath. The need to avoid schism indicates the perceived dangers of the religious movements around this time which led to the first Great Awakening,[3] such that in 1723, the Mason is abjured to be *no innovator in religious affairs.*[4]

By 1725, he is advised merely to *serve god according to the best of his knowledge*, perhaps recognising that the divergence in belief has already occurred. In 1735, we get what sounds like a bit of Deism,[5] with the comment that *religious disputes are never suffered in lodge* [because] *we pursue the universal religion of religion of nature.* By 1765, we find *Shibboleth* simply saying of Masons that ... *with respect to particular notions, modes of faith and worship and the like they are left to judge for themselves.* A long way from the ardour of the *Dumfries* MS. Today we are merely told *not to be an enthusiast, persecutor, slanderer or reviler of religion*, which means no more than that we should not get over-

---

[1] Doney (2).

[2] From the Apostles' Creed. The word *catholic* here does not mean 'Roman' Catholic but *orthodox*.

[3] Starting first in New England and then spreading back to the UK via John and Charles Wesley, it is usually dated to the 1730s but elements pre-date this, for example in the work of Benjamin Keach, Thomas Secker (whose portrait by Joshua Reynolds hangs in the National Portrait Gallery) and Matthew Henry.

[4] The number of protestant beliefs increased almost exponentially in the 18th century.

[5] I describe this in West (5).

excited about religion (*an enthusiast*), not upset a believer (*a persecutor*), not make incorrect accusations about religion (*a slanderer*) nor speak abusively of it (*reviler*). An atheist would have less trouble with this than a Jesuit.

Freemasonry and religion

The statement *Freemasonry is not a religion* is unhelpfully negative. To make sense of it we would need to define a religion, not easy to do. On many definitions, the practice of Freemasonry does indeed resemble the practice of religion: the use of ritual, a required belief in a god, petitionary prayers and the reward of an afterlife. A more helpful and positive version of the statement would be to say that *Freemasonry is compatible with any religion*.

Perhaps the best way to look at the relationship of Freemasonry to religion is to say that our order offers much that a religious context might offer but, since it requires no specific form of belief, it speaks as powerfully to those who have little connection with religion, as to true believers. (The phrase *no specific form of belief* is mostly true of the Craft but not of the Royal Arch whose ritual is heavy on the notion of original sin, a belief unique to specific types of Christianity.[1]) Freemasonry does not compete with religion but accepts, if it also regrets, religion's decreasing relevance in the modern world. I have spoken earlier about the questions we ask candidates. There are an increasing number whose affirmative answer to the question *Do you believe in a Supreme Being?* is the result only of earnest coaching by their proposer. Since 50% of the population profess no religion, the alternative question I propose *Are you happy to participate in prayers in lodge?* seems more honest.

Catch-all clauses

Since the ritual says that the *Charge after Initiation* must be given to the initiate, we could be forgiven for considering its contents to be the definitive list of the excellences demanded of us. Almost all the content of the modern charge appears in Smith's *Companion* of 1735 but the modern[2] version adds two new clauses:

> *Indeed no institution can boast a more solid foundation than that on which Freemasonry rests, the practice of every moral and social virtue.*

and

> *As an individual, I further recommend the practice of every domestic as well as public virtue.*

These catch-all clauses act like the words *and more* in poor quality company advertisements. They seek to imply that if anyone comes up with a virtue that the

---

[1] For example, neither Judaism, Eastern Orthodox, Islam, Shintoism, Buddhism nor Hinduism have a concept of original sin.

[2] Probably written around 1820.

ritual does not mention (or desires a product which the advert does not list) then it will be found within, notwithstanding. The idea that an institution would instruct its members to do everything that anyone, anywhere might approve of, is as daft as the idea of a shop that sells everything.

Truth, honour and virtue

The *Charge after Initiation* lists other excellences of character to which our attention is particularly and forcibly directed. Some of these – secrecy, fidelity and obedience – are more or less bylaws of our order and so I will focus on another 19th century addition to the ritual, the instruction to *indelibly imprint on* our hearts *the sacred dictates of Truth, of Honour, and of Virtue*. This sounds lovely but its meaning is not immediately apparent. The problem is with the capitalisation. We discussed *truth* and *virtue* earlier so let us now focus on the word *honour*. While it often occurs in the ritual, it is a tricky concept, as Falstaff implies:

> *Honour pricks me on. Yea, but how if honour prick me off when I come on? How then? Can honour set to a leg? No. Or an arm? No. Or take away the grief of a wound? No. Honour hath no skill in surgery, then? No. What is honour? A word. What is in that word 'honour'? What is that honour? Air. A trim reckoning. Who hath it? He that died o'Wednesday.*[1]

In *our ancient and honourable institution* it means *respectable*. It is a mark of regard in *honoured this afternoon by the presence of Grand Officers* and a term of religious reverence in *the honour and glory of thy holy name*. These uses are connected through the concept of *esteem*: to be honoured is to receive esteem from others and to honour someone is to esteem them. In the description of Freemasonry as a society of men *who prize honour and virtue above the external advantages of rank and fortune*, the word acts in direct contrast to Boesky's praise of greed. The Freemason is one who would never put material reward above the requirements of the moral life. A Freemason would never take a bribe, never avoid paying his due, never take advantage of anyone nor accept undeserved preferment. As the *Taylor's Lectures* put it:

> *The man of honour scorns to do an ill action ... deeming vice as something beneath him ...*

A man who acts from greed is dishonourable. He loses the esteem of others. The *Lectures*, however, introduce a much grander use of the word, perhaps one worthy of a capital H and involving an Aristotelian use of the word *magnanimity*:

> *The man of **true honour** will not content himself with a literal discharge of his duties as a man and a citizen, but raises and dignifies them to magnanimity, giving where he might with propriety refuse, and forgiving when he might with justice resent, ever deeming it more honourable to forgive than to resent an injury.*[2]   (emphasis added)

---

[1] *Henry IV Part One*: Act 5 Scene 1.

[2] First lecture, seventh section.

147

Supererogation

Here the word *honour* refers to actions going beyond giving what is due, beyond duty. A word used in moral philosophy is *supererogation:* behaviours not required by morality and which only a saint (in a loose use of the word) would undertake. For example, some legends describe Sir Galahad as the personification of purity. He abstained from all worldly pleasures, had total self-control and was resistant to any temptation. As Tennyson writes:

> *My good blade carves the casques of men,*
> *My tough lance thrusteth sure,*
> *My strength is as the strength of ten,*
> *Because my heart is pure.*

In the search for the grail, Galahad travelled alone and having found it and thus achieved his life's ambition, he asked for his death. His views on purity were certainly supererogatory. He would not have been found at the Ladies' Festival:

> *How sweet are looks that ladies bend*
> *On whom their favours fall!*
> *For them I battle till the end,*
> *To save from shame and thrall:*
> *But all my heart is drawn above,*
> *My knees are bow'd in crypt and shrine:*
> *I never felt the kiss of love,*
> *Nor maiden's hand in mine.*
> *More bounteous aspects on me beam,*
> *Me mightier transports move and thrill;*
> *So keep I fair thro' faith and prayer*
> *A virgin heart in work and will.*[1]

To demand of our brother Freemasons that they always go beyond the call of duty, would contradict the warning notice: *that not being detrimental to myself or my connections.* So, while we may enjoy the fantasy of a sacred dictate of Honour, the reality is that we do not expect supererogation of ourselves or of our brethren. We are not a society of saints and heroes but of ordinary and human men with responsibilities and ties, doing our best. For us, honour has no capital H. It is about mutual esteem, a lesser but a more achievable standard.

We have spent enough time on the notion of virtue and truth to understand that there is no meaningful capital-V nor capital-T use of these words and while we may have discovered a capital-H use of the word *honour*, it is not one for

---

[1] Ricks.

Freemasonry. Why such dictates are described as sacred is a mystery. I can find no relevant religious connection and I suspect that whoever inserted the triplet into the ritual thought it sounded beautifully spiritual and tried to enhance it by adding the spurious word *sacred*, accompanying it with the sign of reverence. Sadly, the words carry no meaning other than the prosaic if important:

> *Be genuine and honest, maintain the esteem with which others hold you and be good.*

Like the triplet, the phrase *society of men who prize honour and virtue* does not appear before the re-write of the ritual following the union of the two grand lodges. Both are innovations. That is neither surprising nor regrettable in itself. The ritual has always been subject to change[1] and you may well think that I have made a lot of fuss about three words. However, the triplet, the catch-all clauses and the shift from relief to charity, indicate an increasing desire to be liked by the popular world, even at the cost of meaning.

The new Master

The first charge instructs the new Master *to be a good man and true, and strictly to obey the moral law*. What counts as a good man will change with the context as we have discussed earlier: what was good and right in Homer's time was not the same as that in the time of Aristotle and each had a view different from that of St Francis. Even in our own era, attitudes towards divorce, pre-marital sex and LBTG partnerships have changed, such that what was seen as very wrong in 1900 is perfectly normal in 2000. In place of obedience to a static moral law, we might be better advised to follow *good man and true* with … *and seek to live the moral life*. The new Master is also charged to:

> … *avoid private piques and quarrels, and to guard against intemperance and excess … to be cautious in carriage and behaviour, courteous to your brethren, and faithful to your Lodge … to promote the general good of society, to cultivate the social virtues, and to propagate the knowledge of the art.*

It is worth emphasising that, even when others appear to be acting irrationally, the Freemason is charged with avoiding quarrels, being cautious in the way he presents himself and cultivating the social virtues. In other words, good manners really matter, even if courtesy will result in a sub-optimal result.

A summary of Masonic virtues

The Five Points of Fellowship are of supreme importance. To live by them is to be trustworthy. To act upon them is to trust. The five points indicate a personal relationship between Masonic brethren and, while the habit of loving our

---

[1] Haunch.

brethren makes us more loving of mankind, the principle of brotherly love was originally (but not solely) directed towards our brethren in Freemasonry.

Brotherly love may be partly defined by the phrase *all in it together*. Being brothers, we cannot pick and choose when to take sides. The word we use is *relief*, not charity. The target of relief is an individual and, in its original meaning, relief is about helping a fellow Mason or someone known to the lodge. Relief may be about money but it is more often about behaviour, acting from the heart. Charity is an act of love and only an act of love is an act of charity. Giving money is giving alms, only if given out of mercy, compassion, or pity. Giving for political reasons is not giving alms. A *true* Mason is unfeigning and genuine; he is true to our ideals, a true and constant friend whose love of his brethren is truly demonstrated. Being true to each other, Masons set an example in society. Truth in this sense is sincerity and the Masonic use of the word *true* connotes loyalty, legitimacy and fidelity.

Let prudence direct you, is an instruction to use reason and logic, to think about moral issues, and to be open to advice. *Fortitude* is about acting for the right motives, and maintaining our principles in the face of threat or persuasion to act otherwise. *Temperance* calls us to a life managed by reason, resisting temptations while experiencing human desires and feelings. In Freemasonry, a *just* action is one that is tested for impartiality, made without fear of popular opinion, unmotivated by hope of personal reward and positively consistent with our principles.

There are modes of behaviour implied by our excellences, including obedience to the spirit as well as the letter of the law, guarding against shows of excess, exhibiting courtesy and the social niceties and having conservative views on sexual morality. The decencies of a Victorian gentleman will generally be admired within the order and Freemasons are peaceable and patriotic. We do not expect supererogation of ourselves. We are not a gathering of saints and heroes, but an order of ordinary men with responsibilities and ties, doing our level best.

Practice and institution: managing our future

Shortly before her death in 1943, Simone Weil wrote *The Need for Roots*, a response to a request from the Free French government in exile for a programme of regeneration for France after the war. Her basic premise was that:

> *... we must first of all choose everything which is purely and genuinely good, without the slightest consideration for expediency, applying no other test than that of genuineness ... Naturally, everything which is concerned only with evil, hatred, meanness must in like manner be rejected ...*

There must be no contradiction between what we say and what we do. Being a moral order, the principles we hold must be reflected in the way we manage.

In April 2015, the Pro-Grand Master of the United Grand Lodge of England, Peter Lowndes, said:

> *... At my Annual Briefing meeting yesterday, the Metropolitan Grand Master, Provincial Grand Masters, District Grand Masters and Grand Superintendents were brought up to date on the various initiatives that have been taken to make Freemasonry fit to celebrate its Tercentenary with confidence in its future. This confidence will show that Freemasonry is as relevant today as it has been over all of the last 300 years. To achieve this, we will continue to work closely with Provincial and District hierarchy to develop a clear strategy on sound leadership, the involvement of the membership with clear focus on future needs, all backed up by sufficient factual information. I am determined that this level of involvement and cooperation, which is already showing great benefit, continues to succeed.*

Tinkering

Let us get the irrelevances out of the way. It is true that in the day-to-day administration of our order, small improvements add up. As Tom Peters says:

> *... I have long observed that one of the primary distinguishing characteristics of the best leaders is their personal thirst for and continued quest for new/small/practical ideas ... They long ago gave up on believing in miracles; instead, they depend upon a mass of small innovations – from everyone – to raise every element of their operations to stratospheric levels of performance.*[1]

However, the revitalisation of Masonry itself is not a matter of tinkering at the periphery. None of the following have been of any help in reversing our decline:

---

[1] Peters (2).

- the introduction of magazines.
- the formation of research lodges.
- public relations activity directed at the popular image of Freemasonry.
- efforts to improve communications between brethren and grand lodge.
- education booklets and education officers.
- funds to enable improvements to Masonic buildings.
- change of 'proper solicitation' to 'invitation to apply.'
- recruitment drives with advertisements placed in newspapers.

Nor does it matter whether:

- meetings start early or late.
- meetings are held on weekdays or Saturdays.
- we offer extravagant or simple festive boards.
- dining costs are included in lodge dues or paid separately.
- we have high or low cost dues.
- we use ceremonies with single or multiple candidates.
- candidates are asked to learn a lot or just a little.

Reflecting on such data, Harry Kellerman commented:

> *Are we asking the right questions? Are we clear on what the central core of Freemasonry really is? Why should we seek to preserve it?*[1]

Peter Thornton has argued that it is not Freemasonry that is in decline but the institution that surrounds it:

> *... the moral and ethical teaching [Freemasonry] espouses has not altered and will always be part of a democratic, civilised society. What is in decline is the ... membership ... The distinction must be made or we will continue to advocate fixing something that is not broken.*

Kirk C. White writes:

> *The lessons of Freemasonry are meant to be lived and not simply learned ... In order for Freemasonry to reach its stated goals it needs to be a daily part of each brother's life. Not just once a month for two hours plus an occasional fundraiser.*

Andrew Hammer suggests that for some brethren, Masonry is about:

> *... simple brotherhood, good times and philanthropy, and should not be bothered with contemplating anything beyond what can be easily and completely understood by all. If [so] it is respectfully suggested to you that you have gone through all of Masonry in as much darkness as when you started, and that your understanding of the Craft is not any different from that of any service organisation or mutual benefit club.*

---

[1] Kellerman 1992.

He adds:

And here is the greatest danger facing the craft today.

Perhaps most significantly, R. Pottinger remarked:

The task is not to impose yesterday's 'normal' on a changed today, but to change the organisation to fit the new realities ... Freemasonry ... has its roots in traditionalism and conservatism set in an autocratic environment in which decisions flow down the chain to be obeyed and few real avenues exist to pass messages back through the hierarchy, and with a generally low-perceived benefit from trying. ...

[Freemasonry] must create an environment where new and possibly radical thought is encouraged and two-way communication is considered essential. Only then can the process of renewal and renaissance start.

I find myself in agreement with all these commentators.

Engineering

I have argued that our relevance to society lies in being a community in which the moral life can be continued, even as the virtues are lost elsewhere. I have argued that our role is to be a reservoir of social capital and a moral stronghold in the face of the attacks of the new barbarians, and that almost alone in our order can the virtues find universal traction. Only by focusing on the meaning of Freemasonry can we bring about a reverse in the trend of membership.

As an analogy, consider the commercial organisation that focuses solely on profit and thereby fails. It has forgotten that profit is the reward, not the product itself. On the whole, British companies have been run by accountants and have focused on cost saving and short-term profit. We have no motor industry. German management has focused on engineering. BMW, Mercedes, Volkswagen and Porsche are industry leaders.

Our tinkering to date has ignored the need for engineering. Tinkering assumes that the old audience is still there and that minor adjustments can be made to attract it again – but we really must recognise that the source of candidates which sustained us for a hundred years years has dried up. Our challenge now is to reach a new audience, one that is quite unlike the middle class we have been used to.

More self-possessed, better educated and more egalitarian, it has a different relationship with time and is often in employment that is temporary and shifting, apt to change at short notice. Given the poor state of management in the UK today, this audience has little upward loyalty and has had enough of autocracy. It will expect its opinions to be heard. Much of what happens in the modern organisation actively disengages people and this audience will not accept similarly bad behaviour in voluntary organisations.

Our own management practices must therefore be in tune with our professed values or this new audience will turn its back on us. Behaviour acceptable to the old middle class is not so acceptable to the new audience. With the decline of job satisfaction and engagement at work, together with the decline of religion in society, this new audience is actively seeking meaning and fellowship which the old middle class took for granted.

A firm stance on *Brotherly Love, Relief and Truth* will be a welcome beacon in the darkness, but our new candidates want to see a positive message that actually guides our behaviour. Words alone will not do. Organisations' mission statements are often inconsistent with their actions. It is vital that we show we are different.

Hard questions

Donald Schön differentiated between *theory-in-use*, what we actually do, and *espoused theory*, what we like to believe we do. For example, many company reports say that people are their greatest asset. This is *espoused theory*. Actions that cut training spend demonstrate *theory-in-use*. Organisational learning starts with surfacing current theories-in-use and identifying the gap between them and espoused theory.

To become a bastion for morality, Freemasonry must ensure that the protection of the moral life truly becomes our guiding spirit and that the spirit of brotherhood guides all our actions. We must promulgate a community in which every action is based on trust; where our giving is truly of alms motivated by love; and where all our actions show that we are true to one another. Is this our current reality or just an espoused ideal? It is vital that we avoid defensiveness. Poor organisations hide from problems, denying their existence; good organisations embrace them.

In *The Future of Management*, Gary Hamel invites organisational leaders to consider some hard questions. Slightly reworded, two such questions run:

- *Can you create an organisation where the spirit of community binds people together?*
- *Can you create a sense of mission that motivates extraordinary contributions?*

To help answer these big questions, lets us start with some lesser ones. Accepting Hamel's challenge, we might ask:

Where are the biggest gaps between the rhetoric and reality in our order?
  What are the values we have the hardest time living up to? Does ego ever interfere with our ideals? What most turns brethren off?
Do we have a vision of what we want to be?
  Do we communicate a vision? How do we resolve conflict; by reference to our principles and vision or by politics?

Is our leadership remote or approachable?

What is the most common leadership style? With whom do our leaders participate? Do we actively seek ideas from our lodges? Are we genuinely open to new thoughts?

How do we promote?

What are the criteria we use in appointing brethren to senior positions? What do we do to discover talent throughout the order? What do we do to develop that talent?

You will have your own answers to these questions but here are some comments that I have collected from festive boards near and far. I would argue that they form enough of a consensus to be worrying.

The biggest gap between the rhetoric and reality in our order is to be found in statements that the order is in good heart, while numbers continue to decline. We seem to believe in the dictum, 'That hasn't worked, so let's do more of it.'

We do not communicate a vision; our response to criticism is primarily defensive. With no ruling vision, conflict can only be resolved by political means. Our most common leadership style is top-down; we issue edicts and rules. The answer to questions about ego must be given in the light of the constant hunger for grand honours.

There are enough executive bars and grand officers' changing rooms to suggest that leadership maintains a distance and participation would appear to be limited to a tight circle of intimates. Appointments have the appearance of a merry-go-round. Promotion seems to be an arcane science and the behaviour of those desperate for honours increasingly resembles that of a cargo cult.

The values we have the hardest time living up to arise in the management of our institution; brethren in private lodges are rarely consulted, often ill-informed and frequently isolated from decision-making.

Understanding how this can be turns upon the distinction that MacIntyre makes between *internal* and *external* 'goods'.

Internal and external goods

The *practice* of Freemasonry is about what MacIntyre calls *internal 'goods'* which can only be recognised by the experience of participating in the practice. No one lacking actual experience of what we do, is competent to judge what happens in lodge because they cannot understand how what we do matters. Mystified by many of the things that go on, outsiders will latch on to something out of context – hence the boring and constant rubbish about rolled-up trouser legs.

Not understanding what we are, people outside Freemasonry are tempted to look for financial or other external gains provided by being a Freemason. Such gains would be what MacIntyre calls *external 'goods'*, things having a tangible value. People can understand these and, in a (justifiably) cynical world, many argue that Freemasonry *must* offer external goods: it must be a mutual benefit club, that men must join for business contacts and that it must be a way to get on. When we say that none of these are true, people are mystified and ask, *Well, what do you do it for?*

True, there are some external goods in Freemasonry. We all recognise what happens to a new and often shy brother as he joins the lodge, participates in the progressive offices and finally reaches the chair of King Solomon. In my earlier book, *The Goat, the Devil and the Freemason*, I wrote of the alchemy that Masonry:

> *... can take an ordinary chap and turn him into a Master of the Lodge: capable of running a meeting, making a speech, learning and delivering from memory a part in the ritual at least the same length as Hamlet, and handling with aplomb such tricky words as* acquiescence, corporeal, immemorial *and even* parallelopipedon. *It enables everyone to shine, to take a place in the sun, to be recognised and congratulated and to feel good about themselves.*

In principle, a man might gain many of these skills by attending classes on public speaking, networking and the English language. The gaining of such skills has a value external to Freemasonry; it is an external good, and there are other external goods: medical help, financial support when down on one's luck, loans of equipment to make ageing more bearable and a room in a Masonic home when one cannot manage on one's own. There is no doubt that these have a value and no doubt at all that we value them. Nevertheless, they are incidental to the real and *internal* goods of Freemasonry.

- It is wonderful when a shy brother blossoms but the internal good is the *wonder*, the fact that we *find it wonderful*.
- The efforts of the Preceptor may result in applause but that is incidental to his efforts: his efforts are an *expression* of brotherly love.
- When the ritual is done well, it is a *gift* to the lodge and to the candidate.
- When the meaning of the words shines through, and when the rubric is exact and when the supporting players are perfect, *magic* occurs.
- When a brother needs help, the lodge will *dip into its savings* for him, because it *cares* about him.

The internal goods are the wonder, the expression, the gift, the magic and the caring, none of which have any external value nor could they be recognised or valued by anyone who is not a (good) Freemason.[1] These internal goods are simply not available to (and have no meaning for) a non-Mason or a Freemason who joined for the wrong (external) reasons. Only a Mason who really

---

[1] The savings themselves do have a financial value but they are not the internal good; it is the *act of saving*, and *dipping into them* when a brother needs help, that is.

understands and gives himself to Freemasonry would be able to experience the *wonder*, the *expression*, the *gift*, the *magic* and the *caring*. Even to understand what I am saying requires you to be a good Mason.

Internal goods are valuable for their own sake, not for what one can get for them. The motivation to achieve them is intrinsic, not extrinsic. (I will talk about intrinsic and extrinsic motivation a little later.) Something like this is displayed in Kevin Garside's comment on the state of Newcastle United as:

> ... *the appalling disintegration of a great footballing institution* [barrelling] *further towards its grim conclusion.*

This, he says, is what happens:

> ... *when you rip the heart from a place predicated on the passion of its supporters and run it instead as an abstraction on a balance sheet ... In the years of post-industrial decline, the Toon have come to mean even more to supporters starved of purpose and significance elsewhere in their lives,* [an] *expression of a truth not easily measured but easily felt.*

The owner's financial management may yield an external good for him – revenue minus cost equals profit, which can be taken by the owner or be part of a further equation of value when the club is sold[1] – but the description of St James' Park as *a repository of hope and desire* for the fans indicates an internal good which, Garside seems to suggest, the owner cannot feel or understand.

Practice and institution

MacIntyre argues that no practice *can survive for any length of time unsustained by an institution*. In all practices, there is a need for administration. The famous meeting of the four lodges in 1717 turned out to be a decision to form an institution to govern the practice of Freemasonry. One output of that decision was the 1723 *Book of Constitutions*, but the BoC is no more about the practice of Freemasonry than the *Rules of Golf* are about the internal goods of golf.

The *Rules* govern the manner in which golfers compete. They say nothing about how to hit a golf ball; nothing about how to read a putt and nothing about the joy of seeing a soaring 5 iron drop gracefully on the green. Most golfers enjoy their rounds with little or no reference to the rules, even making up their own as the occasion demands. During their weekly four ball, few golfers go back to the tee to hit another when the first ball goes out of bounds. They would unnecessarily delay their fellow club members if they did.[2]

---

[1] The value of a company is usually a multiple of its earnings or its profit.

[2] The great Patrick Campbell, third Baron Glenavy, said that golf is the only game in which an excellent knowledge of the rules earns one a reputation for bad sportsmanship.

In a like manner, our *Constitutions* are largely about the external administration of Freemasonry, about whether a lodge meeting should be abandoned *(yes, if no Installed Master is present)*, adjourned *(no)* or cancelled *(no)*; about how wide the collar of a Provincial Grand Steward shall be *(2.5 inches)* or what happens if a brother has not paid his dues for two years *(he is automatically excluded although lodge treasurers and other brethren will go to great lengths to avoid this, at some cost to themselves)*.

The internal goods of Freemasonry and golf are unaffected by the rules and the rules say nothing about them. This is not to say that rules are unnecessary. The R&A (now separate from the Royal and Ancient Golf Club) and a grand lodge exist, or should exist, to facilitate the love of the practices they administer but, as MacIntyre says:

> *Institutions are characteristically and necessarily concerned with what I have called external goods. They are involved in acquiring money and other material goods; they are structured in terms of power and status, and they distribute money, power and status as rewards.*[1]

In owning property, managing investments, seeking and returning favours with other institutions, maintaining a standing in the public world, institutions have a life of their own, much of which is unconnected with, and may be inconsistent with their central purpose of facilitating the love of the practice. The cost of an event may include entertainment from which ordinary members are excluded; the need to avoid public embarrassment may mean that a building is sold for far less than it is worth; the desire not to upset another institution may result in a description of a practice as less significant than it is; the desire for recognition may result in charitable donations having a PR purpose.

The corrupting power of patronage

The institution may offer external goods in exchange for behaviours protective of itself but injurious to the practice. MacIntyre calls this the *corrupting power* of the institution. In seeking to protect the life of its own, there is always a danger that the institution will act against its real reason for existence.

> *Concerns about costs or profitability might impinge upon the practice of medicine or automobile manufacturing. The political ideology of the regulatory body may put it at odds with the policies of a professional organisation.*[2]

A grand lodge may give out grand honours, external goods incidental to the practice of Freemasonry, which may motivate behaviours even at variance to the practice. Instead of brotherly love, we may see competition; instead of alms motivated by love, we see charity collected as 'points' towards honours; instead of

---

[1] MacIntyre (4).

[2] Lutz.

equality, we see courtship of those with the power to grant honours. At Installed Masters' Lodges and other places in which the hierarchy gathers, many Masons will have experienced the attempt to hold a conversation with a brother who is looking around for others more important to them in their search for honours.[1]

The power of patronage would not lightly be given up by an institution but it is an example of the tension that can exist between institution and practice.[2] The honours system may prevent difficult messages being communicated upwards; filter out new ideas deemed unacceptable to the powerful and disable disagreement. Many problems persist in organisations because people are not willing to tell the Emperor that he is wearing no clothes.

There is always a tension between institution and practice. It is this tension, this variance between the internal goods of Freemasonry as a practice and the external goods of Freemasonry as an institution, which is so dangerous. It could prevent us from becoming that moral stronghold, able to combat the horrors of the modern dark age, sustaining civility and the moral life, which should become our reason for existence.

A structural way to reduce the damage would be to increase the number of grand officers, just as the way to reduce the cost of houses is to build more of them. In times of crisis, we need more representation on the ground rather than less and so, for example, instead of reducing the number of Assistant Provincial Grand Masters[3] as membership declines, we should increase their number. Promotion may be a matter of thanks for past services but, given our serious need for leadership, it is perhaps more important that we promote brethren with the necessary skills, dedication and ethics. (Change management is an acquired skill.) We should at least double the number of grand officers.

Experiment

Are we ready to change? Let's try an experiment. Overleaf is a short questionnaire. Choose one from each of seventeen pairs of statements.

---

[1] This problem is more prevalent in the United Grand Lodge of England and other grand lodges which award past grand ranks.

[2] The Honours (Prevention of Abuses) Act of 1925 made the sale of knighthoods and peerages illegal following David Lloyd George's activities but accusations of honours being given in return for donations to political parties are still frequent.

[3] A rank used in UGLE provinces to enable visits by the executive to private lodges. The number of APGMs is related to the number of lodges.

FREEMASONRY OUGHT TO ...
Choose <u>one</u> statement (left or right) from each pair.

Promote brethren already known............	.... Search for brethren to promote
Control what brethren can say	.... Encourage free speech
Keep disagreement private	...........................…. Let dissent flourish
Re-appoint	.... Change often
Promote by seniority	........................…... Create a meritocracy
Centralise	.... Decentralise
Save costs	.... Find new revenue
Maintain strong central governance	...... See the centre as a support function
Restrict decisions to the hierarchy	.... Get everyone involved
Marginalise misfits	.... Praise misfits
Avoid defeat ....…...	.... Obsess about victory
Strive for uniformity	.... Prize local creativity
Observe best practices	.... Seek new practices
Honour tradition	.... Welcome the future
Put planning first	.... Put action first
Carry out risk analysis	.... Create excitement
Batten down the hatches	.... Fling open the windows

Look at the statements you have chosen (one from each pair).[1]

The number of *left* statements chosen = ...

The number of *right* statements chosen = ...

The more you choose *left-hand* statements, the more you may favour *control*. The more you choose *right-hand* statements, the more you favour *change*.

14+ left — You are a traditionalist, valuing control.
14+ right — You are a change agent, valuing experiment.
11–13 left — On balance you favour tradition over change.
11–13 right — On balance you favour change over tradition.
Other scores may mean that you are undecided.

How would the brethren of your lodge complete this exercise? Would they be traditionalists, change agents, sceptical or don't knows?

---

[1] Modified from Tom Peters, *Liberation Management*

The need for change

Schön argued that it is in the nature of organisations to maintain a belief in a stable state. Most demonstrate what he called *dynamic conservatism*: an active struggle to remain the same, despite change occurring all around them. My one-time colleague, the OD practitioner Professor Robin Stuart-Kotze,[1] has said:

> *Up to the middle of the 20th century, the economic environment in the Western world had remained relatively stable, arguably since Victorian times – stable in the sense of steady growth (barring periodic and temporary depressions), steady progression of technology and steady increase of knowledge.*

> *A relatively stable environment is compatible with stewardship which aims to keep things on course, maintain consistency, protect the investment in procedures and systems that form the backbone of the stable organisation and make things run as they were designed to run. Stewards take the given and make it work optimally.*

> *However, as the pace of change quickened and unpredictability became normal in virtually all walks of life, it became clear, at least to some, that new behaviours were necessary. Managing the changing, the unknown, and the unpredictable requires vision and leadership. Leadership behaviour is about doing things differently. One tends to lead people and manage things.*

As Peter Senge writes, *the organisations who succeed now and in the future will be those that harness the imagination, spirit and intelligence of all their people*, and what Jonas Ridderstråle and Kjell Nordstrom say about the modern knowledge organisation, bears noting:

> *The most critical resource wears shoes and walks out of the door 5 o'clock every day.*

In the knowledge organisation, the staff make the difference between success and failure. The knowledge workers are the only stock in trade of such organisations and since they can find other jobs with greater ease than most, their commitment must be maintained if the organisation is to prosper. The theories of Taylor and Fayol are simply not relevant and if an incompetent management applies them, the organisation suffers, as Apple under John Sculley showed. Substitute *member* for *knowledge worker* and the same applies to Freemasonry. Our members do not have to stay with us, and unless the management of our order maintains their commitment and enthusiasm, they will leave as they please.

Management theory and brotherly love

Harnessing the imagination, spirit and intelligence of all our brethren is not only a matter of brotherly love, it is also good management. Today management theory calls for behaviour which turns out to be in line with our values.

---

[1] Not a Freemason.

To take an example, most mergers and acquisitions fail. In the 1980s, the *Harvard Business Review* (HBR) reported that 80% of mergers and acquisitions achieved no business success at all and nothing has changed since. In the March 2011 issue of HBR, Clayton M. Christensen et al. write:

> ... *companies spend more than $2 trillion on acquisitions every year. Yet study after study puts the failure rate of mergers and acquisitions somewhere between 70% and 90%.*

They fail most commonly because there is little business need or product fit and employees in the companies involved cannot understand or see any reason for the merger. Frequently the cultures[1] of the merging companies are so different that they operate independently, long after they were supposed to have become one.

Good decisions are commonly the result of people becoming committed to making them work. If people support their leaders, are engaged with them, believe that they are doing their best, believe that their own efforts are respected and that they themselves are truly valued, then they will get behind decisions and make them come right. Most M&As are driven by ego at the top and so have little support from those actually faced with making the change.

Ego-driven decisions are emotionally based and it is true that emotions drive much of our behaviour, despite the fact that we say we value reason more. A character in *The Fall,* a novel by Albert Camus, says: *It hurts me to confess it, but I'd have given ten conversations with Einstein for an initial rendezvous with a pretty chorus girl.* We tend to ignore evidence contrary to and exaggerate evidence in favour of our own opinions. Involvement acts as a brake upon decisions by subjecting them to the test of the opinions of others. You will remember Aristotle's word *phronesis:* often translated as wisdom – about knowledge but also the ability to consult others and seek advice: practical wisdom.

Ridderstråle and Nordstrom write:

> *The boss is dead. No longer can we believe in a leader who claims to know more about everything and who is always right.*

Responsibility in successful companies is shared among the experts in one or more fields of knowledge and endeavour. Involving them is a sensible use of all the resource available. In our lodges, we will almost certainly find the knowledge and skill needed in such areas as organisational development, change management, information technology, social media, management development and leadership training, with no necessary correlation between rank and knowledge. Autocracy disengages the brethren. Involvement is brotherly love.

---

[1] Culture is a vital part of organisational life: the way we do things around here.

Leadership style

A diagram frequently met in leadership discussion is one with two axes: the horizontal axis indicating a greater or less amount of giving orders (telling) and the vertical axis indicating a greater or lesser degree of taking account of people's feelings (relating). This provides four basic styles of management.

- *Management by command* is about telling, with little concern for the emotional needs of those commanded; there is little support or encouragement. It is appropriate, for example, to soldiers on a parade ground but at neither grand nor private lodge level is management by command appropriate to Freemasonry.[1] The research shows that autocratically led groups have far higher attrition than democratically led groups.[2]
- *Management by objectives* (MbO) is about telling but also aims at a form of participation. The manager decides on the objectives but helps the subordinate to decide how to achieve them. This style can play a part in Freemasonry, for example when coaching future officers.
- *Management by communication* assumes that people know what to do, can set their own objectives and recognise their own outputs but may not be completely confident in doing do. The manager thus concentrates upon giving information, support and encouragement. In Masonry, this style should be common. It is an obvious form of brotherly love and a style particularly adapted to the preceptor of a lodge of instruction.

---

[1] The commands given in the ritual are purely formal, ritualistic one might say.

[2] Vugt.

- *Management by vision* assumes fully competent experts (brethren) who create their own roles. The manager participates with his colleagues (brethren), flying high cover when necessary.[1] This style is what we aim for in Freemasonry. It is the end point, the reward of good management, the result of inspiring the brethren with a vision of the possible and encouraging them to achieve it.

Masonic leadership exists to bring out the best in brethren; to develop, coach, facilitate, and communicate; to give the brethren a sense of achievement, recognition, responsibility and opportunities for personal growth. In Gary Hamel's words, we seek to create an organisation in which the spirit of community binds people together, where all brethren share a common mission and make extraordinary contributions to achieve it. As Anita Roddick said:

> *There aren't many motivating forces more potent than giving your people an opportunity to exercise and express their idealism.*[2]

We will frequently have to ask the brethren to sacrifice their own immediate interests for the good of the order and the research[3] shows that brethren will give greater loyalty to leaders who are themselves prepared to make sacrifices. That same research shows that an active and visible commitment to the brethren or lodges under their care will be the most important asset a leader can have. Interpersonal distance or demands for special treatment will dissipate loyalty. It should be obvious that the voluntary organisation needs a spirit of community and sense of mission even more than the commercial organisation.

This does not mean anything goes. One of the most important phrases in management is *loose-tight*, as used by Peters and Waterman in their first book, *In Search of Excellence*.[4] We must remain *tight* on our landmarks and values and on (a few) important rules but maintaining control is not an end in itself – nor is protecting one's ego. Paraphrasing the words I quoted from Simone Weil, everything we do must be completely in tune with the three grand principles and the four cardinal virtues.

Our aims can only be achieved with exemplary values, a culture of honesty and openness, an orientation towards achievement and a sense of ownership among all brethren. We need shared values, maximum trust and minimal controls. We need leadership that can capture hearts and minds, and instil the need for change. This demands *management by walking around* – in ordinary, private lodges as well as

---

[1] I have always thought that this term comes from the Battle of Britain during which the Hurricanes would attack the enemy bombers while the Spitfires flew high to spot and attack enemy fighters.

[2] Roddick.

[3] Vugt.

[4] Peters (1).

grand ones. Such leadership was not available in the 19th century but we cannot rely on serendipity again.

Talent

Observers say that the talent is usually no more than 15% of the organisation. You have to go look for it. Gwyn Williams, the scout who discovered England captain John Terry, said:

> I spend almost every night of the week out and about, looking at games at different levels. On a Monday, I might watch Chelsea reserves to monitor how the next generation at the club was coming along. On Tuesday I could go to a lower league club and see who they had got there. Sometimes I would get a tip-off about a player or an agent would ring me to recommend a lad. In the space of a week, I could be at an under-20 tournament in Toulon, an under-17 event in Luxembourg and then an under-21 tournament in Portugal.[1]

To stretch the analogy with football, by talent we mean game-changing ability; those relatively few people who can provide leadership in uncertain and changing times; who can turn around organisations and inspire others to greater heights.

The search for talent in Freemasonry ought to be as conscious and planned as the activity of the talent scout. The danger is that the institution seeks to promote establishment figures while the practice needs change agents. (It is worth remembering the research findings that members will be willing to make more effort if they have a say on a new leader, even if their favourite is not elected.[2])

Motivation

Motivation is a massive subject, but the aspect most relevant for us is the distinction between intrinsic motivation *(the motivation to complete a task for the sake of its interest or value)* and extrinsic motivation *(the motivation to complete a task for rewards external to the task.)* Edward L. Deci reports findings that:

> ... contingent tangible rewards and other extrinsic factors such as competition and evaluations can be detrimental to outcomes such as creativity, cognitive flexibility, and problem solving, which has been found to be associated with intrinsic motivation ...[3]

It is to intrinsic motivation that we must appeal: the love that the brethren have for Freemasonry and a desire for solutions to its problems. We make a mistake in thinking that brethren will respond only to extrinsic motivation. We give pretty jewels for them to wear to show how much they have given to charity and we offer grand titles to lodges for the same reason. A real problem is that extrinsic

[1] 'Scouting mission', Sarah Holt, *BBC Sport*, July 2006.
[2] Vugt.
[3] Deci (1). See also Deci (2).

motivation is often, and indeed usually, the victim of the law of unintended consequences.[1] We have seen this in the health service where target setting has caused statistics to be falsified and in education where it has caused teachers to cheat over students' exam results, in each case to make it appear that (often irrelevant) targets have been reached.

The most significant danger with extrinsic motivation is that it reduces intrinsic motivation. One would expect that people would be drawn to jobs in health and education by a desire to do something worthwhile and this has been very largely true. However, people working in health find that achieving non-professional outcomes, and making things sound good when they are not, is the route to promotion. Teachers find that exam results and lesson plans produce promotion rather than children's learning. Such disconnect is now causing a haemorrhage of talent the medical and teaching professions.

Poor management has seen the extrinsic drive out the intrinsic. Promotion to grand rank is the main extrinsic motivation in Freemasonry and it has to be used with very great care if it is not to damage our order. Promotion shows what we value and every wrong promotion is a slap in the face to the order. We must ensure we do not reward ambition, self-interest or flattery.

We need new ideas. The old ones have failed us. Creativity requires the establishment of a culture in which lateral thinking is normal, accepted, encouraged and supported. One cannot command creativity. One can only encourage it to flourish. New ideas should not need a dispensation. As Gavin Kotze has written, creative people tend to share certain traits:

> *They have an interest in the abnormal. They cast aside existing assumptions and look at things from new perspectives. They are open to different ideas, always being willing to change tack to find a new route to success. They subscribe to the notion that security is for sissies; a leap of faith can land one in a whole new realm. They exhibit endurance and perseverance, accepting the struggles and strife that litter the road to success.[2]*

A new paradigm

Management has undergone considerable change since the Second World War, during which the US government undertook research to find ways of getting things done better and faster. In the first half of the 20th century, the management paradigm included 'facts' such as:

Control must be maintained at all times.

---

[1] The best book on this is *Freakonomics*, by Dubner & Levitt. One example they give is of a day nursery where parents were late collecting their children. So the nursery started to charge for late pick-up. Lateness increased because parents no longer felt guilty about being late. Think about it!

[2] For The Working Manager Ltd.

Decisions must be made at the top and cascaded down.
Communication must follow the chain of command.
Obedience is due from the lower level to the upper level.

I dare say that these beliefs are still taken as common sense in some places today. Nevertheless, in the eyes of modern management, such beliefs may be common but they are not sense. Management is at a crossroads and successful organisations have switched to a new paradigm, which holds that:

Control is a matter of shared vision.
Creativity and imagination are more important than respecting a chain of command.
Empowerment matters more than obedience.
Caring and ethics are critical parts of decision-making.

Making change

It goes without saying that any change requires the support of the brethren but if the three rules of real estate are *location, location and location*, the three rules of change are *energy, energy and energy*. To believe in a change is to make a commitment to action and people without energy seek (politely) not to believe.

In any lodge, province or other Masonic body, energy for change will be concentrated in a small number of the brethren. The number of *true believers*, those ready and willing to change, is usually matched by the number of *nay sayers*, those committed to *not-changing* and many lodges contain brethren who would rather see the lodge go under than accept change.

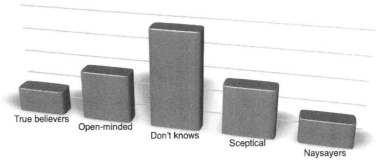

True believers   Open-minded   Don't knows   Sceptical   Naysayers

Many change agents make the mistake of trying first to convince the *naysayers*. This rarely succeeds and simply drains energy away from the change. The most effective route is to appeal to the *open-minded*. If you can move a good number of those into the camp of *true belief*, you cause a ripple effect and a good proportion of the *don't knows* will become open-minded.

167

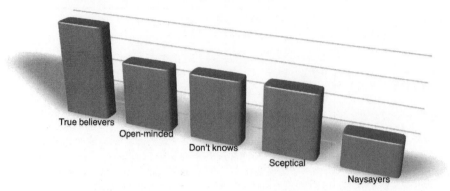

The *don't knows* are of broadly two types: the *don't know but might* and the *don't know but probably won't*. If the open-minded move to the left, the *don't know but might* will almost certainly do so as well. Thus, the weight of the argument shifts and the change will often make itself.

Convincing brethren is not about haranguing them. Successful change requires brethren engaged in the ideals of our order and organisational research shows that the only correlation with engagement is a culture which genuinely prizes people and their involvement – a matter of brotherly love.

Reminder of the main points

This is a reminder, not a summary. It carries little supporting argument.

The central message

There are periodic intervals in human experience when scientific, religious or economic events demand new ways of understanding moral relationships. During such upheavals, moral relativity seeks to take over. This time, it is our turn to respond. As Freemasons, we must maintain a community in which the moral life is continued, even as it is lost elsewhere. We must be a moral stronghold, preserving the virtue of trust and becoming a reservoir of social capital.

The world that we face now may seem less than welcoming to the ideals of Freemasonry but there are large numbers of men in our society hungry for the fellowship and moral meaning that our institution offers. Our challenge is to bring our ideals to the attention of a new and very different audience. We know little about that audience and it will require hard work, open-mindedness, creativity and above all leadership to reach it.

The optimism that runs through this book depends upon a willingness and an ability to change. Holding on to the past will be the last thing our order does.

A summary of main points

History and society

- Membership has been in decline for over 60 years and the reversal of that trend will not be immediate. There is no pill we can take to make things better nor will our problem go away on its own. Until we accept that the problem is systemic, we cannot solve it. Complacency is the enemy. As Will Murray says, the ability to believe exactly what you want to believe, despite evidence to the contrary, is the last refuge of those in denial.

- Freemasonry is not isolated from society and effective management of our institution requires a grasp of what has been happening around us. It is not clear that this has consistently been achieved. We cannot understand the new audience for Freemasonry, unless we understand the social changes that have given rise to it.

- The changes since the 1950s have made Freemasonry unfashionable but in trying to reverse this, we have endangered our core values. In particular, we have neglected the fact that Freemasonry is *a peculiar system of morality, veiled in allegory and illustrated by symbols*. This is certainly not an empty phrase.

169

- Our secrets and rituals really do matter. The secrets satisfy a need for affiliation and create group cohesion. Our rituals teach important lessons. They are delivered *by* brethren, but also *for* brethren. The effort of learning and the perfection of delivery is a *gift* given by brother to brother. The practice of ritual is brotherly love in action. As Kirk C. White writes:

  Ritual causes mental change and that is its purpose … ritual accomplishes that change … by bracketing the time spent as 'special' and unlike our ordinary mundane lives … Our opening and closing rituals mark the time in lodge as different from our daily lives.

- The 19th-century offers useful parallels with today. Freemasonry went into almost terminal decline and it was not until the serendipitous rise of the middle class that the decline was reversed. Facing unforeseen social and economic changes, Freemasonry walked blindfold into a perfect storm with an almost complete lack of leadership. History is now repeating itself but we cannot rely on serendipity again.

Middle class

- For 100 years, the middle class provided our candidates. As a recruitment source, it could not have been bettered, but it became habit forming. We were hooked on it as the source of candidates. We must now recognise that the middle class has gone away.

- The continuity and predictability which characterised middle-class life no longer applies. We now see employment conditions reminiscent of the pre-Victorian era: pay often below a living wage, high unemployment and underemployment, longer working hours for less money, fear of redundancy, disappearance of job security and the end of the career. Life has become harder edged, less caring and with fewer spiritual values.

- Brethren and candidates now have less control over their time. Zero-hours contracts and increased self-employment mean that many do not know when, or indeed if, they will work the following week. Lacking the ability to plan ahead, they cannot easily commit to attending meetings, and cannot even give notice of their intentions. The often-heard Past Master's remark, *When I was initiated* … has no relevance today.

Management

- Respect for and trust in senior management is at an all time low. The myth of the CEO, the absence of a relationship between pay and performance, crime and dishonesty within the finance industry, expenses fiddles and cash-for-access in parliament, sex crimes among media personalities, racial gang rape, organised paedophilia and too many other sins to mention have created an amoral world. The establishment has shown that it cannot be trusted. Work has lost much of its meaning and job satisfaction is at an all-time low.

- We must demonstrate we are different: that our senior management does understand the conditions of the ordinary Masons who form the bulk of our membership; that it does seek and is ready to listen to their views; that it does not reward itself in ways that contrast badly with the experience of the ordinary Mason; that it is not a mutually congratulatory clique isolated from reality and that it does deserve the salutes and ovations it is given.

- Our leadership must demonstrate that morality matters and that in all our actions we place moral considerations first. This goes not just for major crimes but also for the lesser sins of arrogance, pride and self-aggrandisement.

Positive statement

- The false gods of PR have pushed us in the wrong direction. In seeking to be accepted by the popular world, we have tried to portray Freemasonry as a harmless, if eccentric, hobby. If we were to be successful in this, we might (but probably would not) gain acceptance in the popular world, but at the expense of our reason for being. We would lose our attraction to those who are seeking meaning, purpose and the moral life.

  We need a clear and positive trumpet call to show what Freemasonry is and what we stand for. Given such a statement, the public can agree or disagree with us, but at least they will not rely on gossip, rumour or slander for information.

Our role

- A role for Freemasonry today is to become a guardian of trust and a reservoir of social capital. We enable men to trust others and to be worthy of trust, virtues that are in decline in the popular world. We are one of the few organisations in the social capital manufacturing business. Recruitment into Freemasonry is an investment in social capital.

- More than this, Freemasonry offers a purpose-to-life from which moral virtues can be derived. Our order is one of the few communities able to sustain the moral life in an amoral world. By taking on the duty of sustaining civility and the moral life through the new dark ages, our order will become one of MacIntyre's local forms of community in which the moral life can be continued, combatting the horrors of the modern dark age.

- Safeguarding the moral life is the main function of our order and our greatest challenge. We must become a bastion for the virtues, and thereby save ourselves.

- On a parallel with the Rule of St Benedict, a man may choose to be a Freemason and in doing so commit himself to a set excellences by which to live: a life governed by the principles of brotherly love, relief and truth.

- To be a *good* Freemason is to exemplify brotherly love, relief and truth. There is no sense in which a man can say *I want to be a Freemason but not a good one* because Freemasonry is a moral practice.

Engineering

- The revitalisation of Masonry is not a matter of tinkering with the periphery of our order. Only by focusing on the meaning of Freemasonry, can we reverse the trend of membership.

- The analogy that is drawn in this book is of the commercial organisation that focuses solely on profit and thereby fails. It has forgotten that profit is the reward, not the product itself.

- Tinkering obscures the need for engineering.

Excellences of Freemasonry

- *The Five Points of Fellowship* are of supreme importance. To live by the five points is to be trustworthy. To act upon them is to trust. The five points indicate a personal relationship between Masons and, while the habit of loving our brethren makes us more loving of mankind, the principle of brotherly love was originally and primarily directed towards our brethren in Freemasonry.

- Brotherly love may be partly defined by the phrase *all in it together*. Being brothers, we cannot pick and choose when to take sides.

- The word we use is *relief*, not charity. The target of relief is an individual. In its original meaning, relief is about helping a fellow Mason or someone known to and in the vicinity of the lodge. Relief may be about money but it is more often about behaviour, acting from the heart.

- Given the issues that we face today, the original meaning of relief is more important than ever. Giving for political or PR reasons is not giving alms.

- A *true* Mason is unfeigning and genuine: true to our ideals, a true and constant friend whose love of his brethren is truly demonstrated. Being true to each other, Masons set an example in society. The Masonic word *truth* connotes loyalty, legitimacy and fidelity.

- *Let prudence direct you* is an instruction to use reason and logic, and be open to advice. *Fortitude* is about maintaining our principles in the face of threat or persuasion. *Temperance* calls us to a life managed by reason, resisting temptation while experiencing human desires and feelings.

- A *just* action is one that is tested for impartiality, made without fear of popular opinion, unmotivated by hope of personal reward and positively consistent with our other principles.

- The decencies of a Victorian gentleman will generally be admired within our order and Freemasons are patriotic and peaceable. We do not expect supererogation of ourselves. We are not an order of saints and heroes, but of ordinary men with responsibilities and ties, doing our best.

Practice and institution

- Honours are external goods, incidental to the practice of Freemasonry, and often motivate behaviours at variance with it. Instead of brotherly love, we see competition; instead of alms motivated by love, we see charity collected as 'points' towards honours; instead of equality, we see courtship of those with the power to grant promotion.

- The desire for honours prevents difficult messages being communicated upwards, filters out new ideas deemed unacceptable to the powerful, and disables disagreement. Many problems persist in organisations because people are unwilling to tell the Emperor he is wearing no clothes.

- There is always a tension between *institution* and *practice* but we must minimise it within our order. The power of patronage would not lightly be given up but we can reduce the damage by doubling the number of grand officers, just as to reduce the cost of houses we need to build more of them.

- In difficult times we need more leadership visibility, not less. If a gulf opens between the worries of the ordinary private lodge and the concerns of those wearing chains, we shall find it nigh on impossible to turn things around.

Management and brotherly love

- Much of what happens in the modern organisation actively disengages its members. Given the poor state of management in the UK today, the audience we seek has little upward loyalty and has had its fill of autocracy. Our own management practices must be in tune with our professed values or this new audience will turn its back on us.

- In Gary Hamel's words, we seek to create an organisation in which the spirit of community binds people together, where all brethren share a common mission and make extraordinary contributions to achieve it. Harnessing the imagination and intelligence of all brethren is both a matter of brotherly love and good management.

- Successful management, like a successful marriage, does not just happen. It needs to be worked at. Organisational learning starts with being honest about the gap between what we actually do and what we like to think we do.

Organisation culture

- We need a culture in which lateral thinking is normal and actively encouraged. Control must be vested in a shared vision rather than in a hierarchy. Creativity and imagination are more important than the chain of command; empowerment matters more than obedience and brotherly love is vital to decision-making.

- Our aims can only be achieved by a sense of ownership among all brethren. If the brethren feel engaged and involved in decisions, they will get behind those decisions to make them come right.

- There is no correlation in our order between rank and the knowledge necessary to create such a community. Within our membership there will be skill in organisational development, change management, information technology, social media, training and organisation design.

- We should assemble a team of experts with these skills to advise on and direct our change. We must train our future leaders in OD.

Recruitment

- Brethren are unlikely to invite friends into a lodge they feel bad about. Brethren will not talk about dull, grey lodges but they will talk about lodges that are busy, vibrant and exciting – and excitement is infectious.

- The better a lodge feels about itself, the more likely it is to attract candidates and retain members. There is ample evidence that candidates are attracted to energetic lodges. Such lodges retain their members.

- In the past, almost all candidates were friends and family of existing members but as a source of candidates, our members are now a declining force. Getting to know the new audience requires much more than a stilted committee meeting.

- We need to spend significant time with candidates prior to initiation. Every lodge now needs a social life in which the brethren can meet and chat to candidates, and *vice versa*.

- The questions we ask in interviews describe a society which has ceased to exist. The relationship between the sexes has changed. Freemasons will continue to drink the loyal toast but monarchism now does not warrant an interview question.

- No theologian accepts the *old man in the sky*. On the pattern of *Are you happy to drink the health of Her Majesty?* we would be better advised to ask, *Are you happy to participate in prayers in lodge?*

- The statement *Freemasonry is not a religion* is unhelpfully negative. A more positive statement would be *Freemasonry is compatible with any religion.* Our order offers much that a religious context might offer but speaks equally powerfully to those who have little religious belief. Freemasonry does not compete with religion but it accepts, if it also regrets, religion's decreasing relevance.

A brief summary of the philosophical argument

- We cannot derive a moral statement (an *ought*) from a factual statement (an *is*) but moral judgements are more than enunciations of feelings. They are supported by argument and there is a rationality to such argument.

- Sartre argues that to be *authentic*, a moral judgement implies an individual choice of *who to become.* In deciding that thus-and-such an action is acceptable today, we choose to become the person who accepts thus-and-such in general.

- Sartre argues that authentic moral judgement must be a rational act, not a matter of habit (schema) or obedience to uncritically accepted rules. We must think about morality.

- The tradition of the virtues that stems from Aristotle does not start from facts. It assumes a purpose-to-life, the description of which is in itself a moral statement. (The use of the words *purpose-to-life* is dangerous. It is a technical term. It does not imply that there is only one purpose to life.)

- *Life is all about …* is not a factual statement but a value judgement. It implies or discounts certain actions. The moral life is in danger today because it is almost impossible to find a context, a purpose-to-life, which can support it. With no context, the moral life must wither and decay, hence the *end of decency*. How do we choose?

- The problem is eased if we think of something like the Rule of St Benedict. To be a Benedictine is to live by the Rule. The candidate for the Benedictine life chooses to accept the Rule after much examination, discussion and debate. He makes a rational choice to live by the Rule, an authentic choice. The candidate defines himself as a person who accepts that form of moral life, and becomes a Benedictine.

- On a parallel to St Benedict and his rule, Freemasonry offers a purpose-to-life from which a moral life can be derived. The rational choice to become a Freemason is also an authentic choice. Making a choice to become a Freemason is, *ipso facto*, making a choice to live by the principles of the order.

- One cannot be a Mason unless one does live by these principles. One can only pretend to be one. Many men seek a purpose-to-life, a context in which the moral life finds traction. To provide it becomes our duty. It is also the way we will save ourselves.

175

Recommended actions

Many of the principles set out by Warren Bennis are still relevant:

> *Build trust. Maximise collaborative efforts. Increase a sense of ownership. Grow self-control and self-direction. Create an open, problem-solving climate. Get decision-making and problem solving as close to the information sources as possible. Recognise the authority of knowledge and competence as opposed to rank.*

Be open to change

Accept the existence of the problem.

Cease making statements that all is well when it isn't.

Study the historical parallels.

Study the impact of social changes on our institution.

Focus on the ordinary Mason

Think in terms of the average Mason, what affects his life.

Recognise his financial position.

Recognise the time demands on him.

Help brethren understand the new audience.

Teach brethren about social and economic change and how it affects us.

Create an open, problem-solving climate

Explain the executive decision making process.

Explain proposed decisions before they are made.

Actively invite dissent, comment and questions.

Recognise the authority of knowledge as opposed to rank.

Communicate to and involve the ordinary Mason, not just the executive.

Explain our order's strategy to turn things around.

Remember that the phrase *distinctions among men* refers only to the ritual.

Recognise the importance of leadership

Manage by communication and vision.

Make a statement about leadership intentions: control is a matter of shared vision; creativity and imagination are more important than a chain of command; empowerment matters more than obedience.

Train current and potential grand officers in leadership.

Cease the practice of senior brethren gathering in executive bars and private dining rooms, away from the ordinary Mason.

Ensure that the members of the executive are regularly seen in private lodges, talking to and getting the views of ordinary Masons.

Explain and propagate what we are, not what we are not

Clearly explain the nature and meaning of Masonic virtues.
Teach the *allegory* and *symbols*.
Explain the internal goods of Freemasonry.

Learn from successful lodges

Call such lodges together and identify what makes them successful.
Enable successful lodges to work with less successful ones.
Create a handbook to help less successful lodges.
Help lodges create websites and use social media.
Dramatically reduce approval time.

Go out to look for talent in the order

Recognise that specialist know-how exists at all levels in our order.
Actively search for leadership potential among all brethren.
Promote only those capable of leadership and change management.
Involve brethren in the appointment of the executive.
Explain appointments and the criteria for promotion.

Reduce extrinsic motivation

Reduce the power of patronage.
Double (at least) the number of Grand Officers (and increase APGMs[1].)

Recognise that we are a moral order

Put morality at the front of every decision.
Ensure that every decision is compatible with our principles.
Explain to brethren the need to protect the moral life.
Explain the demands that this makes in ordinary life as well as in lodge.

Recognise that, like it or not, we now have a social duty

The barbarian attacks on decency must be resisted.
That is what we are here for.
Take a public stance against immorality in society.
Adopt causes.

---

[1] Assistant Provincial Grand Masters.

Grow social capital

Explain the need for trust.

Explain how Freemasonry is a reservoir of social capital.

Teach brethren about creating social capital within the private lodge.

Encourage civic engagement.

Teach brethren how to become engaged.

Charity

Ensure that all charity is given for the right motives.

Ensure each lodge has funds to help its own brethren and community.

Women

Work with women's Freemasonry to help them grow.

Learn from them about feminism and how it affects Freemasonry.

Learn from the Women's Institute how to support causes.

The de-christianisation of the Craft is not complete

The Royal Arch still has Christian beliefs at its centre.

(It has been argued that orders restricted to one religion are not genuinely part of Masonry.)[1]

---

[1] Hammer.

List of illustrations

Bibliography

Alexander, Caroline, *The Endurance*, Bloomsbury, 1998.

Alfes, Kerstin et al., *Creating an engaged workforce; findings from the Kingston employee engagement consortium project*, CIPD 2010.

Anderson, James, *The Constitutions of the Free-Masons*, 1723 & 1738, *Quatuor Coronati* facsimile edition 1976.

Andrews, Lyman, 'Lampedusa', *Fugitive Visions*, White Rabbit, 1962.

Anouilh, Jean, *Antigone*, Random House, 1946.

Aquinas, St Thomas

  (1) *Summa Theologica*, Ave Maria Press, 2000.

  (2) *Commentary the Nicomachean Ethics*, transl. C.I. Litzinger OP, Henry Regnery Co., 1964.

Armstrong, *History of Freemasonry in Cheshire*, 1901.

Arndt, H.A., 'The Trickle-Down Myth', *Economic Development and Cultural Change*, Vol. 32, No. 1, 1983, The University of Chicago Press.

Barsacq, Jean-Louis, *Place Dancourt: la vie, l'oeuvre et l'Atelier d'André Barsacq*, Gallimard, 2005.

Batham, C.N. (ed), *The Collected Prestonian Lectures 1961-1974*, Lewis Masonic, 1983.

Bennis, Warren, *Organizational Development: its nature, origins, and prospects*, Addison Wesley Longman, 1969.

Beresiner, Yasha, 'Robert Crucefix, a man and a mason to be proud of', *250th anniversary celebrations of Burlington Lodge*, 2006.

Bizzack, John, *For the good of the order*, Autumn House Publishing & Consulting Group, 2013.

Blandy, Sarah et al., *Gated Communities: A Systematic Review of the Research Evidence*, ESRC Centre for Neighbourhood Research, 2003.

Bragg, Melvyn, *The Book of Books: the radical impact of the King James Bible, 1611-2011*, Hodder & Stoughton, 2011

British Social Attitudes Survey, various years, Sage Publications.

Brown, Callum, *The Death of Christian Britain*, Routledge, 2001, 2nd edition 2009.

Brown, Richard, *Change and Continuity in British Society 1880-1850*, Cambridge, 1987.

Buck, Keith S, *Provincial Grand Lodge of Essex 1776-1976*, privately printed in aid of the Redevelopment & Modernisation Fund of the Royal Masonic Hospital, 1976.

Busfield, Alan, 'The Last Forty Years of Freemasonry', *Proceedings of the United Masters Lodge No. 167*, Auckland, New Zealand, Vol. 26, 1986.

Byrne, Patrick, *The membership crisis in Freemasonry*, hinchley-wood-lodge.com.

Calderwood, Paul R., 'Architecture & Freemasonry in 20th-Century Britain', *AQC*, Vol. 126, 2013.

Castells, Francis de Paula, *The Genuine Secrets in Freemasonry prior to 1717*, A. Lewis, 1971, (first pub. 1930).

Chafe, William H, *The Unfinished Journey: America Since World War II*, Oxford University Press, 2006.

Church, The Catholic, *Compendium of the Catechism of the Catholic Church*, Libreria Editrice Vaticana, 2005.

Cleckley, Hervey, *The Mask of Sanity*, Literary Licensing LLC, 2011, (first pub. by The CV Mosby Company, 1941).

Clough, Arthur Hugh, *Poems*, Everyman, 1998.

Cockcroft, George (writing as Luke Rhinehart), *The Dice Man*, Talmy Franklin, 1971.

Coleman, James S, 'Social capital in the creation of human capital', *American Journal of Sociology*, Vol. 94 Supplement 1998, University of Chicago Press.

Dabney, Robert L, *Systematic Theology*, 1878. Published online at pbministries.org.

Davies, Gareth, 'The Duke of Sussex lays a Foundation Stone,' *The Square*, June 2015.

Day, Caroline et al., *A Literature Review into Children Abused and/or Neglected Prior Custody*, Youth Justice Board, 2008.

Deci, Edward L.

(1) *Intrinsic Motivation*, Plenum Press, 1975,

(2) 'Self-determination theory and work motivation', *Journal of Organizational Behaviour*, 2005.

Dixon, William, *Freemasonry in Lincolnshire*, Forgotten Books, 2014 (first pub. James Williamson 1894.)

Doney, Keith

(1) *Freemasonry in France during the Nazi Occupation*, Keith Doney, PhD Thesis for the University of Aston in Birmingham, May 1993.

(2) 'French Freemasonry and the Resistance 1940–1944', *Freemasonry Today*, April 2002.

Donne, John, 'Devotions, Station 17, Now this bell tolling softly for another...', *Devotions upon Emergent Occasions and Death's Duel*, Vintage Spiritual Classics, 1999.

Dubner, Stephen J. & Levitt, Steven D., *Freakonomics*, Penguin, 2007.

Dyer, Colin

(1) *Symbolism in Craft Masonry*, Lewis Masonic, 1976.

(2) *William Preston and his work*, Lewis Masonic, 1987.

Fine, Cordelia, *A Mind of its Own*, Icon Books, 2007.

Francis, Thomas, *History of Freemasonry in Sussex*, Forgotten Books, 2013, (first pub. 1883.)

Fraser, George MacDonald, *Quartered Safe Out Here*, HarperCollins, 1995.

Fryer, D. and Stambe, R., 'Neoliberal austerity and unemployment', *The Psychologist*, Vol. 27, No 4, April 2014.

Fulford, Roger, *The Royal Dukes: the Father and Uncles of Queen Victoria*, Collins, 1973.

Gorbachev, Mikhail, *Perestroika: New Thinking for Our Country and the World*, Collins, 1987.

Griffin, Jo, *The Lonely Society*, Mental Health Foundation, 2010.

Gunn, Simon & Bell, Rachel, *Middle Classes: their rise and sprawl*, Cassell & Co, 2002.

Halpenny, Frances G. & Hamelin, Jean, *Dictionary of Canadian Biography*, Vol. 5, University of Toronto Press, 1983.

Hamel, Gary, *The Future of Management*, Harvard Business School Press, 2007.

Hammer, Andrew, *Observing the Craft*, Mindhive Books, 2010.

Han, Byung-Chul, *The Burnout Society*, Stanford University Press, 2015.

Hare, Robert D, *Psychopathy: Theory and Research*, John Wiley & Sons Inc., 1970.

Harker, Lisa et al., *How safe are our children?*, NSPCC, 2013.

Harrison, David, *The Transformation of Freemasonry*, Arima Publishing, 2010.

Haunch T.O., 'It is not in the Power of any man: A Study in Change', Prestonian Lecture for 1972, *The Collected Prestonian Lectures, Volume Two, 1961–1974*, Lewis Masonic, 1983

Henderson, Kent and Belton, John, 'Freemasons – An Endangered Species?', *AQC*, Vol. 113, 2000.

Herzberg, Frederick, *Motivation to Work*, John Wiley & Sons, 1959.

Hobbes, Thomas, *Leviathan, or The Matter, Forme and Power of a Common Wealth Ecclesiasticall and Civil*, 1651.

Hooke, Andrew et al., *Cost benefit analysis of traffic light & speed cameras*, Home Office Police Research Group, Crown Copyright 1996.

Hume, David, *Treatise of Human Nature*, 1738.

Jackson, A.C.F., *English Masonic Exposures 1760–1769*, Lewis Masonic, 1986.

James, P.R., 'The Grand-Mastership of HRH The Duke of Sussex, 1813–1843', *The Collected Prestonian Lectures 1961–1974*, Lewis Masonic, 1983.

Jones David M. & Molyneaux, Brian L., *Mythology of the American Nations*, Hermes House, 2009.

Kalam, A.P.J. Abdul, *Indomitable Spirit*, Rajpal & Sons, 2012.

Kearsley, Mike, '1814 – Consolidation and Change', *AQC*, Vol. 127, 2014.

Keiningham, Timothy & Aksoy, Lerzan, *Why Managers Should Care about Employee Loyalty*, American Management Association, 2009.

Kellerman, Maurice, *The Challenge of Changes in Membership in New South Wales*, given at the first biennial AMRC Conference, 1992.

Kennedy, Paul, *Rise and Fall of the Great Powers*, Random House, 1987.

King, Steven, *Poverty and welfare in England 1700–1850*, Manchester University Press, 2000.

Knoop, Douglas et al., *The Early Masonic Catechisms*, Quatuor Coronati Lodge, 1943.

Lane, John, *Masonic Records 1717-1894*, United Grand Lodge of England, 1895.

Larkin, Philip, 'This be the verse', *High Windows*, Faber & Faber, 1979.

Levitt, Stephen D. & Dubner, Stephen J., *Freakonomics: A Rogue Economist Explores the Hidden Side of Everything*, William Morrow, 2009.

Lewin, Kurt, 'Group decision and social change', in Newcomb, T. and Hartley, E. (eds), *Readings in social psychology*, Holt, 1947.

Lewis, C.S., *The Four Loves*, Geoffrey Bles, 1960.

Loftus, Donna, *The Rise of the Victorian Middle Class*, BBC History, 2011.

Lutz, Christopher Stephen, *Reading Alasdair MacIntyre's After Virtue*, Continuum, 2012.

MacIntyre, Alasdair

(1) *Against the Self-Images Of the Age: Essays on Ideology and Philosophy*, University of Notre Dame Press, 1989.

(2) *Three Rival Versions of Moral Enquiry*, Duckworth, 1990.

(3) *Dependent Rational Animals*, Carus Publishing, 1999.

(4) *After Virtue*, University of Notre Dame Press, 2007.

Marks, Mitchell Lee, *Charging Back Up the Hill*, Jossey-Bass, 2003.

Maslow, Abraham, 'A Theory of Human Motivation', *Psychological Review*, 1943.

Mason, Paul, *Post-capitalism: a guide to our future*, Allen Lane, 2015.

McBride A.S., *Speculative Masonry*, Macoy Publishing, 1971, (first pub. 1924).

McGregor, Douglas, *The Human Side of Enterprise*, McGraw Hill, 1960.

McInnes, Tom et al., *Monitoring Poverty and Social Exclusion 2014*, Joseph Rowntree Foundation, 2014.

Mitchell, B.R., *British Historical Statistics*, Cambridge University Press, 1988.

Mitre, Bartolomé, *Historia de San Martín y de la emancipación sudamericana*, 1869, translated and abridged by William Pilling as *The Emancipation of South America*, Chapman & Hall 1893, re-printed Kessinger Publishing 2009.

Murray, Roy, 'The four cardinal virtues and the tassels in the lodge room', *AQC*, Vol. 107, 1999.

Murray, Will, *Corporate Denial*, Capstone Publishing, 2004.

Newman, John Henry, *Newman Reader*, The National Institute for Newman Studies, 2007.

Nink, Marco, 'Employee Disengagement Plagues Germany', *Business Journal*, April 2009.

Noll, Thomas et al., 'A Comparison of Professional Traders and Psychopaths in a Simulated Non-Zero Sum Game', *Catalyst*, Vol. 2, Issue 2, 2012.

Nordström Kjell, and Ridderstråle, Jonas, *Funky Business*, Pearson, 2000.

Novak, Michael, *The Spirit of Democratic Capitalism*, Simon & Schuster, 1982.

Oliver, Dr George, *The Book of the Lodge*, introduction by Richard Sandbach, The Aquarian Press, 1986, (first pub. 1864).

Padelford, Frederick Morgan, 'The virtue of temperance in the Fairie Queene', *Studies in Philology*, Vol. 18, No. 3, 1921.

Payne, Brian & Dorothy, *Extracts from the Journals of John Deakin Heaton, M.D. of Claremont, Leeds*, Publications of the Thoresby Society, Miscellany 1973, Vol. 15.

Peters, Thomas J.

(1) with Waterman, Robert H. Jnr, *In Search of Excellence*, Harper & Row, 1982.

(2) *Thriving on Chaos*, Macmillan, 1991.

(3) *Liberation Management*, Ballantine Books, 1995.

Pottinger, R, 'New Zealand Freemasonry in 2005', *Transactions of Masters and Past Masters Lodge No. 130,* Christchurch, New Zealand, 1997.

Price, Richard, *A Discourse on the Love of our Country,* The Constitution Society, 1789.

Putnam, Robert D., *Bowling Alone,* Simon & Schuster, 2000.

Rampton, Martha, 'The Three Waves of Feminism', *Pacific Magazine,* Fall 2008.

Raven, Simon, *Alms for Oblivion,* Vintage, 1998.

   (1) Vol. I

   (2) Vol. II

Reynolds, Keld J., 'The Lautaro Lodges', *The Americas,* Vol. 24, 1967, published by the Academy of American Franciscan History.

Richardson, Sarah, *The Domestic Impact of the Napoleonic Wars,* University of Warwick.

Ricks, Christopher (ed.), *Tennyson: A selected edition,* Longman, 1989.

Ridley, Jasper, *A Brief History of the Freemasons,* Robinson, 2008.

Riley-Smith, Jonathan, 'Revival and Survival', in Jonathan Riley-Smith (ed.) *The Oxford History of the Crusades,* Oxford University Press, 1999.

Roddick, Anita, *Business as Unusual,* Thorsons, 2000.

Sacks, Jonathan, *The Politics of Hope,* Random House, 1997.

Sandbach, R.S.E., 'Robert Thomas Crucefix 1788-1850', *AQC,* Vol. 102, 1989.

Sandel, Michael J., *Justice,* Allen Lane, 2009.

Scase, Richard and Goffee, Robert, *Reluctant Managers,* Routledge, 1989.

Schön, Donald

   (1) *Beyond the Stable State,* Norton, 1973.

   (2) with Argyris, Chris, *Organizational learning: A theory of action perspective,* Addison-Wesley, 1978.

   (3) with Argyris, Chris, *Theory in practice: Increasing professional effectiveness,* Jossey-Bass, 1974.

Senge, Peter M., *The Fifth Discipline,* Random House, revised edition 2006.

Shelley, Percy Bysshe, *1819,* in *Percy Bysshe Shelley,* poems selected by Fiona Sampson, Faber and Faber, 2011.

Smiley, Jane (ed.), *The Life and Death of Cormac the Skald,* Penguin Classics, 2001. (Written 1250–1300 CE, Icelandic author unknown.)

Smith, Tom W., *Beliefs about God across Time and Countries,* NORC/University of Chicago, 2012, Report for ISSP and GESIS.

Social Issues Research Centre, The, *Future of Freemasonry,* 2012, A report for the United Grand Lodge of England.

Stevenson, Charles L., *Ethics and Language,* Yale University Press, 1944.

Stout, Martha, *The Sociopath Next Door,* Broadway Books, 2005.

Taylor, Frederick W., *Principles of Scientific Management,* Harper & Brothers, 1911.

Thatcher, Margaret, *The Downing Street Years,* HarperCollins, 1993.

Thompson, F.M.L. (ed), *The Rise of Suburbia*, Leicester University Press, 1982.

Thornton, Peter, 'Nine out of ten Freemasons would attack Moscow in Winter', *Proceedings of the 1992 Australian Masonic Research Council Conference.*

Tolkien, J.R.R., *Return of the King*, Allen & Unwin, 1955.

Trevelyan, G.M., *History of England*, Longman, illustrated edition 1973.

Vallance, Edward, *A Radical History Of Britain*, Abacus, 2010.

Varney, Dr Justin et al., *Public Health England: Everybody Active, every day, an evidence based approach to physical activity*, Crown copyright, 2014.

Verschoor, Curtis C., 'New Survey of Workplace Ethics Shows Surprising Results', *AccountingWEB*, April 2012.

Vugt, Mark van, 'Follow the leader', *The Psychologist*, 2004.

Weightman, Craig, *A Journey in Stone*, Lewis Masonic, 2015.

Weil, Simone, *The Need for Roots*, Routledge & Kegan Paul, 1952.

West, David

(1) *St Laurence Working* (ed), privately published for St Laurence Lodge, No. 5511, stlaurencelodge.org.uk, 2010, second edition 2013.

(2) *Employee Engagement - and the failure of leadership*, Amazon, 2012.

(3) *The Devil, the Goat and the Freemason - a study in the history of ideas*, Hamilton House, 2013.

(4) *Things to do when you have nothing to do - how to find those candidates who have been looking for you all this time*, Hamilton House, 2014.

(5) *Deism - at the time of the founders of the Premier Grand Lodge*, Hamilton House, 2015

White, Kirk C., *Operative Freemasonry: a manual for restoring light and vitality to the fraternity*, Five Gates Publishing, 2012.

Williams, Karel, *From Pauperism to Poverty*, Routledge and Kegan Paul, 1981.

Wilson, David, 'How psychopaths hide in plain sight – a psychological analysis of serial killer Dennis Rader', *Independent*, 18 August 2015.

Winn, Ray, *Running the Red: An Evaluation of Strathclyde Police's Red Light Camera Initiative - Research Findings*, The Scottish Government Publications, 1999.

Wittgenstein, Ludwig

(1) *Tractatus Logico-Philosophicus*, transl. D.F. Pears & B.F. McGuinness, Routledge, 1961.

(2) *Lecture on Ethics*, from notes taken by Rush Rhees, *Philosophical Review*, Vol. 74, 1965.

World Health Organization (*WHO*), *The Global Burden of Disease, 2004 Update*, 2008.

Zeldis, Leon, 'Freemasonry's Contribution to South American Independence – a Factual Approach,' *AQC*, Vol. 111, 1998.

Printed in Great Britain
by Amazon